It's Hard to Have a Mouse-free House

"But with God all things are possible."
(Matthew 19:26)

BY Mary Ellen Stewart

CONTENTS

Discipline #6: Unforgiveness

PART THREE: BATTLEFIELDS OF LIFE

Discipline #7: Finances

Discipline #8: Health

Discipline #9: Prayer

PART FOUR: GOD'S TOOL FOR OVERCOMING

Discipline #10: Perseverance

MAINTAINING A MOUSE-FREE HOUSE

INTRODUCTION

A Mouse in the House

In October of 1992, my husband Andy and I opened our California home for a backyard wedding ceremony and reception. Two days later, we started out on a three-week car trip to see the fall leaves changing colors in my hometown of St. Louis, Missouri, and Andy's hometown of Omaha, Nebraska. Though we had a wonderful experience, the many miles of traveling made us weary and eager to get home.

As we entered our house, the first thing that caught our attention was the mound of mail littering Andy's desk. Then we noticed a small burlap bag next to the stack of envelopes. The bag contained peanut brittle—a special treat left for us by Sue and Denny, Andy's newlywed daughter and son-in-law. A jagged hole in the side of the burlap indicated that someone had already helped themselves to some of the sweet treat inside. So instead of bothering to loosen the wire and open the bag from the top, we slipped pieces out of the little hole and munched on it while we went through our mail.

Later that day, as I was preparing sandwiches for a snack, I noticed peculiar holes in the slices of bread we'd just bought. While puzzling over this, I found a large hole in the side of the bread wrapper. Suddenly I realized the identity of the culprit who had freely shared our candy, and now the bread. It had to have been a mouse!

I scouted around and discovered the mouse had made a trail in every cupboard, drawer, and closet, and around every baseboard in every room. I surmised that he must have come in through a door that had been left open to accommodate the wedding reception caterers. That little guy had survived in our house for three weeks with nothing to eat except peanut brittle until we added fresh bread to his diet.

Andy and I set out a trap with cheese. Within minutes we heard it snap. Deciding the incident was too funny to keep to ourselves, we informed our family. They were horrified to learn we'd gobbled up a sack of peanut brittle a mouse had been playing around in. But when we told them that we enjoyed the candy as much as the little mouse did, they all laughed with us.

Some months later, I was feeling overwhelmed and discouraged about various problems in my life. As I prayed about them, I realized that I was berating myself and despairing over my failures instead of trusting God the way I should.

In my spirit, I heard a message from the Lord: *"It's hard to have a mouse-free house. But with God all things are possible."* I thought of the impudent little rodent that had sneaked into our house while Andy and I were away and brazenly violated our home.

As I meditated on the "mouse-free house" concept, I remembered a message the Holy Spirit gave me in 1983, when I was asked to prepare a lesson for our weekly women's fellowship meeting. It was on the ten areas of discipline: *worldliness, words, thoughts, pride, fear, unforgiveness, finances, health, prayer,* and *perseverance.*

Shortly after teaching that lesson, the Holy Spirit led me into a deep three-year study of the disciplines to facilitate my own spiritual growth. He showed me that *worldliness, negative words,* and *negative thoughts* are things that come against us; *pride, fear,* and *unforgiveness* are emotions that come against us. When Satan keeps us in a negative mode, he can affect our *finances, health, and prayer life.* The good news is, God has given us the tool we need to help us overcome physical and spiritual battles: *perseverance.*

If we don't heed God's advice in these ten areas of discipline, Satan will creep in and spoil our lives—just like a mouse, when given the opportunity, will sneak in and defile our homes.

I resented having to clean up the messes that mouse made. However, that kind of drudgery is nothing compared to cleaning up the messes that worldliness, negative thoughts, and negative emotions create in our lives.

Following these ten disciplines will enable us to obey the Ten Commandments and fulfill the commandment Jesus gave to walk in love. Then, when Satan launches his barrage of attacks, we will have the confidence we need to make them boomerang away from us. As we learn to walk daily in God's disciplines, we will produce more fruit for His kingdom and better enjoy our journey in life.

As I further contemplated the "mouse-free house" concept, I sensed the Lord was compelling me to put His ten disciplines into a book for instruction and meditation.

When I told my eight-year-old grandson, James, that I was writing a book, he asked, "What's it gonna be called?"

"*It's Hard to Have a Mouse-Free House*," I said.

In response to his confused look, I explained why I chose that title.

"I understand what you're trying to do, Grandma," he replied with enthusiasm. "You want to help people live a trouble-free life." Even at that tender age, James understood.

That is indeed my goal. And so, dear reader, find a comfortable spot to curl up with this book. As you read it, meditate on the Scripture passages sprinkled throughout the text. Ask the Holy Spirit to fill your spirit with His insights, and enjoy God's unique sense of humor. Let Him show you how to maintain a mouse-free house by plugging the holes and crevices in your spiritual home with the wisdom and Word of God.

DEDICATION

This book is dedicated to the Holy Spirit, our Counselor, Comforter, and Friend.

Acknowledgments

I feel that I have just birthed a healthy child with the assistance of the Lord and my family and friends. Now I have to turn it over to the world, and I pray it's treated well—much the same feelings I had with the children God gave me to nurture until they were no longer in my care.

I want to thank my husband Andy, his three daughters, Dwnell, Terrie, and Sue, his son-in-law, Denny, my two daughters-in-law, Elaine and Cindy, plus our extended family of grandchildren and great-grandchildren, other family members, and friends for their encouragement and support during the many years I spent learning how to organize and write this book.

I am grateful to my granddaughter Ashley Anders for her artwork on my book cover. She has drawn pictures for me since she was a small child. I am happy to see her enjoy art as a profession.

Thanks to my children, Mary Catherine, Mark, Jane, and Norman Jr., for encouraging me to buy computers, for helping me to get acquainted with the unfamiliar computer world, and for getting this book printed and distributed.

A very special thanks to my friend Robyn, who encouraged me to get my work edited and published after it sat on a shelf for over a year. She went with me to my first meeting with my editor. She also helped me get adjusted to my new computer when I started my rewrites.

A special thanks to my editor, Kathy Ide. She took on the task of helping a person with no experience to fulfill her goal of writing and publishing a book. Her perseverance and dedication to the task is second only to the Holy Spirit, whose gentle nudging for many years inspired me to put God's ten disciplines into a book that will help strengthen the body of Christ.

Thanks especially to my heavenly Father for His Word, and for the blessing of writing this book.

PART ONE: NEGATIVE THINGS THAT COME AGAINST US

PART ONE

NEGATIVE THINGS THAT COME AGAINST US

God's disciplines help us fight against negative things that
keep us from bearing fruit for God's kingdom.

Worldliness
Negative Words
Negative Thoughts

So God created man in His own image;
in the image of God He created him;
male and female He created them.
(Genesis 1:27)

Discipline #1: Worldliness

God uses covenants to help mankind
fight spiritual and physical battles.

The rainbow shall be in the cloud,
and I will look on it to remember
the everlasting covenant between God and
every living creature of all flesh that is on the earth.
(Genesis 9:16)

Chapter 1

Walking in Worldliness or Fellowship

Many Christians consider *worldliness* to be carnal pleasures such as smoking, drinking, or gambling. But as I researched and studied this word, the Holy Spirit gave me the following definition: *Worldliness is anything that keeps people from fellowshipping with God.*

There are many things in life that can distract us from spending time with God and keep us from getting to know Him better. But fellowshipping with God is a necessity if we want to successfully navigate the storms of life. As we commune with Him we can be led by His wisdom.

If we neglect our quiet times with the Lord, we will fall prey to the devil's schemes. Satan is the god of this world, so whoever is not following God's ways will inadvertently follow his leading. Most people are unaware of the tremendous influence the world has on their thinking and activities. The apostle Paul says, "For all seek their own, not the things which are of Christ Jesus" (Philippians 2:21).

Paul tells us not to walk in craftiness, to renounce the hidden things of shame, and not to handle the Word of God deceitfully. He says, "But if our gospel be hid, it is hid to them that are lost: in whom the god of this world hath blinded the minds of them which believe not, lest the light of the glorious gospel of Christ, who is the image of God, should shine unto them" (2 Corinthians 4:3–4 KJV).

If we do not choose to walk in the light of the gospel, we will end up walking in the darkness of this world. Christians who do not have continuity in fellowshipping with God become double-minded. The Bible says a double-minded person will not hear from God (James 1:5–8), because faith and doubt are as far apart as the east is from the west. The mind and emotions are Satan's targets, and it is imperative we develop a vigilant watch over them. God gives us assistance in this if we fellowship with Him daily.

Walking in Fellowship

Fellowship means close communication or contact with someone. Fellowshipping with God is just as private and intimate as the interaction you have with your spouse or children.

God uses the Holy Spirit to talk to us through our spirits. If I talk to God like He is somebody, He talks to me like I am somebody, and together we get things done. However, if I talk to Him like He is nothing, I will receive nothing for an answer and nothing will be accomplished.

Some Christians think a minister should fellowship with God for them, speaking to the Lord on their behalf. But no one can do this for someone else. You wouldn't want a minister to fellowship with your spouse for you.

Walking in Agreement

Christians are to walk in agreement with God on a daily basis, with the help of the Holy Spirit. Amos 3:3 says, "Can two walk together, unless they are agreed?" Without agreement, a Christian's walk with God is like a sailboat without wind—dead in the water.

As we continue to walk with God, He teaches us how to sail through the storms of life, when to put into ports of rest, how to stock up on supplies, and when to refuel for spiritual and physical strength.

God has given His children free will. This enables each of us to be the captain of our own ship, but God wants to provide direction as we continue along the journey. The skills we acquire as we sail through our lives, and the number of shipwrecks we experience, will depend, to a large extent, on how much or how little we fellowship with God. If we acknowledge that God is the wind that steadies our sails, we won't be worried when we hit the storms. "Be anxious for nothing, but in everything by prayer and supplication, with thanksgiving, let your requests be made known to God; and the peace of God, which surpasses all understanding, will guard your hearts and minds through Christ Jesus" (Philippians 4:6–7).

Walking in Faith

Sometimes God may seem like an untouchable nothingness. We feel squeezed and smothered by the octopus of worldliness. In those times, we may not have much desire to fellowship with God. But it is in these very situations that such fellowship is the most necessary.

You can jump-start your faith by praying, by reading and hearing and studying the Word of God, and by remembering who you are in Jesus Christ. Then you will hear from God.

At one time in my life, I was so distraught over a situation, I couldn't pray. I felt like I was holding on to God's hand in midair while other people in my life were holding on to me. If I let go of His hand, I feared we would all tumble back to earth.

When I told God how I felt, I heard these words in my spirit: "*My arm is long.*" Those words comforted me. I knew that with God in control, I could relax. I could let Him hold on to my hand, knowing He wouldn't let go.

Isaiah 30:30 tells us, "The Lord will cause His glorious voice to be heard, and show the descent of His arm." Isaiah 59:1 says, "Behold, the Lord's hand is not shortened, that it cannot save; nor His ear heavy, that it cannot hear." As Christians, we can rest assured that whether we are in midair or have fallen into the pits of the earth, our hands are anchored in the Lord's hand.

PART ONE: NEGATIVE THINGS THAT COME AGAINST US

Circumstances beyond my control brought me to my knees and forced me to lean on God's understanding, not my own. Proverbs 3:5–6 tells us to trust in the Lord, not to lean on our own understanding, and let Him direct our paths.

Walking in the Word

Like many Christians, I've memorized the Lord's Prayer. At one time it was the only thing I could pray. But the words in that prayer were sufficient to revive my spirit and bring peace to my soul. Since that time, I have realized how important it is to memorize Scriptures that deal with specific problems. The Word of God offers answers to problems, and it stimulates faith.

Following are some Scriptures I pray daily to strengthen my spirit when I fellowship with God. (I changed the pronouns in the original text to first person, to make them feel more personally applicable.)

- "I have the mind of Christ." (1 Corinthians 2:16)
- "I can do all things through Christ who strengthens me." (Philippians 4:13)
- "Greater is He that is in me, than he that is in the world." (1 John 4:4 KJV)
- "The joy of the Lord is my strength." (Nehemiah 8:10)
- "No weapon formed against me shall prosper." (Isaiah 54:17)
- "God shall supply all my need according to His riches in glory by Christ Jesus." (Philippians 4:19)
- "[I pray that] the eyes of my understanding being enlightened; that I may know what is the hope of His calling, what are the riches of the glory of His inheritance in the saints." (Ephesians 1:18)
- "I shall not die, but live, and declare the works of the Lord." (Psalm 118:17)

The wisdom we inherit through the Word can help us to overcome worldliness and sin.

Jesus knew the Word, and He used it to immobilize Satan. After John baptized Jesus in the Jordan River, the Spirit led Jesus into the wilderness where He fasted for forty days. Then the devil took Jesus up on a high mountain and promised Him all the kingdoms of the world if He would worship him. But Jesus said to him, "Away with you, Satan! For it is written, 'You shall worship the Lord your God, and Him only you shall serve'" (Matthew 4:10).

As we become disciplined in the Word of God, we will win victories over the enemy. Then we will begin to crave intimate fellowship with God. We will no longer be content with a third-party relationship with Him.

As we learn to release our innermost selves into the loving hands of our Father, we will enjoy fellowshipping with Him daily. We will be able to give Him our worry, pain, grief, and even the goals we wish to attain.

God wants to meet our needs. Scripture says, "Delight yourself also in the Lord, and He shall give you the desires of your heart" (Psalm 37:4). If we fellowship regularly with Him and refuse to walk in worldliness, we will receive the rewards of this promise.

Chapter 2

Worldliness in the Old Testament

A brief journey through the Old Testament will give us an overview of how worldliness started and how it has progressed in the world. It all began with the first man and woman's disobedience to God.

Disobedience to God: the Beginning of Worldliness

Adam and Eve lived in a paradise called the garden of Eden. There they experienced a beautiful, perfect relationship with God because they lived a sinless life.

When God created Adam and Eve, He made a three-part covenant with them. He charged them to populate and subdue the earth, to tend and keep the garden, and to have dominion over all living creatures.

God gave them only one commandment: not to eat from the tree in the midst of the garden—the tree of knowledge of good and evil. He warned them that if they ate its fruit, they would die.

God gave Adam this warning before Eve was created. Yet he apparently made no attempt to protect her from the temptation (Genesis 2:16–17). Satan entered a serpent and enticed Eve to eat the forbidden fruit. She then persuaded Adam to eat the fruit and disobey the direct command from God. (Genesis 3:6)

As soon as Adam and Eve ate of the fruit, they realized they were naked. This prompted them to make coverings for themselves out of fig leaves. In the cool of the evening when God came into the garden to fellowship with them, as usual, they were afraid and hid from Him.

Their strange behavior prompted God to question Adam. Adam immediately criticized Eve, saying, "The woman whom You gave to be with me, she gave me of the tree, and I ate" (Genesis 3:12). This was the beginning of man's attempt to blame someone else.

Next God questioned Eve, and her answer was that the serpent had tempted her. Thus began the "devil made me do it" syndrome.

When Adam and Eve's sins were revealed, God performed the first blood sacrifice for the sins of mankind. He used animal skins to make tunics for their clothing in place of the fig leaves they had haphazardly put together.

Afterward, He exiled them from the garden of Eden before they could be tempted to eat of the tree of life and live forever. God placed a flaming sword in front of the tree of life. (See Genesis 3:21–24.)

The sin of disobedience to God caused man to lose his soul (Genesis 2:17, "You shall surely die") and his heavenly body (Genesis 3:19, "To dust you shall return"). God then gave control of the earth to Satan.

After human beings were exposed to Satan's ways, God initiated new covenants to teach them how to live in a hostile atmosphere until He was ready to put His final plans of redemption and restoration into operation.

The Adamic Covenant

Everything changed when Adam and Eve disobeyed God. Curses came upon the world, the animal kingdom, and people. Those curses remain in effect until mankind is redeemed. Some definitions for r*edeem* are: to buy back; to repurchase what was lost; to get or win back; to repair or restore; to free from a lien by payment.[1]

---

[1] *Merriam-Webster's Collegiate Dictionary,* 11th ed., (Springfield, Massachusetts: Merriam-Webster, Incorporated), 2007.

The first man lost his sinless nature and his dominion over the world, and the world became his hard taskmaster. Without God's love and forgiveness, worldliness would have completed the destruction of humankind.

Satan had hoped for the demise of mankind. Nevertheless, God created human beings for companionship. Therefore, He gave His children rules and covenants so that He might continue fellowshipping with them. God's plan from the beginning of creation was to redeem people from sin, give them back domain over the earth, and reconcile them to Himself through the blood of Jesus.

Through the fall of man and his history after he left the garden of Eden, we get a panoramic view of man's struggle with worldliness.

Since Satan indwelled the serpent, the serpent was cursed more than every other beast of the field for his part in causing Adam and Eve to sin. "And the Lord God said unto the serpent, . . . Upon thy belly shalt thou go, and dust shalt thou eat all the days of thy life" (Genesis 3:14 KJV).

Satan, the indwelling energizer of the serpent, was also cursed. "I will put enmity between thee and the woman, and between thy seed and her seed [Jesus]; it shall bruise thy head, and thou shalt bruise his heel" (Genesis 3:15 KJV).

Eve's punishment was to bring forth children in pain. "Unto the woman he said, I will greatly multiply thy sorrow and thy conception; in sorrow thou shalt bring forth children; and thy desire shall be to thy husband, and he shall rule over thee" (Genesis 3:16 KJV).

God cursed the earth with thorns and thistles. He told Adam he had to obtain his food by hard work and sweat until he returned to the earth from which he came (Genesis 3:19).

As human beings multiplied under cursed and adverse conditions, the logical thing would have been for them to seek

God's protection and advice. Instead, they embraced worldliness and became enmeshed with sin.

> There were giants in the earth in those days; and also after that, when the sons of God came in unto the daughters of men, and they bare children to them, the same became mighty men which were of old, men of renown. And God saw that the wickedness of man was great in the earth. . . . And the Lord said, I will destroy man whom I have created from the face of the earth; both man, and beast, and the creeping thing, and the fowls of the air; for it repenteth me that I have made them. (Genesis 6:4–7 KJV)

Though the earth is full of vileness today, it can't compare to the state of humankind before the flood. People became so abhorrent God regretted He ever made humans, animals, insects, or birds. Satan, with the help of the fallen angels who followed him, perpetrated that tragedy. The sons of God (angels) had children with the women of the earth. They were involved in sexual perversion and every detestable sin they could envision. God destroyed the world with a flood to cleanse the earth of their evil influence (2 Peter 2:4–5).

Although the offending angels were chained, other angels who were subservient to Satan still roamed free, so women were encouraged to keep their heads covered as a sign that they were under the authority of men. "And the angels which kept not their first estate, but left their own habitation, he hath reserved in everlasting chains under darkness unto the judgment of the great day" (Jude 1:6 KJV).

First Corinthians 11:10 says, "For this reason the woman ought to have a symbol of authority on her head, because of the angels." We are told in 2 Peter 2:4 that "God did not spare the angels who sinned, but cast them down to hell and delivered them into chains of darkness, to be reserved for judgment."

Job 1:6 tells us that Satan is still allowed to present himself to God with the sons (angels) of God. Satan uses his authority to accuse the brethren day and night (Revelation 12:10). However, during the thousand-year reign of Christ here on earth, Satan will be bound in chains like the angels who await judgment. Then he will be freed for a season to exercise his evil influence on the world for the last time. After that, he will be cast into the lake of fire and brimstone forever (Revelation 20). The apostle John saw a new heaven and a new earth after the first earth and heaven had passed away (Revelation 21:1).

Despite all the vileness and sin committed on the earth before the flood, one man came forth blameless in his walk with God. His name was Noah, and he had three sons: Shem, Ham, and Japheth. God showed Noah how to build an ark of gopher wood that would save his family and two or more of all living creatures, male and female, from the flood that was to cover the earth.

The Noahic Covenant

After the flood, God made a third covenant with mankind. Though it did not erase the curses, God used it to bless the people of Noah's family. He told them to multiply, replenish the earth, and take dominion over all living things. A rainbow in the sky was the sign of His covenant with Noah that the earth would never be destroyed by water again (Genesis 9:16).

God's covenant with Noah established the sacredness of human life. "Surely your blood of your lives will I require; at the hand of every beast will I require it, and at the hand of man; at the hand of every man's brother will I require the life of man. Whoso sheddeth man's blood, by man shall his blood be shed: for in the image of God made he man" (Genesis 9:5–6 KJV).

The whole earth had one language. But as men grew in number, they began to believe they could accomplish anything, even reaching the heavens and becoming like God. So they built a city, which they called Babel, and in it an enormous tower.

This angered God. He knew men could accomplish whatever they decided to do if they were of one accord. So He confused their language. (*Babbling* came from the word Babel to refer to people talking foolishly or not making sense.) He scattered them across the face of the earth, and they ceased building the city and tower (Genesis 11).

However, the evil being perpetrated in Babel spread across the earth. Some of Noah's descendants from Ham settled in Babylon, a city that came to represent Satan and all of his corruption.

Abraham: the Father of All Nations

Several generations after the flood, God dealt with mankind's sin, rebellion, and worldliness through a righteous man called Abram, later called Abraham. God told Abraham that his descendants would be as numerous as the stars in heaven, and he would teach his children to worship and fellowship with Him. Even though Abraham and his wife, Sarah, were childless, Abraham believed God.

Since Sarah was barren, she encouraged Abraham to father a child with her maid, Hagar. Abraham obeyed her wishes and Ishmael was born. Abraham loved him dearly. He thought God would work through Ishmael's descendants to fulfill His promise. However, God told Abraham that although Ishmael would have twelve sons and become the father of many nations, his wife, Sarah, would have a child in her old age. And that child would be the one who would fulfill God's promise to Abraham.

Several years after Ishmael's birth, Sarah became pregnant and gave birth to a son named Isaac. Great strife and jealousy developed between the two sons and their mothers. God told Hagar to take Ishmael and leave Abraham's family, with His promise to protect and prosper them. The twelve sons of Ishmael became the powerful Arabic nations of today. Yet strife continues between the Arabic nations and Israel, Isaac's descendants.

Sarah set a bad example when she insisted that Abraham help God keep His promise for an heir. Men bring terrible calamities upon themselves when they interfere with God's timing and fail to listen to His advice.

When God revealed that Sodom and Gomorrah were to be destroyed because of worldliness and the great sins in those cities, Abraham, relying on God's great mercy, asked Him to spare the cities if at least ten righteous men could be found. Although ten could not be found, Lot, Abraham's nephew, along with his wife and two daughters who lived in Sodom, were allowed to flee. But they were cautioned against looking back.

Lot's wife allowed worldliness to overcome her. When she looked back to see what was happening to her worldly possessions, she turned into a pillar of salt. Her disobedience caused her early death—a vivid reminder that God insists on obedience to His commandments regardless of how much He loves humankind.

Lot and his daughters fled to the mountains, where they lived a solitary life for some time. The young women were afraid there would be no lineage for their father, and because they were not fellowshipping with God or asking for His advice, they decided to get their father drunk with wine and then lie with him. Each of them conceived and bore a child.

Moab and Ben-Ammi were the sons born to Lot by his daughters. Lot's descendants are the children of the Moabites and the Ammonites in the Jordan area (Genesis 18–19). They are part of the Muslim world.

Ruth was a Moabite, and she became a daughter-in-law to Naomi. After her husband died, Ruth followed Naomi to her homeland. Ruth married Boaz, a kinsman to Naomi. Because of her great love for Naomi and her God, Ruth became part of the lineage of Jesus.

The Covenant of Circumcision

God's covenant with Abraham offered blessings to all those who blessed Abraham and his nations, and curses for those people who cursed Abraham and Israel (Genesis 12:1–3). God required all males to be circumcised from eight-day-old babies to adults (Genesis17:11–12). Circumcision was a sign that the Jews were special and belonged to God—just as being born again of the Spirit of God at the time of salvation makes us special today.

Abraham was faithful to God's commandments and became the father of all nations—not by his seed, but by his faith. Paul explains this in Ephesians 3:6: "The Gentiles should be fellow heirs, of the same body, and partakers of His promise in Christ through the gospel."

After Isaac became a young man, God tested Abraham's faith by asking him to sacrifice his son Isaac on the altar. When Abraham chose to obey and placed Isaac on a sacrificial altar, God intervened and provided an animal for the sacrifice. Then God said, "Blessing I will bless you, and multiplying I will multiply your descendants as the stars of the heaven and as the sand which is on the seashore; and your descendants shall possess the gate of their enemies. In your seed all the nations of the earth shall be blessed, because you have obeyed My voice" (Genesis 22:17–18).

Birth of Two Nations

Because of Abraham's righteousness, God was able to establish His covenant with the Hebrew people. Isaac, Abraham's son, fathered twins: Esau and Jacob. Esau was the firstborn and would have been given the birthright. But when he was hungry and fatigued after a time of hunting, his worldliness caused him to sell his precious birthright to Jacob for a bowl of stew.

Esau's descendants were the Edomites, who lived in what is now called Petra, which was uninhabited for centuries due to the water supply drying up in that area. God became angry at the Edomites because they gloated over the invasion and destruction of Jerusalem when Judah was sent into captivity. So He declared that no survivors were to be left in the house of Esau (Obadiah 1:11–18).

The same kind of jealousy existed between Esau's and Jacob's descendants as had developed between Ishmael's and Isaac's descendants. History reveals the havoc this jealousy has wrought between families and nations.

After God chose to work with Jacob instead of Esau, He gave Jacob a new name: Israel. Jacob fathered twelve sons, whose descendants became known as the twelve tribes of Israel. Joseph, one of the twelve sons, was sold by his jealous brothers as a slave, and his owners carried him into Egypt. Joseph was faithful to God during his years as a slave. As a result, God helped him rise to power.

When God revealed through Joseph that there would be seven years of plenty and seven years of hunger, Pharaoh put Joseph in charge of collecting and storing food for the seven bad years. During the famine, Joseph's brothers left their homeland to buy food in Egypt. Eventually, Joseph made himself known to them. He asked all of his family to move to Egypt to escape the famine. So what Joseph's brothers had meant for evil, God used for good.

God did for Joseph what He often does for mankind. He took a bad situation and caused something positive to come from it.

Moses: a Man the Lord Knew Face-to-Face

The Hebrew people multiplied in great numbers and grew wealthy. After Joseph died, new rulers came to power, and they considered the Hebrews a threat to Egypt. The Hebrew people lost all their wealth, were severely persecuted, and became slaves to the Egyptian people. Since they were multiplying so fast, Pharaoh commanded that all baby boys be cast into the river (Exodus 1:1–16).

When Moses was born, his mother hid him to keep him from being killed. She put her newborn in a tiny ark made from bulrushes (tall plants commonly found in wetlands) and hid it among the reeds of the river. Pharaoh's daughter found him floating in the water. Though she knew he was a Hebrew child, she had compassion on him and accepted him as her own.

Miriam, Moses' sister, arranged for her mother to become a nurse to Moses. After he was weaned, his mother took the child to the palace, where, as the son of Pharaoh's daughter, he lived the life of an Egyptian prince.

When he was a young adult, Moses saw an Egyptian beating a Hebrew. In anger, Moses killed the Egyptian. In fear of his life he fled to the desert. Moses married and had two sons. He lived with his family in the desert until God called him to deliver the people of Israel from their bondage in Egypt (Exodus 2; Acts 7).

God had a new plan of redemption for His children.

The Mosaic Covenant

The Mosaic covenant with the Israelites was made after they left Egypt and moved to Horeb. That covenant consisted of animal sacrifices, laws, and the Ten Commandments. These things were added to the covenant made with Abraham. God promised the Israelites blessings for obedience to His laws and curses for disobedience (Deuteronomy 28). The people were taught through the laws and the Ten Commandments how to conduct their lives until the Messiah came to redeem them from the curses.

God reminded the people, "Ye have seen what I did unto the Egyptians, and how I bare you on eagles' wings, and brought you unto myself. Now therefore, if ye will obey my voice indeed, and keep my covenant, then ye shall be a peculiar treasure unto me above all people: for all the earth is mine" (Exodus 19:4–5 KJV). Moses gathered the people together and told them what God had said, and they all agreed to obey God's new covenant (Exodus 19:7–8).

Moses' and Aaron's Failures

God chose Moses and his brother Aaron to lead the people out of slavery to the land He had promised to the descendants of Abraham. The Hebrew people had a slave mentality, and they wanted to go back to Egypt instead of listening to Moses and learning of God's plan for them. Worldliness and rebellion caused them to be in the wilderness for forty years.

When the people continually complained that they needed water and were going to die from thirst, Aaron and Moses became angry with them. The Lord intervened and told Moses to strike the rock with his rod. Out of it came an abundance of water for the people and animals to drink.

> Then the Lord spoke to Moses and Aaron, "Because you did not believe Me, to hallow Me in the eyes of the children of Israel, therefore you shall not bring this assembly into the land which I have given them." This was the water of Meribah, because the children of Israel contended with the Lord, and He was hallowed among them. (Numbers 20:12–13)

The children of Israel left Kadesh and journeyed to Mount Hor, on the border of Edom. Because of Aaron's anger at the waters of Meribah, God commanded Moses to take Aaron and his son Eleazar up to Mount Hor, then strip Aaron of his priestly garments and put them on Eleazar. Aaron died and was buried on Mount Hor, and the people mourned him for thirty days (Numbers 20:24–29).

The Palestinian Covenant

After Moses led the people to Moab, God gave them the covenant concerning Palestine. (See Deuteronomy 29:10–15.) God knew the people would fail to keep His commandments and laws after they entered the land of Canaan, the Promised Land. So, in the Palestinian covenant, He promised to bring them back from the lands of captivity. God said, "If any of you are driven out to the farthest parts under heaven, from there the Lord your God will gather you, and from there He will bring you" (Deuteronomy 30:4).

> Then Moses called Joshua and said to him in the sight of all Israel, "Be strong and of good courage, for you must go with this people to the land which the Lord has sworn to their fathers to give them, and you shall cause them to inherit it." (Deuteronomy 31:7)

Moses, because of his actions at the waters of Meribah, was not allowed to cross the river Jordan into the Promised Land. God took him up from the plains of Moab to Mount Nebo across from Jericho, showed him the land, then buried Moses secretly in a valley in the land of Moab, and the people mourned him for thirty days (Deuteronomy 34).

Even though Moses allowed worldliness to get him out of fellowship with God at the waters of Meribah, God knew Moses "face to face"—an honor no other prophet of Israel had (Deuteronomy 34:10).

After the death of Moses, Joshua was put in charge of the twelve tribes of Israel. He was chosen because he gave a good report on the land when Moses sent spies to check it out. He said it was a land flowing with milk and honey, and although there were giants, the Israelites could handle them with God's help. The other spies, with the exception of Caleb, were afraid of the giants.

The Israelites' fear of fighting the giants in the Promised Land turned what could have been an eleven-day journey into a forty-year ordeal in the wilderness. God used this time to establish His laws and commandments with the people while He waited for the old generation to die. God led the new generation, under the leadership of Joshua, in its conquest of the Promised Land (Joshua 1:1–3).

God's Mercy and Patience

The Scriptures reveal humankind's struggles with worldliness from the beginning of time, when Adam and Eve were forced out of the garden of Eden. But they also reveal God's magnanimous mercy, His infinite patience, and His consuming desire to fellowship with His children.

In the books of Exodus, Leviticus, Numbers, and Deuteronomy, we learn that God tried to teach the Hebrew people that certain physical laws must be obeyed before His spiritual laws can operate effectively in their lives. He listed all the blessings of obedience, reminded them of the curses of disobedience, and admonished them to choose the blessings instead of the curses.

Then God gave a severe warning. He said, "If ye will not for all this hearken unto me, but walk contrary unto me; then I will walk contrary unto you also in fury; and I, even I, will chastise you seven times for your sins" (Leviticus 26:27–28 KJV).

God gives the same warning to us today. The good news is, we also have access to abundant blessings if we choose obedience and walk in His ways.

Sin and Rebellion in the Land of Plenty

The Hebrew people prospered and grew rich in the land of Canaan, as long as they had Joshua to lead them. But after Joshua died, the people returned to idolatry and rebelled against God's commandments, rules, and regulations. Worldliness overtook them, and they received the curses instead of the blessings. They chose to fellowship with the pagan people who were ignorant of God's ways. They even followed the pagan example of sacrificing their children by fire to pagan gods.

Today, we are not ignorant of God's ways. Yet Satan still destroys Christian children through the use of drugs, alcohol, illicit sex, and the misuse of guns. Satan's goal is to destroy God's families because they are the "apple of His eye" (Zechariah 2:8).

Our lack of fellowship with God and our worldliness have made us just as vulnerable to Satan as the Israelites were.

After Joshua's death, God appointed judges to look after the people. But they asked for a king. They wanted to be like the rest of the world. They had the Creator of the universe to look after them, protect them, and prosper them, but they yearned to enjoy the worldliness they saw in other nations.

So God chose Saul to be their first king.

David, who was from the house of Judah, was their second king. God made a covenant with David that his seed and throne would be established forever (2 Samuel 7:4–17). God was referring to David's lineage, which would give birth to Jesus, the Son of God.

God chose Solomon, David and Bathsheba's son, to be Israel's third king. Israel was a great nation during Solomon's reign.

After Solomon's death, his son Rehoboam became king. He was an ungodly ruler who listened to bad counsel, treated people unfairly, and taxed them heavily. This caused the citizens to rebel against the house of David. They split into two nations. Judah and Benjamin became the tribe of Judah (1 Kings 12).

Exile Prophecy Fulfilled

Israel had nineteen ungodly kings, and Samaria became their place of worship instead of the temple in Jerusalem. As a result of their disobedience to God's commandments, their worship of pagan gods, and their pulling away from the house of David, God allowed Assyria to take them captive (2 Kings 17).

The relative goodness of eight of Judah's twenty kings caused them to fare a little better than the nation of Israel. As a nation, they lived in peace and independence 136 years longer than Israel before they were taken captive by the Babylonians. Regardless of how much God did for the Hebrew people, they refused to listen to His pleadings for repentance. They deliberately chose God's curses instead of His blessings.

After Cyrus, king of Persia, overthrew Babylon, he gave the Hebrew people permission to return from exile and rebuild the temple in Jerusalem (Ezra 1:1–4). At first, only a few thousand returned from the tribes of Judah and Benjamin. Then some Levites and priests joined them. Later, a few others straggled back.

The rest were too comfortable to leave their homes in the pagan lands where they had been scattered during the captivity by Assyria and Babylon. They were content to intermingle with the pagan people and worship pagan gods. They turned their backs on the God who brought them out of slavery into a land of milk and honey. History proves that when people begin to enjoy worldliness and sin, they lose their desire to stay committed to serving God.

The rebuilding of the temple was interrupted many times because of opposition from the pagan people who lived in the areas around Jerusalem. After Darius became king, a controversy arose, and the building of the temple was stopped for some time.

Finally, the Israelites asked for a search to find the original decree given by King Cyrus to rebuild the temple. The decree was found and read to the new king. King Darius issued a warning that all those who opposed the rebuilding of the temple in Jerusalem would be put to death (Ezra 6:11).

Years later, the disciples were worshipping in the temple with Jesus and admiring the impressive structure. He told them the temple would be demolished (Luke 21:6).

In AD 70 the Romans destroyed the temple. A new temple will be built during the reign of the Antichrist; however, he will take away the daily sacrifices and set up the abomination of desolation spoken of by Daniel and Jesus (Daniel 12:11; Matthew 24:15).

When God made the Palestinian covenant with the Israelites, He knew the Hebrew people would not listen to the prophets of God, that they would refuse to separate themselves from the worldliness of the pagan people, and that they would not stop the worship of pagan gods. In Amos 3:2 God admonished them by saying, "You only have I known of all the families of the earth; therefore I will punish you for all your iniquities."

God spoke to the prophet Ezekiel of putting the stick of Judah and the stick of the house of Israel together and making them one nation again. Then God said:

> I will make them one nation in the land, on the mountains of Israel; and one king shall be king over them all; they shall no longer be two nations, nor shall they ever be divided into two kingdoms again. (Ezekiel 37:22)

A New Beginning

The holocaust of World War II caused the Jewish people in German-occupied countries to flee to their homeland in Israel. After centuries of living in foreign countries, the prophecy of Ezekiel was partially fulfilled. The Jews are now permanently established in their own land with their own government. Their persecution is a result of idolatry, worldliness, and disobedience to God's commandments and regulations.

However, God is faithful to keep His promises. "For thus says the Lord: 'Just as I have brought all this great calamity on this people, so I will bring on them all the good that I have promised them'" (Jeremiah 32:42).

Even though God performed many miracles for the Israelites, they wanted to follow the ways of the pagan people. That caused them to lose God's blessings, their independence as a nation, and many lives. As we study the Old Testament, we may wonder why they were so determined to walk in worldliness, ignore God, and worship idols.

Their stories served as a warning to the Gentiles in the New Testament, and they are a warning to Christians today. God said, "The Gentiles shall know that the house of Israel went into captivity for their iniquity; because they were unfaithful to Me, therefore I hid My face from them. I gave them into the hand of their enemies, and they all fell by the sword" (Ezekiel 39:23).

God's Covenants

Throughout the Old Testament, God kept making covenants with His people to teach them His ways, so they could have lives free from sin and disaster. In each new covenant He added specific rules and regulations to assist people in their walk with Him. Regardless of His continual attempts to intervene and help, men and women continued to allow worldliness and sin to permeate their lives.

Satan became the god of this world after Adam and Eve were cast out of the garden of Eden for their disobedience to God's commandment. This led to mankind's problems with worldliness. Our reluctance to fellowship with God allows Satan to creep into our spiritual homes and desecrate them with sin, disease, and poverty, much like a mouse sneaks in to defile a house. Without fellowship with God, we are all vulnerable to Satan's weapons of spiritual warfare.

A Cursed Nation

God chose the Jewish people—a small, insignificant nation—to teach them His ways. He was preparing the world to receive Jesus as the Redeemer. Only the blood of God's own Son could alleviate the power of the curses sin brought on mankind.

God is faithful to help us, but He wants things done His way. "Thus says the Lord: 'Cursed is the man who trusts in man and makes flesh his strength, whose heart departs from the Lord. For he shall be like a shrub in the desert, and shall not see when good comes, but shall inhabit the parched places in the wilderness, in a salt land which is not inhabited'" (Jeremiah 17:5–6).

God allows us to choose whether He will be the wind that steadies our sails. For us to safely navigate the treacherous river of life, it is imperative that we become familiar with our navigating tool: the Word of God.

God's River

Let me drink from God's River,

That flows from the throne above,

Let me drink of God's goodness,

Of His mercy and His love.

O waters may be troubled,

Mountains may swell and shake,

But God has a peaceful river,

Flowing from His holy place.

Chapter 3

Worldliness in the New Testament

Worldliness—lack of fellowshipping with God—began when Adam and Eve were cast out of the garden of Eden. This thread, woven throughout the Old Testament, continues through the New Testament.

The Final Covenant

God's Mosaic covenant failed with the Jewish people because they were unable to walk in God's ways with all the rules and regulations. So He came up with a no-fail plan. He would eliminate the animal sacrifices and provide a continual, ongoing blood sacrifice for the sins of all mankind. "And the Word became flesh and dwelt among us, and we beheld His glory, the glory as of the only begotten of the Father, full of grace and truth" (John 1:14).

God was talking about this final plan when He said, "A new heart also will I give you, and a new spirit will I put within you: and I will take away the stony heart out of your flesh, and I will give you an heart of flesh. And I will put my spirit within you, and cause you to walk in my statutes, and ye shall keep my judgments, and do them. And ye shall dwell in the land that I gave to your fathers; and ye shall be my people, and I will be your God" (Ezekiel 36:26–28 KJV).

Jesus died on the cross to fulfill the law, be a sacrifice for our sins, and teach us how to walk in love. He came that we might have life more abundantly here on earth and to show us how to walk in the Spirit so worldliness will not consume so much of our time (John 10:10). He brought us the final covenant, which allows us to become God's dear children and to fellowship directly with Him through the power of the Holy Spirit.

Insidious Worldliness

It is Satan's ultimate goal to keep us from fellowshipping with God since he knows how vulnerable we are when we lose contact with our heavenly Father. Worldliness is one of his favorite weapons in this battle, and he uses it in insidious ways.

The worldliness that creates obvious sin in the physical world is relatively easy to identify. However, subtler aspects of worldliness—such as distractions, procrastination, wrong priorities, and even busyness—are easily camouflaged.

Worldly Busyness

Busyness got in Martha's way when she and Mary entertained Jesus in their home. Martha was doing the serving by herself. She wanted Jesus to reprimand Mary for not helping her. But He said to her, "Martha, Martha, you are worried and troubled about many things. But one thing is needed, and Mary has chosen that good part, which will not be taken away from her'" (Luke 10:41–42).

I used to feel frustrated by the story of Martha, Mary, and Jesus. I easily identified with Martha, since I am the oldest daughter and the second child in a family of eight. After I got married, I had four children of my own. Because of my background I believed Martha had a legitimate complaint.

During a Bible study many years ago, I heard a minister speak on Mary and Martha. He talked about how his mother stayed home on Sundays and prepared a big dinner for the family, while his father took the children to church. He said his mother would have been better off in church. I then aired my viewpoint: "Well, somebody had to do the work!" The minister smiled.

But he was right. His mother was missing a needful part of Sunday worship: praising God and listening to His Word.

Worldliness kept her from spiritual growth, just as worldliness kept Martha from hearing what Jesus had to say in her home.

Martha's desire to serve Jesus outweighed her desire to listen to His teaching. Her mind was set on getting a particular job done. But Jesus said Mary had chosen the good part, which was the spiritual food He was feeding her as she sat at His feet and listened. There were no Bibles in her day, so she seized the opportunity to listen to His word. What she was learning, no man could take from her. Martha, on the other hand, was distracted by the work of putting food on the table for people to eat. Jesus appreciated Martha's work, but she was missing out on the spiritual food He was serving.

When we spend hours looking after the well-being of other people, we tend to concentrate on them instead of giving proper time to our own spiritual growth. To keep growing spiritually, we need to be like Mary and take time to meditate on Jesus instead of focusing on our many responsibilities.

Jesus could easily have prepared a miracle for Martha if she had sat at His feet the way Mary did. After all, He fed the five thousand. He can prepare miracles for us, too, if we don't allow worldly busyness to keep us from taking hold of the good part: the Word of God.

Later, Jesus did perform a miracle for Martha and Mary. After He heard of Lazarus's death, He tarried awhile before going to Bethany. When Martha heard He was finally coming, she went to meet Him. She said to Jesus, "Lord, if You had been here, my brother would not have died. But even now I know that whatever You ask of God, God will give You" (John 11:21–22). Martha had great faith in Jesus, and she believed He was the Son of God.

Worldly Unpreparedness

Jesus told a parable about ten virgins who were to take part in a wedding ceremony. The five wise virgins took extra oil for their lamps, but the five foolish virgins took no oil. While waiting for the bridegroom, they all fell asleep. When the call came at midnight that the bridegroom was coming, the five foolish virgins found their lamps were going out, so they left to buy oil, but on their return, the doors were shut and locked. (See Matthew 25:1–12.)

The five foolish virgins were not prepared for the emergency of needing extra oil in their lamps at the wedding, and that kept them from entering into a time of great rejoicing. They lost blessings because they were unprepared to serve as bridesmaids.

Christians can lose blessings when we are not prepared to be of service to God. The unsaved lose blessings too—and not only in this lifetime. They will lose eternal life if they are not ready to meet God.

God expects us to be prepared for all crises. Sometimes that necessitates missing meals or losing sleep. However, since sleeping and eating are necessary and natural things, we have to be sensitive to when we should be fellowshipping with God and when we must focus on food or rest.

Worldly Cares

In another parable, Jesus told a story about a man sowing seeds, and He emphasized how important it is to have fertile soil. Our hearts are like rocky, untilled soil: they can keep God's Word from bringing forth fruit in our lives. In Luke 8:14 Jesus said of these seeds, "The ones that fell among thorns are those who, when they have heard, go out and are choked with cares, riches, and pleasures of life, and bring no fruit to maturity."

Producing good fruit takes a lot of time, as any farmer can tell you. I am a farmer's daughter, and I watched my father carefully prepare the soil to receive his precious seeds. He would never put expensive seed into soil that had not been cultivated and fertilized.

The rural people of Jesus' time were well acquainted with planting and harvesting problems. Jesus told them to work while it was day, for night was coming when no man could work.

Although He was speaking spiritually, He knew a farmer would understand His meaning. A farmer's work begins at sunup and ends at sundown, and there are many backbreaking jobs, such as hoeing and weeding, that have to be done before you can bring in a good harvest.

The cares of this world can keep us from spending time fellowshipping with the Father, which helps us grow spiritually. Jesus was reminding His listeners not to allow worldly cares to keep them from producing fruit for His kingdom.

Worldly Sleep

When Jesus was fellowshipping with His disciples at the Last Supper, and afterward on the Mount of Olives, their focus was on worldly matters. They were missing the spiritual connotations of that night.

Jesus warned them that they would be made to stumble before the night was over. Peter said, "Even if all are made to stumble, yet I will not be" (Mark 14:29). But Jesus told Peter that he would deny he knew Him three times before the cock crowed.

Jesus took them to a place called Gethsemane. He asked the rest of the disciples to sit and wait while He took Peter, James, and John a little farther away so that He might pray in private. He said to them, "My soul is exceedingly sorrowful, even to death. Stay here and watch with Me" (Matthew 26:38).

When He came back and found them sleeping, He said to Peter, "Simon, are you sleeping? Could you not watch one hour? Watch and pray, lest you enter into temptation. The spirit indeed is willing, but the flesh is weak" (Mark 14:37–38).

He left them to pray three times. Each time He came back, they were asleep. Jesus was prayerfully preparing for His crucifixion, but the disciples were allowing the worldliness of sleep to interfere with their preparation for the disasters in which they would soon become embroiled.

Earlier in the evening, Peter and the disciples told Jesus they were prepared to die for Him. Yet when the enemy attacked, they ran like rabbits. Later, after Peter denied knowing Jesus three times, he sorrowed deeply.

Worldly Perspectives

Jesus performed amazing miracles and taught many truths through parables, but His disciples did not understand the full impact of what they saw and heard. They looked at things through their five senses: sight, hearing, taste, smell, and touch. This kept them in worldliness.

When they encountered Jesus after the crucifixion before His ascension into heaven, they realized they had been fellowshipping with the power of God all along. Through the anointing of the Holy Spirit, they were able to stop seeing things through man's point of view, and the eyes of their understanding were enlightened (Ephesians 1:18). They became mighty men of God who led many others to the Lord. They even died the cruel death of martyrs because they learned to teach and preach the way Jesus did.

The religious people of His day could not tolerate the teachings of Jesus because He emphasized love while their emphasis was on the Old Testament laws. When the disciples understood the power given to man through the blood of Jesus, they were ready to promote His salvation for mankind, even unto death.

> For we have not followed cunningly devised fables, when we made known unto you the power and coming of our Lord Jesus Christ, but were eyewitnesses of His majesty. For he received from God the Father honor and glory, when there came such a voice to him from the excellent glory, This is my beloved Son, in whom I am well pleased. And this voice which came from heaven we heard, when we were with him in the holy mount. (2 Peter 1:16–18 KJV)

Peter reminded the brethren that the law came from Moses but grace and truth came from Jesus Christ. (See John 1:17.)

Worldly Good Works

By faith, Christians are the seed of Abraham, and we receive all the blessings of Abraham, plus the new covenant we have through the blood of Jesus.

Abraham was not counted as righteous because of his good works according to the law. His righteousness came by faith. "Therefore it is of faith that it might be according to grace, so that the promise might be sure to all the seed, not only to those who are of the law, but also to those who are of the faith of Abraham, who is the father of us all" (Romans 4:16).

Many people today think their good works will get them into heaven. But no one is good enough to enter God's kingdom. "But we are all as an unclean thing, and all our righteousnesses are as filthy rags; and we all do fade as a leaf; and our iniquities, like the wind, have taken us away" (Isaiah 64:6 KJV).

Jesus said that no one enters the kingdom of heaven except those who do the will of the Father. The will of the Father is to receive Jesus as our Savior and to fellowship with Him. With His love and grace, we can learn to walk in His ways.

Worldly Self-glorification

Paul tells us not to glory in anything except the cross of Jesus. "For in Christ Jesus neither circumcision availeth anything, nor uncircumcision, but a new creature. And as many as walk according to this rule, peace be on them, and mercy, and upon the Israel of God" (Galatians 6:15–16 KJV).

Those of us who are new creations in Christ Jesus must walk in the rules and regulations that being a child of God requires. Fellowshipping with God daily will help us reconcile the world to Him through the blood of Jesus. It will also help us maintain a "mouse-free house."

Worldly Condemnation of Others

I lived on the island of Rhodes, Greece, for a short time in the early 1950s when my first husband, Norman, was stationed aboard a United States Coast Guard Cutter. Prostitution was legal on the island, and the wives were concerned that it would cause problems for the men on the ship. Instead of condemning the prostitutes, an older woman commented that when she saw someone in a bad situation, this thought always crossed her mind: *There but for the grace of God go I.*

I was a young married woman at the time, and it amazed me that this older lady could express sympathy instead of condemnation for the prostitutes. Since then, I have noticed many places in the Gospels where Jesus dealt gently with the prostitutes He came in contact with. Because of His great love and grace, they could "go and sin no more" (John 8:11).

Paul said to the Ephesians, "For by grace you have been saved through faith, and that not of yourselves; it is the gift of God, not of works, lest anyone should boast" (Ephesians 2:8–9).

It is by the grace of God and the blood of Jesus that sin can be forgiven.

Worldly Wisdom

Ephesians 5:15–17 says, "See then that you walk circumspectly, not as fools but as wise, redeeming the time, because the days are evil. Therefore do not be unwise, but understand what the will of the Lord is." Paul urges us to be wise with the wisdom of God. While we are in this world, we will be surrounded and influenced by evil. The wisdom of God helps us keep up our guard.

Walking in God's wisdom and His ways requires continual discipline, but this is His will for us.

Worldly Desires

James tells us that we fall into Satan's traps of evil through our uncontrolled desires. "When lust hath conceived, it bringeth forth sin: and sin, when it is finished, bringeth forth death. Do not err, my beloved brethren. Every good gift and every perfect gift is from above, and cometh down from the Father of lights, with whom is no variableness, neither shadow of turning" (James 1:15–17 KJV).

God does not tempt people to sin—Satan does. God gave us a free will, and we make choices based on our own desires. When we are tempted by evil, the choices we make can bring forth sin in our lives; then we are at the mercy of our enemy.

We won't be so easily enticed by the ungodly pleasures of the world if we are fellowshipping with God daily.

The New Covenant

The sacrifice of God's Son, Jesus, for our sins put an end to God's intervention in the lives of people, and He no longer has to make any new covenants. He looks at the world now through the blood of Jesus.

If we walk in God's ways and listen to His Word, we are free from the curse of the law given to men through God's covenant with Moses. Galatians 3:13–14 tells us, "Christ has redeemed us from the curse of the law, having become a curse for us (for it is written, 'Cursed is everyone who hangs on a tree'), that the blessing of Abraham might come upon the Gentiles in Christ Jesus, that we might receive the promise of the Spirit through faith."

The new covenant God made with humankind provides a continual sacrifice for sins. There are no more animal sacrifices, no long list of rules and regulations, no more covenants required of men—just the precious blood of His Son, the price for our redemption from Satan's clutches.

When Jesus was crucified, the beatings He received and the weight of our sins changed His appearance dramatically. (See Isaiah 52:14.) We can't begin to imagine the entire filth of the world poured out on one person.

The Keys to Death and Hell

As Jesus hung on the cross, prepared to leave the presence of God and spend three days in Hades and preach to the dead, He cried out, "My God, My God, why have You forsaken Me?" (Mark 15:34). Jesus felt the enormous affliction sinners will feel on the day of judgment.

Jesus took away that unfathomable experience of being separated from God for eternity for all men who are willing to invite Him to live in their hearts, ask forgiveness for their sins, and accept Him as their Savior. He has paid the price for every horrible sin that people can commit.

> For Christ also suffered once for sins, the just for the unjust, that He might bring us to God, being put to death in the flesh but made alive by the Spirit, by whom also He went and preached to the spirits in prison, who formerly were disobedient, when once the Divine longsuffering waited in the days of Noah, while the ark was being prepared, in which a few, that is, eight souls, were saved through water. (1 Peter 3:18–20)

After Jesus rose from the dead, He made Himself known to Mary Magdalene and the women who were with her at His tomb, to the disciples, and to many others. Before He left the earth, Jesus delegated His authority to us that we might do the works that He did. (See Matthew 28:18–20; Mark 16:15–18.)

In Matthew 16:18 Jesus said to Peter, "I also say to you that you are Peter, and on this rock I will build My church, and the gates of Hades shall not prevail against it." As Christians, we need not fear spiritual death or hell. In Revelation 1:18, John heard these words: "I am He who lives, and was dead, and behold, I am alive forever more. Amen. And I have the keys of Hades and of Death."

Jesus has saved us from spiritual death and hell. But we must follow His teaching before we can have a mouse-free house and enjoy the things God has prepared for us in this life.

The Price

Jesus Christ paid the price when He went to Calvary.

No silver or gold in a treasury could pay the price for you or me.

It took the cross of Calvary to save our souls and set us free.

The price for man was blood, you see.

Unless that blood was shed for thee,

Sin and hell would get the victory.

PART ONE: NEGATIVE THINGS THAT COME AGAINST US

Chapter 4

Worldliness Today

Today, Christians are troubled with the same problems unbelievers face: divorce, drugs, illicit sex, unwed pregnancies, and poverty, to name just a few. If we walk in worldliness, we will reap the things of the world. Most Christians are not overcoming because they think and act as the world does.

Paul talks about this in Galatians. He says, "Walk in the Spirit, and you shall not fulfill the lust of the flesh. For the flesh lusts against the Spirit, and the Spirit against the flesh; and these are contrary to one another, so that you do not do the things that you wish" (Galatians 5:16–17).

To be overcomers, we need to identify the areas of our lives in which Satan tries to convince us to live in worldliness.

Worldly Priorities: Distractions

Each of us consists of a body, a soul, and a spirit. The soul houses the mind and emotions. The body will return to the dust from which it came. The spirit is eternal, because that is where God lives. Yet most of us spend the majority of our time catering to our bodies, educating our minds, and being driven by our emotions. Not much time is spent on spiritual growth or in communication with our Creator.

When we are living in worldliness, our priorities can get out of order. Then we will easily become distracted by the things of the world.

The enemy uses ordinary, commonplace, everyday activities to distract us, cause us to procrastinate, or convince us to sin. This can cause us to lose God's blessings and protection.

Since the daily distractions of this world can be eternally fatal, fellowshipping with God should be our number-one priority.

Worldly Priorities: Pleasures of Life

As I was praying and meditating one night, I heard these words in my spirit: *Life is not about bigger houses and finer cars, it's about relationships*. One of my children had recently earned a master's degree and bought a bigger house and a better car—not knowing that a divorce was imminent. God's warning in my heart helped prepare me for that tragedy.

God's interest is always in people, not things. He wants us to concentrate on our relationships with our families, friends, those we come in contact with on a daily basis, and Him.

Worldly priorities keep us focused on education, possessions, fame, fortune, and pursuing the pleasures of this life. While we are piling up earthly rewards, we may be losing our heavenly rewards. Paul says, "Every man's work shall be made manifest: for the day shall declare it, because it shall be revealed by fire; and the fire shall try every man's work of what sort it is" (1 Corinthians 3:13 KJV). All of our worldly accomplishments and achievements will burn; only the relationships we work on will remain.

Worldly Inattention

Years ago, when I lived in Missouri, a friend of mine kept a lemon tree in her living room near a window. The tree produced many good lemons for her use. When she moved to Greece, she gave me her tree. I was thrilled.

I put it in front of my patio door. About every three months it bloomed profusely. But the lemons grew only to about the size of my thumb before they dropped off. More blooms came, and more tiny lemons grew and dropped off. I moved my unhappy tree to different locations, hoping it would bring more fruit to maturity, but the poor thing kept blooming and bearing thumb-size lemons until it began to lose its leaves. It was dying a slow death. With great sorrow and much regret, I gave it a decent burial in a recycle bin.

One day as I was reading about bringing fruit to maturity, I thought of that lemon tree. During my meditation, this thought came from the Holy Spirit: *You can't raise healthy plants if you don't pay enough attention to them.*

I then recalled a television program I had seen on how to raise healthy plants. The man on the show had said that plants, like people, desire attention and communication. So he talked to his plants every day.

My mother worked diligently with her garden and house plants. She had a "green thumb" and everything grew beautifully for her. She spent many hours with her flowers and her vegetable garden. She gave each plant individual attention—just as she had given to her eight children. My mom examined each of her plants daily to see if they needed fertilizer or water, if they were being bothered by disease, or if they seemed happy with their light. For her this was a labor of love. Love is the principal design in the tapestry of life, for God is love and He created everything (1 John 4:16).

As I meditated on my failure to grow lemons, I realized I had also started to grow fruit for God's kingdom many times, but grew tired and impatient, so the fruit fell to the ground prematurely. This was a revelation to me, and it spurred me on in my desire to produce mature fruit that would abound to my account in heaven.

Now that I live in California, I am able to raise beautiful plants in my home and yard. I have learned to pay attention to their needs. Yet many times, I find myself slipping back into my patterns of neglect.

We need to give God our attention daily; otherwise, we will slip back into old behavior patterns. Bearing fruit for the kingdom is our sacrifice to God. It requires patience and the discipline of hard work. But with patience, we can yield an abundant harvest for our Lord.

Worldly Habits

A simple incident in my early childhood produced in me motivation, desire, and a lifelong habit of good dental hygiene.

When I was in second grade, our teacher emphasized the importance of having clean teeth. She said if we didn't brush the food out at night before going to sleep, little demons with hammers would come in and make holes in our teeth called cavities. Since I had a vivid imagination, I was determined those little demons wouldn't find anything to hammer on in my teeth at night.

My teacher motivated me through her illustration, and I developed the desire to have clean teeth. A habit was established that I still don't break today under any circumstance. Regardless of the late hour at home or on a plane, I brush my teeth before I sleep. No distractions can keep me from my nightly ritual. When dentists look in my mouth, they are amazed at how healthy my teeth are.

We can choose to develop good habits or bad ones, to walk in God's discipline or in the world's discipline. Our Master calls us to be experienced spiritual soldiers who are disciplined, ready to march into battle and carry His banner high. We do not allow the enemy to intimidate us, because we know that "the battle is the Lord's" (1 Samuel 17:47). To be victorious, we must visualize the battle, just as I visualized those little demons hammering on my teeth.

Why We Were Created

Once we identify the areas of worldliness in our lives, we can defeat them by acknowledging who we are and recognizing that we were created by God for His purposes, which bring honor and glory to Him and ultimate joy to us.

Created More than Angels

The Holy Spirit gave me a beautiful revelation one day in church while we were singing songs of praise and worship. I felt the joy of the Lord so strongly in my spirit I thought, *I wish I were an angel.* I thought being an angel would put me closer to God. But the Spirit surprised me with this thought: *You're more than an angel; you are a child of God.*

Romans 8:16–17 says, "The Spirit Himself bears witness with our spirit that we are children of God, and if children, then heirs—heirs of God and joint heirs with Christ, if indeed we suffer with Him, that we may also be glorified together."

After receiving that revelation, I felt a tiny piece of the exquisite ecstasy that will be mine when I am united with my heavenly Father in His kingdom. That lasted for a fleeting moment before I dropped back to reality in this world.

We tend to admire the angels of God because they bask in His glory while we struggle to free our earthly bodies and souls from the tentacles of worldliness. But because we are children of God, we will judge the angels and the world. First Corinthians 6:3 says, "Do you not know that we shall judge angels? How much more, things that pertain to this life?"

The angels do not have the spirit of Christ in them because they were not crucified with Him. Romans 6:4 says, "Therefore we were buried with Him through baptism into death, that just as Christ was raised from the dead by the glory of the Father, even so we also should walk in newness of life."

Created to be Spiritual Warriors

We are to be active warriors in the battle against our enemy, Satan. But before we step out into the world each day, we must put on our spiritual armor. Since we are wrestling against wickedness in heavenly places, we have to put on our helmet of salvation, gird our waist with truth, don our breastplate of righteousness, grab our shield of faith, shod our feet with peace, and take the sword of the

Spirit, which is the Word of God. When we have done all we know to do, we are to stand (Ephesians 6:12–17).

God puts powerful weapons at our disposal for use against the enemy. Yet if we forget to put on our armor in our daily battles, we are blatantly ignoring what God has given us. With salvation, truth, righteousness, peace, faith, and prayers, we can win victories for the kingdom of God.

Created as the Spirit of God

Many years ago on television, I saw a blind, mentally and physically handicapped man who could play anything on the piano if he had heard the music. His mother, who adopted him because of his handicaps, kept praying God would give him a talent, something that would make his life worthwhile. God honored her request.

When I heard him play, I was so astonished I thought of Job 7:17 and asked, *"Lord, what is man that you should exalt him?"* The answer came to me: *He is the Spirit of God.*

Genesis 2:7 tells us, "The Lord God formed man of the dust of the ground, and breathed into his nostrils the breath of life; and man became a living being."

The great Holy Spirit dwells in each of us. That tiny piece of God's breath that comes into us separates us from the animal kingdom. The human spirit is eternal because God is eternal. When we allow the Holy Spirit to come into our lives through the blood of Jesus and teach us how to live according to God's rules and regulations, that piece of God's breath returns to Him forever.

Created for God's Enjoyment

Once, as I was thinking about the evil things people do and how loving and kind God is to us in spite of our failures, I asked God why He created man. In my spirit I heard, *When people create things with their talents, what do you think gives them the most pleasure?*

After some reflection, I answered, "Sharing our talents and creations with others."

God created the world for the same reason. He loves to create.

He also created man to enjoy His creation; He gave man gifts for creating and the enjoyment of sharing those gifts. He created us to be like Him. His desire for us is "to know the love of Christ which passes knowledge; that you may be filled with all the fullness of God" (Ephesians 3:19). When we are filled with the fullness of God, we can enjoy the beauties of this life and His creation.

Our Creator has gone to so much trouble to show His love for mankind, even the angels sometimes wonder about it. One said, "What is man, that thou art mindful of him? or the son of man, that thou visitest him? Thou madest him a little lower than the angels; thou crownedst him with glory and honour, and didst set him over the works of thy hands" (Hebrews 2:6–7 KJV).

Though we are often awed by the glory angels have, they wonder in amazement about the great love God has for us.

Created to Be Heirs

Angels were created to be servants of God, but men were created to be sons of God. We are heirs, not servants, because in us the old spirit of self has been replaced with the Holy Spirit. Paul said to the Galatians, "For ye are all the children of God by faith in Christ Jesus" (Galatians 3:26 KJV).

"Therefore you are no longer a slave but a son, and if a son, then an heir of God through Christ" (Galatians 4:7).

Created to Evangelize

God gave us rules and regulations, including the Ten Commandments, to help us live as children of His. But He knew we would have to be redeemed from the curses of disobeying those rules, so He sent His Son to be crucified for our sins. When we become mature enough, the glory of God will fall over us and the world will want what we have.

PART ONE: NEGATIVE THINGS THAT COME AGAINST US

God has special jobs for each of us to do for His kingdom, and He doesn't want us trying to delegate these jobs to other people we think might be more spiritual. Every Christian can be an evangelist.

Several years ago, when a few big Christian ministries were having serious trouble, I asked God what was happening. I received this message in my spirit: *Some will increase and others will decrease.* The Holy Spirit informed me that God was not relying on big ministries to spread His Word. He wants every corner of the world evangelized by individual Christians so the name of Jesus will be heard under very rock, in every hole, and behind every tree.

Every Christian is responsible for whatever ground his or her feet tread on. In order to take our territory for Jesus Christ, we will need the kind of sacrificial love that comes only from God.

When our spirits are fully connected to His Spirit, we will know the love that passes knowledge: Christ's love for us (Ephesians 3:19). That understanding will give us victory in our battle against the enemy. If we put worldly achievement first in our lives, we will miss opportunities to bring fruit to God from His vineyard (the world), and that will affect His rewards for us in heaven.

Created to Be His Children

Many years ago, after the Holy Spirit taught me many things about God's disciplines, I felt depressed because I knew I had allowed Satan to rob me of blessings. I wondered how God could stand His children sometimes.

As parents, we can identify with God's problems. Our hearts grow heavy when we watch our young people put their time and energy into worldliness, not paying attention to their spiritual growth until they become vulnerable to Satan and sin.

In answer to my questions, the Holy Spirit used the same technique Jesus used in His day. To help me understand God's ways, He taught me parables about the everyday experiences of life that relate spiritual things to physical things.

The Lord urged me to recall memories concerning my firstborn child. When Norman saw our baby girl minutes after she was born, he asked what was wrong with her. The doctor laughed at his concern. He told my husband that our baby was covered with scum from childbirth, and she would look different after she was cleaned up.

The Holy Spirit explained to me that just as newborns are cleaned up from the scum of physical birth, we are cleaned up from the scum of the world when we are born again spiritually. After we become Christians we are clean in God's eyes.

While I was meditating on the comparison of physical birth and spiritual birth, I received a series of startling questions through the Holy Spirit. He asked if I would be angry with a child who was one year old and didn't act like he was two. Of course I replied no. He said, *I wouldn't either.*

Next He asked if I would be angry with a three-year-old who didn't act or think like a six-year-old. Again I answered no. His answer was the same: *I wouldn't either.*

Then He asked if I would be angry with a twelve-year-old who didn't act or think like an adult. My answer was still no, and His was still *I wouldn't either.*

God's children have spiritual ages just as our children have physical ages. Some of His children never reach maturity, but He fellowships with them according to their spiritual stages, just as we fellowship with our children according to their physical stages of life.

That reminded me of a question I had asked Him some years earlier, when through a dream I saw the head of Jesus on each step of a ladder reaching up as far as I could see. At that time, He explained that Christians are on the ladder of life, and as they climb the spiritual rungs, Jesus is there for each individual. We are not hurried up the ladder of life but climb according to our spiritual growth and ability.

God is looking at the world through the blood of Jesus, so He does not get angry with us, regardless of the level of our spiritual maturity, any more than we would get angry with a mentally or physically handicapped child who can only reach a certain level of maturity.

Christians are hard enough for God to deal with because of their rebellious hearts, but I wondered how He felt about unsaved people.

The Holy Spirit then reminded me of a spontaneous abortion I'd experienced. I went to the doctor one day and he told me I was pregnant, but he explained that my symptoms indicated I would probably lose the pregnancy. I lost it the next day. A friend of mine asked how I felt about the loss of the baby. I told her that I had not formed a relationship with the child. So while I felt some sadness, it wasn't near as shattering as if I'd gone through a partial or full-term pregnancy and then lost the baby.

As I considered my feelings, I realized that God thinks of people who have not been "born again of the Spirit" as aborted children. Though they are still His children, they are in the womb of the world, and He doesn't develop a relationship with them until they are born again.

His sadness is tempered by the fact that He never knew those who are aborted into hell. Jesus said, "And then I will declare to them, 'I never knew you; depart from Me, you who practice lawlessness!'" (Matthew 7:23).

God has done everything He can to keep men and women out of hell, but it is up to us to accept His reconciliation. "All things are of God, who has reconciled us to Himself through Jesus Christ, and has given us the ministry of reconciliation, that is, that God was in Christ reconciling the world to Himself, not imputing their trespasses to them, and has committed to us the word of reconciliation" (2 Corinthians 5:18–19).

PART ONE: NEGATIVE THINGS THAT COME AGAINST US

Created to Walk in the Spirit

The Holy Spirit leads us by reminding us of the Word of God and giving us revelation knowledge of the Scripture according to our experiences. We cannot walk in the Spirit without following the commandment given by Jesus that we love each other the way He loves us (John15:12).

Paul was worried about the gospel being distorted by false teachers among the Galatians, so he said, "If we live in the Spirit, let us also walk in the Spirit. Let us not be desirous of vain glory, provoking one another, envying one another" (Galatians 5:25–26 KJV).

If we take our eyes off Jesus and look at our circumstances, we will fall into worldliness, which results in the fruit of the flesh. The fruit of the Spirit gives us the peace, joy, and love that help us become profitable servants for God's work in His kingdom.

The Word tells us that the results of the harvest depend on the type of seed that is sown. Paul said God cannot be mocked or deceived. "For he that soweth to his flesh shall of the flesh reap corruption; but he that soweth to the Spirit shall of the Spirit reap life everlasting" (Galatians 6:8 KJV).

Satan can't take away our salvation, but he can keep us from receiving blessings or from being a blessing to others. He can cause us to be immature Christians instead of the spiritual warriors God needs for His end-time army.

Created to Walk in Fellowship

Men may be able to accomplish every goal they desire, including wealth, fame and glory. But without fellowshipping with God through the blood of Jesus, they remain miserable. The spirits of men cry out to be connected to the Spirit that gives them life.

The first step we must take in fellowshipping with God is to accept the blood of Jesus for our salvation. Then the Holy Spirit comes to dwell in us, and through Him our spirits are reborn and renewed. As our counselor, teacher, and friend, He reminds us of God's Word, illuminates the Word for us, and convicts us when we sin. Though Satan tries to condemn us before the Lord, Jesus stands at the right hand of the Father and intercedes for our transgressions.

When we face a big battle against Satan, we seem to be able to gather the necessary strength to endure. But the continuous barrage he launches against us with worldliness leaves us weary, battle scarred, and discouraged. However, Jesus left us the Holy Spirit to assist us in all battles of spiritual warfare.

We are warned about Satan in 1 John 3:8: "He who sins is of the devil, for the devil has sinned from the beginning. For this purpose the Son of God was manifested, that He might destroy the works of the devil."

God wants us to fellowship with Him so He can show us how to "fight the good fight of faith" and "lay hold on eternal life" (1 Timothy 6:12).

Chapter 5

Battling Worldliness

When my granddaughter Ashley was very young, I promised her I would get her a dog when she turned ten years old. As her tenth birthday drew near, she reminded me of my promise. But at that time her mom and dad were divorced, and her mother didn't have the time or facilities to care for a dog. Since she lives in Missouri and I live in California, I got Ashley the dog when she came to visit me during the holidays in December. We agreed that I would train the pup and keep her until Ashley's family could take care of her.

Ashley named her dog Nicole, after her favorite teacher. She is a beautiful gold-and-white Shih Tzu with warm brown eyes, black-tipped ears, and a long pink tongue that hangs out of her mouth most of the time. She has bloodlines that would satisfy royalty, with ancestors winning several prizes in various dog shows.

However, Nicole is a barbarian and a renegade. She spent her first six weeks in a huge cardboard box with three other puppies, where she learned to climb and claw the box like a cat—a habit she continued with my patio door and furniture. She chewed on everything, even metal objects. I constantly thrust bones in her mouth, hoping to distract her for a while, the way a parent sticks a pacifier in a baby's mouth to keep him from crying. But nothing seemed to quench Nicole's insatiable appetite for chewing.

At the time I brought this dog into my home, I didn't realize what I had agreed to. She certainly has been a handful! But through her antics, I have learned several lessons about battling worldliness.

Being What We Were Created to Be

I spent hours during the winter months in the backyard trying to train Nicole and picking up after her and my other dog, Annie. Nicole's personality was quite different from Annie's. To her, discipline was a game. Whenever I thought she had gone too far, she escaped by outrunning me. Scolding caused her to bark or growl in a way that made me think she was attempting to justify her actions.

Her greatest joy seemed to be in pulling the little plastic bag containing her "nuisances" out of my hands. When she tired playing with it, she'd gleefully run ahead and play with the feces, expressing the same delight children display when hunting Easter eggs. Any deposits I overlooked she brought to our patio door. I think this was her way of saying she was better at the game than I was.

The veterinary clinic gave me a chemical that was supposed to have such a bad odor that dogs would not enjoy the feces. But that didn't affect Nicole.

I fretted, ranted, and prayed about her problems. Finally, the Lord impressed on my spirit that Nicole didn't really understand what I wanted. Just like His people don't always understand what He wants from them because they are used to doing things the world's way. Nicole was doing a natural thing that many dogs do, not knowing that I found it extremely objectionable. I needed to exercise patience and remember that she was being what the Lord created her to be: a dog.

Fretting

One day, as I was complaining to my husband about Nicole, the Lord interrupted me with this thought: *Stop trying to think like a dog.* I laughed and told my husband about the message. But later I meditated on this gentle reprimand.

After thinking about it for a while, I realized I was allowing Nicole to consume too much of my time and attention. I was letting her harass me to the point where my mind was constantly on her. God considered my fretting about Nicole's wrongdoings a form of worldliness.

Psalm 37:8 says, "Cease from anger, and forsake wrath; do not fret—it only causes harm." When we are fretting about worldly problems, we are actually stirring up more evil around us.

Enjoying the Filth of the World

Another day, while I was again meditating on the problems I was having with Nicole, I received this revealing message in my spirit: *Nicole enjoys playing around in the filth of her world just as some of My people enjoy playing around in the filth of their world. You want Nicole to adjust to your ways and your desires. That is what I want from My people too. With patience and love, they will eventually respond to Me.*

What a mighty God we serve! His mercies are new every morning (Lamentations 3:22–23). All He wants from us is to walk in agreement with Him, not in agreement with the world. "Wherefore come out from among them, and be ye separate, saith the Lord, and touch not the unclean thing; and I will receive you, and will be a Father unto you, and ye shall be my sons and daughters, saith the Lord Almighty" (2 Corinthians 6:17–18 KJV).

God does not want us to wallow in the ways of the world any more than I want Nicole to play in the filth of her world. I want her to be obedient and disciplined, to live by rules and regulations that conform to my desires.

Accepting Consequences

Nicole is slowly learning that trouble is something she doesn't like. When I reprimand her, she does a quick spread eagle that would satisfy any policeman. Then, to make sure all is well, she does a belly crawl to me.

Nicole is coming to realize that there are consequences to pay for acts of rebellion. She desires my love and acceptance.

The war isn't over, but at least we have some moments of peace in the course of a day. Eventually, her disobedience will stop. Then we can have peace and love—the same desire God has for us. He wants us to respond to animals and people the way He does; with infinite patience instead of anger and frustration.

Looking at the Heart

With all of Nicole's shortcomings, she has one outstanding feature: a good heart. She demonstrated this while on an evening walk. She was pulling me, trying to catch up with Annie and my husband, Andy. Suddenly, my foot slipped on the damp grass. As I tumbled down the hill, I lost her leash.

"Nicole!" I cried.

She ran back and licked my ear and my face. Andy was concerned about my fall, but all I could do was lie on the ground and laugh while Nicole treated my tumble the best way she could: with her tongue.

Many Christians are like Nicole: untamed, but with big hearts. And the heart is what God looks at. He is teaching me through Nicole how short I am on patience and how I can learn to love the seemingly unlovable. He has used this little dog to remind me how much I allow worldliness to consume my time and affect my thinking.

Finding Sufficiency in Grace

After rearing four children and training their various pets, I thought I could operate spiritually under pressure. But Nicole often reminds me that old habits die hard.

One day I complained to the Lord about a problem I was dealing with, and these words came to me: *I have given you wisdom to rise above it.* And so He has. But it's up to me to use that wisdom.

Paul pleaded with God three times for the messenger of Satan to depart from him. God answered by saying, "My grace is sufficient for you, for My strength is made perfect in weakness" (2 Corinthians 12:9). God's grace is sufficient for us regardless of how we are persecuted by the enemy. He gives strength and wisdom through His Word to help us rise above the problems we face.

Learning to Adapt

When Nicole was almost a year old, she and Ashley took their long-awaited trip to Missouri. Our biggest problem was trying to get Nicole calm enough to ride in her little carrier on the plane. The veterinarian suggested we try half the usual dose of a strong tranquilizer. All it did was make her legs wobble. She was as hyper as ever.

The next morning we gave her the full dose and off they went. Nicole never slept, but she was relaxed. She climbed out of her cage and sat calmly in Ashley's lap during most of the plane ride.

Her first night in her new home was fine. However, the family had planned one last outing for the summer, and they felt that Nicole might be a problem on the trip. So they left her in a shelter overnight. When they picked her up the following evening, they discovered she had developed a bladder infection. The veterinarian said it was due to stress.

After speaking to Ashley about the problem, I asked to talk to Nicole. When Nicole heard my voice, she made a strange sound. "Grandma," Ashley exclaimed, "did you hear that? She cried!"

With lots of love from Ashley, Nicole got over her trauma and adjusted to her new environment. Her boisterous behavior returned, and she continued to wreck havoc doing the usual tricks that always got her into trouble.

Like God's rebellious children, Nicole continued in her bad behavior until she got caught. Then, for a moment, she stopped her pilfering and plundering. But she always returned to her familiar behavior patterns.

Making Adjustments

Nicole was a great companion for Ashley, but her antics kept Ashley very busy. Autumn is rainy in Missouri, and Nicole loved wallowing in the mud around trees and flowerbeds. Nicole had to be left outside when the family was gone because she couldn't be trusted in the house. Ashley had to give her a bath two or three times a day.

As winter approached, Ashley's mother expressed concern that Nicole might not adjust to being left all day, in some cases all night. We decided that Ashley should bring Nicole back to California when she came to visit me in December.

Nicole was glad to be back in her California home with her canine friend, Annie. And Ashley enjoyed her visit with me. When she had to leave without her precious pet, it was a sad parting. Still, we both knew it was better for Nicole to be with me. I told Ashley that Nicole would always be our love dog—a bond that ties the three of us together.

Changing Hearts

Even though Nicole has a barbaric nature, she has become a loving dog. When she is in the house, she stays at my side when I'm standing and nestles against me every time I sit down. (Andy and I never allowed dogs on couches or chairs in our homes before we had Nicole.) If I leave a room, she looks frantically for me. If I go outside when she is in the house, she cries until I come back and let her out to be with me.

Nicole has won a special place in my heart. Andy once commented that if something happened to him, I would probably allow Nicole to sleep with me. But that would be difficult for me. I have always believed in the old cliché that cleanliness is next to godliness, and sleeping with dogs doesn't fall into that category.

Andy gets as miffed at Nicole's wrongdoings as I do, but he has not escaped the little pup's ability to reel him in with love.

My husband has always loved fast, dangerous rides. At sixteen, he hopped freight trains from Nebraska to California. In World War II, he joined a glider division. The gliders did not have engines, so they were towed by large planes to strategic spots, then cut loose from the plane and allowed to glide to the ground with men and cargo (a dangerous feat—the gliders were never used a second time).

At the age of seventy-nine, Andy rode in a police car with one of our grandsons, complete with sirens.

Andy has always wanted to take a wild fire truck ride with horns blaring. That fantasy now includes Nicole riding by his side, her ears flapping in the wind.

Forgiving Trespasses

As much as Annie loves Nicole, she refuses to let that pup get away with any shenanigans. One night, as I gave them their biscuits before bedtime, I got distracted and forgot which dog had received the first one. So I threw the other biscuit into the air. Of course, Nicole got it. A few minutes later I heard the short barks Annie makes when she wants to remind me that I have forgotten something important to her. My first reaction was to scold her. But as she walked away with head bent low, I thought of the biscuits. When I gave her the coveted biscuit, she forgave my trespasses and went quietly to bed.

Showing Patience and Love

Nicole has taught me that love does cover a multitude of sins. Each night as my husband and I pray, Nicole curls up under our feet while Annie lies in front of the fireplace. As we pray, we forget all the distractions and ill will the day has produced. We know our heavenly Father is pleased to see us worshipping Him in peace and love.

Nicole may never be able to change her obnoxious behavior, but she desires to be loved and she tries to please us. Just as we strive to become disciplined to walk in God's ways and so experience

His blessings, Nicole is slowly changing as we use patience and love—God's keys for success in His kingdom.

Seeing Life from Nicole's Point of View

I was penned up for weeks in a cardboard box with three other noisy puppies. They were adopted before I was. That's because I had a problem. Since my mom chewed on my belly button after I was born, I developed a hernia that needed surgery. My hyperactive personality also discouraged people from wanting to adopt me. (Maybe Mom chewed on my belly button because I made her nervous too.)

God finally found me a good home. My new home already had another dog. Annie is a prim and prissy poodle who doesn't like rolling in the dirt or getting her feet wet. She wants to stay out of trouble, but I love excitement and adventure.

When I get caught causing problems, I want to justify my actions by explaining that I need to explore to learn. But it's hard to present my viewpoint to people because their doggy language is limited.

Even though my outdoor adventures cause me to get yelled at, I still like to see what is going on in the world. I recently found a way to see the street from inside the house. The padded window seat in front of the living room window gives me a good view of the neighborhood. But the other day I chewed on the windowsills and barked at people. It made Grandma angry, and she closed the shutters, so I can't sit in my favorite spot anymore.

I had a great adventure when I flew on a plane to Missouri to be with Ashley. I lived with her for a few months. Guess I bothered people there, too, because Ashley brought me back to California. Annie and I both love Ashley, and we look forward to her visits with us.

Although I miss Ashley, it is good to be home with Annie, Grandma, and Grandpa. Evenings are the best part of the day for Annie and me. We always go for a walk with Grandpa before dinner. During prayer time, we curl up under the table at their feet. Later, when we watch TV, Annie takes a nap in front of the fireplace while I snuggle up on the couch with my grandma, or I sit by her chair while she works at the computer. Then it's bone time! And off to bed we go.

I love the family God gave me. I want God to help my family adjust to my doggy traits, and I want to make them happy by getting rid of my bad habits.

Sometimes when they pray, I hear them ask God to help them get rid of their bad habits too. That makes me very happy.

Appreciating Uniqueness

Nicole still plays in the loose dirt around trees or flowers, and with her blonde hair, she looks like a dirty ragamuffin regardless of how often she is groomed. Annie has dainty feet and hates to put them in wet grass, but Nicole thrives in getting muddy.

Our Creator has given each animal its own personality, just as He has done with people. He never creates two things identically. There is always something distinctive about each of His creations, whether human, animal, or flora. Each petal of a rose, each shape of a leaf, has His special stamp on it. So does each human being and animal.

Uniqueness has become a lost art among people today. Their focus is on production. If they make something good, they want to produce a lot of it, exactly the same way.

When I tried to change Nicole's audacious personality into the tranquil personality of my little poodle, God was not pleased. He is equally displeased when we try to make all of our children fit into one mold. That struggle for the perfect mold is an attempt in futility. It will never happen in this lifetime.

The curses Adam and Eve brought to mankind and to the earth, through disobedience to God's commandment, affected all forms of life. Animals, like people, have a hard time living in this world God cursed. He desires that we nurture and protect His animal kingdom. They are just as essential to our survival as we are to theirs.

All of creation is waiting to be redeemed.

> For we know that the whole creation groans and labors with birth pangs together until now. Not only that, but we also who have the firstfruits of the Spirit, even we ourselves groan within ourselves, eagerly waiting for the adoption, the redemption of our body. (Romans 8:22–23)

When Christ returns to restore His kingdom to its original state, the wolf, lamb, leopard, goat, calf, and lion will all lie down together. A little child shall play around a viper's den; a nursing child shall play by a cobra's hole; nothing shall hurt or destroy. The cow and the bear will graze together. The lion will eat straw like the ox. The physical world is waiting and groaning for that time. (See Isaiah 11:6–9.)

Letting the Holy Spirit Be Our Guide

God has prepared a way for people to escape from the grip of the strong arms of the worldliness octopus. Instead of being pulled in by its many tentacles, God wants us to reach out and grab hold of the hand that can save us. The Holy Spirit can teach, motivate, and inspire each individual Christian through his or her own experiences—if He is allowed to—until the desire to fellowship with God becomes as natural as the desire to sleep and eat.

Jesus says in John 14:26, "The Helper, the Holy Spirit, whom the Father will send in My name, He will teach you all things, and bring to your remembrance all things that I said to you."

With the help of the Holy Spirit, a Christian can encounter the storms of life and not be anxious. He can be a wise, experienced captain of his ship, focused on God and His Word, knowing his soul and his fate are in the Master's hands.

The Holy Spirit can help us maintain a mouse-free house.

Father, we thank You for the beauties of the world You created for our enjoyment. We thank You especially for the great spiritual lessons You teach us in Your animal kingdom. We pray we will be good caretakers of that kingdom and not be abusive or destructive with any part of it. We look forward to the day when all creation is redeemed from the curses brought upon the earth by worldliness and sin. Amen.

To the Lord: An Ode of Praise

To my Shepherd, gentle and brave, I will sing an ode of praise.

You're my Savior, and with pride, under Your wings I hide.

Hallelujah, hallelujah, hallelujah, praise the Lord!

You're my Master and my Guide, in You I trust and confide.

When the storms of life prevail, You're the port to which I sail.

Hallelujah, hallelujah, hallelujah, praise the Lord.

O You're the rock to which I cling, and of Your grace I sing.

And throughout eternity may my praises ring for thee.

Hallelujah, hallelujah, hallelujah, praise the Lord!

Discipline #2: Negative Words

Negative words have the power to curse.
Positive words have the power to bless.

Let the words of my mouth and the meditation of my heart
be acceptable in Your sight, O Lord, my strength and my Redeemer.
(Psalm 19:14)

Chapter 6

Satan's Lie or God's Truth

The Greek myths are ancient stories describing relationships between men and gods, highlighting good vs. evil. According to one Greek myth, evil was contained in Pandora's Box; when it was opened, evil escaped. However, the Bible tells us the true story of how evil was let loose in the world.

Satan is evil personified. He knew that disobedience to God's Word would allow evil to rear its ugly head to entrap, enslave, and persecute human beings. So his first lie was told to Adam and Eve to convince them that God did not mean what He said. They accepted Satan's lie over God's truth and ate the forbidden fruit. The process of physical death entered their bodies. God cursed what He had created.

Satan's curses still prevail against men today through unbelief. The Bible says in Proverbs 26:2, "Like a flitting sparrow, like a flying swallow, so a curse without cause shall not alight."

After God listed the blessings and curses in Deuteronomy 27 and 28, He asked the Israelites to obey His word, to choose the blessings instead of the curses. Then He added, "I call heaven and earth as witnesses today against you, that I have set before you life and death, blessing and cursing; therefore choose life, that both you and your descendants may live" (Deuteronomy 30:19).

Inheriting the Curses

Years ago, the expression "bad seed" was commonly used in connection with children who continued with problems of immorality generation after generation. The problems were often related to such things as rebellion, drug addiction, alcoholism, trouble with the law, or having illegitimate babies. If the children dropped out of school, their illiteracy usually generated poverty, which caused them to live unproductive, unhappy lives.

Weaknesses in the character of a person are actually curses. These curses predispose us to inherit certain undesirable physical or mental traits, or influence us to make bad choices, as Adam and Eve did. These curses were instituted in the Ten Commandments when God said, "I, the Lord your God, am a jealous God, visiting the iniquity of the fathers upon the children to the third and fourth generations of those who hate Me" (Exodus 20:5).

God showed the Israelites how they could be free of the curses in Deuteronomy 30:14. He said, "The word is very near you, in your mouth and in your heart, that you may do it."

God in His great mercy has always desired people to be free from the curses of sin. The Scripture says Jesus was the Word made flesh, and He came and dwelt among us (John 1:14). Even though He was crucified for our sins, and His death sets us free from the curse of the law, we still have to walk in the discipline of God's Word; otherwise, curses can plague us, because we live in a cursed world. Instead of following the ways of the world, we must focus on the Word of God. Our words and God's Word must be in agreement before we can reverse the power of His curses.

Inheriting the Truth

The Scriptures teach us the truths of God's Word and how we are to apply them in our daily walk with Him. If we continue to ignore God's Word, Satan's first lie will keep rolling its destruction against us like a bowling ball knocking down the pins. We will never be free from the entanglements of sin in this world unless we use God's Word and walk in His ways.

John 8:32 says, "You shall know the truth, and the truth shall make you free." We can be blessed instead of cursed.

The following Scriptures proclaim the truth in God's Word.

- "Forever, O Lord, Your word is settled in heaven" (Psalm 119:89).
- "My covenant I will not break, nor alter the word that has gone out of My lips" (Psalm 89:34).
- "The words of the Lord are pure words, like silver tried in a furnace of earth, purified seven times" (Psalm 12:6).
- "The entirety of Your word is truth, and every one of Your righteous judgments endures forever" (Psalm 119:160).
- "Every word of God is pure; He is a shield to those who put their trust in Him. Do not add to His words, lest He reprove you, and you be found a liar" (Proverbs 30:5–6).
- "Heaven and earth will pass away, but My words will by no means pass away" (Matthew 24:35).

Since God and Jesus are eternal, the Word is eternal. Jesus came to earth and made the Word flesh and blood by being born of woman so that He might be able to better understand the problems of men. He redeemed our sins by going to the cross, then He returned to heaven and is alive today. So the Word is alive!

Putting Truth in Action

When circumstances do not line up with God's Word, we need to examine the source of our trouble. If we don't continually increase our faith in God's Word, Satan will pawn His lies off on us. For our faith to be profitable in our lives, we must accompany God's Word with actions. We are reminded of this in James 2:26: "For as the body without the spirit is dead, so faith without works is dead also."

Abraham believed God's Word when he was told his descendants would be as numerous as the sands of the seashore. Even when God asked him to sacrifice his son on the altar, Abraham was willing to do that. He knew God would honor His Word regardless of how the circumstances looked. Abraham's faith was accompanied by action. God honored him by making him the father of nations. For us to receive the blessings of Abraham, our faith must be accompanied by actions too.

Chapter 7

Power in God's Word

Many years ago, as I was pondering the failures of Christians to receive answers from God, He illuminated Scriptures that Jesus used when He spoke about the problem and said, "Hypocrites! Well did Isaiah prophesy about you, saying: 'These people draw near to Me with their mouth, and honor Me with their lips, but their heart is far from Me. And in vain they worship Me, teaching as doctrines the commandments of men'" (Matthew15:7–9, quoting Isaiah 29:13).

As I meditated on the Scriptures in Isaiah, my thoughts turned to the power in a gun. When you put bullets in the chamber, aim at your target, and pull the trigger, power goes forth. However, if you put those same bullets in the barrel, the bullets will fall to the ground. The gun barrel is only a vessel the bullets go through. The bullets have to be in the chamber to give them power.

The mouth is the vessel that words go through. If words originate from the mouth and not the heart (spirit), there is no power behind them. If God's Word is to be effective in our lives, our spirits must be connected to God's Spirit, where the power lies. If His word goes no further than the mouth, there will be no answer, "for the kingdom of God is not in word but in power" (1 Corinthians 4:20).

Electricity has been around since the beginning of time. However, people lived many centuries before they learned how to harness the power of electricity with generators and make use of that power through electrical gadgets. Now our way of life is so plugged into electricity, if we have a power failure, many things we take for granted grind to a halt. When that happens we become uncomfortable because we miss the blessings electricity brings us.

God is the vital source for our spiritual power. Our hearts are the generators that He uses to harness power for His words. Just as we got along for centuries without the power of electricity, we can get along without being plugged into God's power; however, if our spirits don't plug into the power of God's Spirit, Satan can keep us from enjoying the blessings God has planned for us. It's comparable to going back and living in the days before Jesus came to become the Light of the world.

Power to Create

When God spoke to the waters, the light, the darkness, the seas, and the dry land, His Word brought the earth and heavens into existence (Genesis 1:1–31). God's Word creates power and has power.

God explains how His Word operates:

> For as the rain comes down, and the snow from heaven, and do not return there, but water the earth, and make it bring forth and bud, that it may give seed to the sower and bread to the eater, so shall My word be that goes forth from My mouth; it shall not return to Me void, but it shall accomplish what I please, and it shall prosper in the thing for which I sent it. (Isaiah 55:10–11)

God compares His Word to the rain and snow, both of which make water. When water is withheld for long periods of time, the earth becomes barren. Trees don't bud; therefore, seeds can't grow and regenerate life. Man and earth will perish without water. God's Word to us is like the rain is to the earth. We will perish without it.

When people choose to believe Satan's lies, the Word cannot water their souls, regenerate new spiritual life, or help them reap the benefits and blessings God's Word was meant for them to have. God says, "Incline your ear, and come unto me: hear, and your soul shall live; and I will make an everlasting covenant with you, even the sure mercies of David" (Isaiah 55:3 KJV).

Power for Binding and Loosing

We can tie God's hands as well as the hands of angels sent to help us. Jesus shows us how we do this in His lesson on binding and loosing: "Assuredly, I say to you, whatever you bind on earth will be bound in heaven, and whatever you loose on earth will be loosed in heaven" (Matthew 18:18).

This power to loose or bind can work for or against us. Since the power for good and evil exists around us, we can loose evil by speaking negative things, or we can loose good by speaking God's Word. We can bind evil by speaking God's Word, or we can bind God's Word by speaking negatively.

One day as I was praying in the Spirit, I was going to pray the Scripture concerning God's Word, but to my surprise out popped these words: "Let my mouth bring forth live fruit, not dead fruit." The Spirit was emphasizing to me that our mouths can bring forth live fruit for God's kingdom or dead fruit for Satan's kingdom. We choose our fruit with our mouths.

After Jesus had spent forty days in the wilderness and was hungry, Satan said to Him, "If You are the Son of God, command that these stones become bread" (Matthew 4:3). Jesus answered, "It is written, 'Man shall not live by bread alone, but by every word that proceeds from the mouth of God'" (Matthew 4:4).

Satan is insidiously clever. Therefore, we, like Jesus, must be aware of the enemy's ploys against us. Satan can make us think we're in charge of situations even if we're not living and speaking God's Word. When we are walking or talking in the ways of the world, however, we are under Satan's dominion because he is the god of this earth.

God warns us in Malachi 3:13 that our words have been harsh against Him. If we speak critical or negative words about people or situations, that makes it harder for God to help us. He is constantly fighting the enemy on our behalf. We need to use our weapon of warfare, the Word of God, to help Him win the battle for us, just as Jesus did.

Power in Agreement

In 1986, my first husband, Norman, and I were walking on the grounds of the PTL (Praise the Lord) Club before the park was closed and the program went off the air. As we walked, we noticed that a lot of Scripture had been chiseled in the sidewalks. Norman's attention was drawn to a quote from Matthew 18:19, which said, "Again I say to you that if two of you agree on earth concerning anything that they ask, it will be done for them by My Father in heaven." He commented that it would be great if that Scripture worked, but he couldn't see it in the lives of the Christians he knew.

My reply to him was that God's Word is true even if we can't see the manifestation of it. When God makes a contract, He stands behind it. He has stood behind every covenant He ever made with humankind. However, Christians today do what the Israelites did: make contracts with God and then allow Satan to get them into unbelief.

Unbelief voids any contract we make with God. The Scripture warns us against unbelief when it says, "Take heed, brethren, lest there be in any of you an evil heart of unbelief, in departing from the living God. But exhort one another daily . . . lest any of you be hardened through the deceitfulness of sin" (Hebrews 3:12–13 KJV).

The people in Nazareth were offended by Jesus because they thought of Him as a carpenter, not a prophet. He was unable to do "many mighty works" there because of their unbelief (Matthew 13:57–58 KJV). Unbelief with God is the same thing as reneging on a written or verbal contract in the world. It takes all parties involved to honor a contract.

As I prayed about my husband's observation concerning the word of agreement, I asked the Lord to give me some revelation on the subject. His answer was to *meditate on the Scriptures.* As I studied verses concerning God's Word, I realized that all knowledge is given through meditation. There are no gimmicks or quick answers. But if we persevere in the study of the Word, it will eventually get to our spirits, where it receives power.

In John 15:7, Jesus said, "If you abide in Me, and My words abide in you, you will ask what you desire, and it shall be done for you." Jesus knew the Word has to take up residence in our hearts before it receives power from God.

Jesus also said, "I am the vine, you are the branches. He who abides in Me, and I in him, bears much fruit; for without Me you can do nothing" (John 15:5). Unless the Word is abiding in our spirits, we have no power to receive the many blessings the Word promises us. Nor can we be the mighty source of power necessary to help God establish His kingdom here on earth.

Power to Give Rest

After God created heaven and earth, He rested. He desires that we learn how to rest in Him through faith in His Word.

Once, when I had urgent prayer requests, I questioned God about them. Then I heard in my spirit, *It's My job to get things done. I leave criticism and condemnation up to the world.* We may think God criticizes or condemns us, but He is always for us. It's our common enemy who causes us to criticize and condemn ourselves and one another.

The Word says, "Rest in the Lord, and wait patiently for Him; do not fret because of him who prospers in his way, because of the man who brings wicked schemes to pass" (Psalm 37:7).

If we rest in God we allow Him to do the work instead of fretting about getting it done. He knows our weaknesses, and His desire is to make Himself strong on our behalf. He knows the power that lies in His Word, and He will take care of His promises.

In one week, God answered three of the four requests that I had considered urgent. I had to rest about eight months in the Lord before the fourth one was answered. It may take years for a request to be granted. Regardless of the time it takes, God wants our spirits to rest, knowing the problems are in His hands, not ours.

"For he that is entered into his rest, he also hath ceased from his own works, as God did from his. Let us labour therefore to enter into that rest, lest any man fall after the same example of unbelief" (Hebrews 4:10–11 KJV).

The worldliness, worries, and anxieties of the world keep us from entering God's rest. We tend to focus on problems, devise our own solutions, then try to come up with answers according to the world's way. If we truly rest in God's Word, He will help us arrive at the right decision. When we let our frustrations cause us to speak forth corrupt communication, we make God's Word void, and we perpetuate our own failure to enter into God's rest.

Chapter 8

Preparation for a Bumper Crop

A farmer cultivates land by breaking up the ground. He tills the soil to keep it loose, hold moisture better, and get rid of weeds and rocks. If he doesn't break up the soil, thorns and weeds will choke the seed.

When a farmer plants the seed, he follows the instructions given for planting that specific kind of seed. A good farmer refuses to waste his seed on unprepared soil or the wrong kind of soil.

He improves the quality of the soil by fertilizing it. Different seeds require different soil and fertilizer. The kind of harvest he will receive from the seeds he sows will depend on the work and preparation that went into the soil preparation and planting.

Jeremiah 4:3 speaks of the heart as soil: "Thus says the Lord to the men of Judah and Jerusalem: 'Break up your fallow ground (untilled ground or idle hearts), and do not sow among thorns.'" Jesus also talked to the multitude about the problems of sowing seeds in the wrong kind of soil (Matthew 13:3–8).

Planting Good Seed

The heart requires a lot of preparation for God's seed (the Word) to produce good fruit for His kingdom. Before we can produce a bountiful harvest for God, we have to follow the instructions and patterns Jesus laid out for us. John 8:28–29 gives us an illustration:

> Jesus said to them, "When you lift up the Son of Man, then you will know that I am He, and that I do nothing of Myself;

but as My Father taught Me, I speak these things. And He who sent Me is with Me. The Father has not left Me alone, for I always do those things that please Him."

Jesus prepared Himself, with the help of the Holy Spirit, to speak and do the things that pleased His Father. God wants us, too, to learn, with the help of Jesus and the Holy Spirit, the things we can speak and do that will give us good seed to plant. If we walk in God's wisdom and do what His Word says, He will remove the thorns, rocks, and weeds, and prepare the soil of our hearts.

For a heart to produce excellent fruit for the kingdom of God, it must start off with good seed (the Word of God), planted in good soil that can be cultivated with God's wisdom, fertilized with prayer and watered with His love.

Protecting the Crop

God wants us to be free from the influence of Satan. For us to receive the good gifts our Father has promised us, we must follow the one commandment given by Jesus: "This is my commandment, that you love one another as I have loved you" (John 15:12).

In Matthew 7, Jesus mentioned the "golden rule" of doing to other people what we would have them do to us. He cautioned us to be aware of false teachers, warned us about the perils of judging one another, and mentioned the narrow gate that leads to life and the wide gate that leads to destruction. He further warned that if we don't use the Word of God as our foundation, our houses will be built on sand, and floods will destroy them. However, the houses (lives) built upon the rock of God's Word will be able to stand the adversities and storms of life.

If we follow Jesus' teachings, we can use the Word to eliminate the daily problems that seek to exterminate our spiritual fruit, like the grasshoppers, bugs, and worms that seek to devour our crops. Just as certain precautions free us from insects that would gorge on our plants, God's Word will free us from the spidery web of sin and worldliness that Satan weaves around us.

Chapter 9

Power to Justify or Condemn

As a child, I heard these taunting words many times: "Sticks and stones may break my bones, but words will never hurt me." However, words do have power, both positive and negative. That power comes either from the Holy Spirit or from Satan.

Benjamin Franklin knew the power in words. He said, "The pen is mightier than the sword." A sword can wound or kill. Words have the power to build up or tear down, create battles or stop battles, bring hope and increase our faith, or cause us to walk in unbelief until we enter the realm of despair. Our words bring rewards or curses, condemnation or justification.

God's words do not return void, and ours don't either. They usually bring the opposite of what we desire because of the way we use them. People do not understand and respect the power words have.

I still hear the old phrase, "Words are cheap, so put your money where your mouth is." Words are never cheap. On the contrary, they can be very expensive. Words can affect our health, our finances, and our relationships.

Jesus taught about the power in the spoken word when He cursed a fig tree. Peter got excited when he noticed the fig tree had dried up and was withering away. Jesus said to him, "Whatever things you ask when you pray, believe that you receive them, and you will have them" (Mark 11:24).

The idea the world has placed in our hearts that God's Word doesn't mean what it says didn't work for the Israelites when they walked in disobedience to God's Word, and it won't work for Christians either. God's Word requires faith and action to be profitable.

Positive Words Can Create Trouble

When "positive thinking" became popular and many books were written on the subject, I became interested in the power of words in our lives.

God, through the Holy Spirit, taught me a great lesson, albeit a painful one, when my husband Norman and I decided to take two of our children on a float trip with other members of my family. Since we had taken short canoe trips down a tranquil river with our church group several times, we thought we were canoe veterans. But we were unaware of the treacherous qualities of the river we were getting ready to float on.

As we loaded up our canoes, my sister told me the river was rocky and suggested I wear tennis shoes because thongs would not protect my feet if the canoe turned over. Because I was involved in positive thinking at the time, her warning fell on deaf ears. "We are not going to turn over," I said. "If I thought we were going to turn over, I wouldn't go." My sister didn't argue with me. I felt smug that I could have whatever I claimed.

The Bible warns against overconfidence in our words. Proverbs 10:19 says, "In the multitude of words sin is not lacking, but he who restrains his lips is wise." At that time, I was unaware that there are two sources of power for our words: the Holy Spirit and Satan.

All the canoes on the float trip had two people in them except ours. I sat between my husband and our twelve-year-old son, Norman Jr., because old injuries to my neck and back kept me from trying to row. I felt like Cleopatra floating down the Nile River. As I basked in the beauty of the view, my escorts laboriously rowed the canoe. The first two hours were wonderful, and then we enjoyed a leisurely lunch.

The river was running low in many places, due to the lack of summer rain, so more rocks than usual protruded. With the weight of three people, our canoe sat low in the water. When we hit the first rapid waterfalls, our canoe dragged on the rocks, turned over, and landed on my foot. I lost my thongs in the river, but we recovered most of our belongings. Even though the excruciating pain made me think I had broken my foot, we had to travel on.

When we came to shallow rapids again, the canoe turned over a second time and landed on the same foot, bringing me to tears. For me the fun was gone. But the worst was yet to come.

As we approached the third rapids, huge rocks jutted out of the water. When I saw the water was deep after the falls, I panicked and jumped out of the canoe. As I sat there in the shallow running water, I watched the canoe turn over the third time. It floated gracefully down the river—after it plunged my son, my husband, and our food and cargo into the deep.

As he struggled to keep from drowning, my husband managed to grab a tree branch sticking out of the water. Norman Jr. climbed out on the opposite side of the river, then took a path that led back to where I was. After resting awhile, my husband swam down the river to join the others.

My son stood on the bank and called out to me, encouraging me to come out of the water. Self-pity took over, and I began to cry. I was worried about my husband because of his recent lung surgery. I was also suffering agonizing pain in my foot and ankle. The cold river water helped me bear the pain, but I knew I couldn't walk on sharp rocks without shoes. If anyone tried to carry me over the jagged rocks that covered the uneven river bottom, he would risk injury to himself.

It is strange how the mind tends to wander when you are faced with a crisis. There I sat among rocks in icy-cold water. I thought of the salmon in Alaska that fight the swift water on their upstream journey for spawning. Many meet their deaths as they try to jump over rocks, but others move valiantly upstream, struggling to reach their destination. As I thought of them, I was determined to conquer the river and reach the safety of the shore.

My twelve-year-old son, who had recently received Jesus as his Savior, cheered me on by reminding me of my faith. "Mom," he said, "you believe in prayer. Pray!"

I felt chagrined at his reprimand because prayer had never entered my mind. However, as I sat alone in the cold river, I heard these words in my spirit: *Satan is having a great time with you today, isn't he?*

"I guess so," I muttered. My thoughts were so fragmented with pain and worry that my focus was on the problems, not the solutions.

As I began to pray, I realized I could get out of the water only one way: by crawling on my hands and dragging my wounded foot. I began my torturous journey to the riverbank, trying to keep my flesh from being jabbed by the sharp rocks.

While my son stood on the shore, waiting for me, I clawed and dragged my body out of the water to the safety of the river's bank. When my feet touched dry ground, I sent God a prayer of thanks and breathed a sigh of relief. Then, with my son leading the way, I limped down the river to where our group had gone ashore.

We still had the big problem of crossing the river to the side where the trucks were ready to load up our canoes and cars were ready to take us home. My daughter and her friend tried to help me get into their canoe. However, when I tipped the canoe to one side, almost spilling their equipment into the river, I realized I didn't have the strength to climb into the canoe. So I swam across the river.

My husband and family were happy to see me safely ashore. In spite of my pain, I assured them I was okay. We went back to my mom and dad's house, where we enjoyed a big family dinner. We spent the evening in laughter and in sharing the float trip experiences. All in all, it had been a day of fun, even for me.

However, that night I kept waking up to pain and with the sensation of water roaring around my head. Once, while I was awake, I heard these words: *Positive thinking without prayer is a dangerous thing. Speaking positive words is a good thing, but to be effective, they must be accompanied by the power of prayer.*

The Holy Spirit reminded me that the kingdom of God is not in word but in power. He brought to my attention the things I had said earlier in the day to my sister: that I would not turn over in the canoe and that I didn't need tennis shoes. He also reminded me that I had not prayed when I made those statements. I had not asked for His protection.

Words Defile or Defend

Jesus spent a lot of time teaching the disciples about words and their power. "I say to you that for every idle word men may speak, they will give account of it in the day of judgment. For by your words you will be justified, and by your words you will be condemned" (Matthew 12:36–37).

I suffered greatly for my rash words. I was on crutches for six weeks. My ankle and foot continued swelling and hurting for a year. I was condemned by my words, not justified.

When Jesus addressed the multitude and the Pharisees, He said, "Hear and understand: not what goes into the mouth defiles a man; but what comes out of the mouth, this defiles a man" (Matthew 15:10–11).

The Pharisees were offended and Jesus' disciples didn't understand the message. So He admonished them further. "Do you not yet understand that whatever enters the mouth goes into the stomach and is eliminated? But those things which proceed out of the mouth come from the heart, and they defile a man" (Matthew 15:17–18).

The condition of our hearts determines the kind of words that come out of our mouths. We can't bring forth God's Word if our spirits are full of the world's garbage. We are justified when we speak forth God's Word and walk in His ways; however, Satan is allowed to persecute us when foolish and idle words proceed from our mouths.

When God chose Solomon, David and Bathsheba's son, to become Israel's third king, Solomon was overwhelmed at the prospect of leading such a large nation. God appeared to him in a dream one night and asked him what he needed. God was pleased when Solomon asked for wisdom to lead the people who were "like the dust of the earth in multitude" (2 Chronicles 1:9).

Since Solomon asked for wisdom instead of wealth, God gave him the knowledge he wanted, plus wealth in amounts greater than any king before or since. Kings from far-off lands visited Solomon to see his wealth and hear his wisdom.

In Ecclesiastes, Solomon gives us wisdom he gleaned from God.

> Do not be rash with your mouth, and let not your heart utter anything hastily before God. For God is in heaven, and you on earth; therefore let your words be few. For a dream comes through much activity, and a fool's voice is known by his many words. (Ecclesiastes 5:2–3)

Ecclesiastes 5:6 says, "Do not let your mouth cause your flesh to sin, nor say before the messenger of God that it was an error. Why should God be angry at your excuse and destroy the work of your hands?"

I had been a fool with my words, rash with my mouth, and hasty when uttering my opinion instead of listening to the wisdom of my sister, who had been on that river many times. I caused my flesh to suffer a lot of pain because I refused to take advice on how to float down a river that was known to be extremely rocky, swift, treacherous, and full of rapids.

I said I wouldn't turn over in a canoe and didn't need tennis shoes. Both of those statements were made without prayer, the power of God, to back them up. Therefore, the enemy pounced on my words with the power he had to make my radical statements untrue. Satan can persecute or harm us when we leave an opening for him through our negative words.

We are capable of loosing evil with our mouths or loosing good. We can bind evil with our mouths, or we can loose evil, the way I did on my ill-fated canoe trip. It is important to preface our binding and loosing with prayer that originates from our spirits, so the power of the Holy Spirit will be behind our words.

We don't want to start blazing away at the enemy like a child playing with a toy gun. Our spirits require proper assimilation. Then God's Word through us will be accompanied by His power instead of Satan's power.

Chapter 10

Developing a Clean Spirit

James observed that a ship is controlled by a small thing (a rudder), a horse obeys by a small thing (a bridle), a forest can be burned by a little fire, and the tongue (a small thing) boasts of big things. "The tongue is a fire, a world of iniquity. The tongue is so set among our members that it defiles the whole body, and sets on fire the course of nature; and it is set on fire by hell" (James 3:6).

James says that man can tame the animal kingdom, but he can't control his tongue. "With it we bless our God and Father, and with it we curse men, who have been made in the similitude of God. Out of the same mouth proceed blessing and cursing. My brethren, these things ought not to be so" (James 3:9–10).

Scripture tells us that even a good man can sin in his heart. "For many times, also, your own heart has known that even you have cursed others" (Ecclesiastes 7:22).

James 3:2 says, "We all stumble in many things. If anyone does not stumble in word, he is a perfect man, able also to bridle the whole body."

We know there are no perfect people, because John tells us, "If we say that we have no sin, we deceive ourselves, and the truth is not in us" (1 John 1:8).

The unbridled tongue creates hell on earth. If we don't want to walk in God's curses, we must control the words that come from our mouths. "Put away from you a deceitful mouth, and put perverse lips far from you" (Proverbs 4:24). When things seem to be getting out of control, we need to check our mouths to see whether evil has been allowed to escape through our words.

Many years ago, Nellie, my mother-in-law, developed Alzheimer's disease. She had always been a prayer warrior and spent many hours in prayer for our family. When we realized she had developed this disease, we moved her from her home in Springfield, Missouri, to St. Louis, Missouri, to be close to us.

Before we moved her into an apartment, she spent a few months living with us. I had hoped she could eventually stay with us, but regardless of what we did or how hard we tried to please her, we couldn't make her happy. She constantly complained about everything my husband and I did for her.

While we were going through that terrible time, not knowing what we were doing wrong, I asked the Lord for wisdom. I received these words in my spirit: *Don't answer evil with evil.* Even though it is hard to be pleasant to someone when everything you do is criticized, we must not allow evil to pollute our spirits.

The Scripture tells us to be courteous, compassionate, and loving, "not returning evil for evil or reviling for reviling, but on the contrary blessing, knowing that you were called to this, that you may inherit a blessing" (1 Peter 3:9).

The only way we can curb our tongues is by consistently walking in love. That is why Jesus insisted we "turn the other cheek" instead of getting into an argument. Most of the time, people prefer to answer evil with evil. However, if we wish to develop clean spirits, we cannot meditate on the evil things we hear.

God's Words Control Anger

When my husband and I first pondered my mother-in-law's reactions to us, we thought she had just grown old and grumpy. As I prayed for understanding, I asked the Lord why old people become so angry with the ones who are trying to help them, especially those closest to them. He answered with one word: *control.*

I was reminded how little children are eager to become self-sufficient. As they grow older, they become unruly when they are being taught certain rules and regulations. During the teenage years especially, they want to be free from authority. It is common for teenagers to think they are old enough to be in charge of their lives; hence, some become rebellious and defy anyone who attempts to control them, including law enforcement, parents, or guardians. Those who defy authority can suffer disastrous consequences for disobedience.

However, as time goes on, we eventually feel that we really are in control of our lives. For about forty years we believe the world is our oyster, and we stay busy looking for the pearls. Then we discover that we are becoming elderly. Someone is trying, again, to put limitations on us, usually health or business related. The longer we live, the more control we are likely to lose in our personal affairs. These periods are known as the cycle of life.

Even if we are aware that we need that control, our anger may surface against our caretakers, as it did when we were small children trying to become adults. That is why the very old and the very young often develop rewarding relationships—they sympathize with each other's feelings.

God wanted man to have dominion in this world and control over his environment. He gave Adam charge over his family, even though Adam, through disobedience to God, allowed Satan to become the god of this world. Men, with the help of God, are supposed to maintain control and be the heads of their families. However, relinquishing control of their lives to God and letting Him be the head of the family is difficult for men. The world reinforces that controlling spirit in them by making them think they have to be in charge of every situation.

The unquenchable desire for control causes some men to become abusive to their families. They do not understand that they are being controlled by the decisions they make, either for Satan or for God.

When men do not realize that they are controlled by their choices, they may complain that they have lost control over their lives, especially after retiring from their jobs. Those men were probably never able to give God the complete control necessary to keep them feeling secure in the seasons of their lives. Otherwise, retiring would just be another part of the cycle of life, a process of making good choices, thus eliminating the insecurity of losing control.

In every stage of our lives, we are faced with choices. A spirit of anger will surface whenever we are forced into situations we don't like.

After my first husband died, I discovered that anger is a natural part of grieving, as is a feeling of losing control. When I asked the Lord why anger is part of the grieving process, He said it is the safety valve that vents our feelings of despair. Venting anger keeps us from becoming immobilized by grief or loss of control. However, anger is a danger zone that can lead to bitterness or depression.

When we are grieving, our anger may be directed at specific people or at certain situations that have developed in our lives, such as the death of a loved one, loss of a job, poor health, divorce, or other catastrophe. We can even become angry at something as common as retirement.

Regardless of the specific circumstances, we must go through all the stages of grief in order to continue our lives as healthy, happy individuals. However, we can't get bogged down in prolonged grief that will cause us to become bitter. With God's help, we can adjust to any change. We can even use anger in a constructive rather than destructive way.

God's Words Hinder Alzheimer's

Not many people want to look after patients with Alzheimer's disease. But with fervent prayer and by the grace of God, my husband and I found someone to look after his mother. Virginia, a widow, who had experience working in a nursing home, decided she wanted to be home with her children. So she took two or three patients into her home. She kept most of her patients until they died or required hospitalization.

Norman died before his mother did. I was thankful he didn't have to watch her suffer. The disease progressed until she lost her memory of family and friends and seemed to have forgotten the name of her only child. To make things worse, she became totally blind.

However, we had some good moments with her. One day, when Virginia told her I was coming to see her, her face lit up and she said, "My little Mary?" That was a term she'd used many times in years past when referring to me. She always thought of us as Ruth and Naomi, the mother and daughter-in-law in the Old Testament. After her son's death, that longstanding bond of "Ruth and Naomi" respect and love helped us face the most turbulent days of our lives together. I was thankful that her connection to me was not completely severed by her disease.

Even though Nellie became cantankerous toward Norman and me, she was always obedient to Virginia and never complained to her about her situation. Virginia had known Nellie for only seven years when she died, but she gave her the greatest of all compliments by saying, "Nellie had Alzheimer's with grace."

Alzheimer patients exhibit strange traits, including paranoia and foul language. Nellie lived many years with Alzheimer's disease and had periods of paranoid thinking, but a foul word never proceeded from her mouth. Virginia had another patient with Alzheimer's who used atrocious language continually, and she was also a Christian.

At Nellie's funeral, her long-time minister spoke of the grace with which Nellie lived her life. Even though her mind failed her in her last few years on earth, Nellie was able to control her mouth from her spirit.

Nellie spent her last three weeks of life in the hospital, apparently unaware of people or her surroundings. Yet each day, I spent time with her, reading from the Bible and sharing special prayers from my prayer book. One day I became distraught and disheartened since she seemed unresponsive to my presence. I told her I was going home, even though I had intended to spend more time with her. When a frown crossed her face, I reassured her I would stay longer. As I continued to read and pray, her face relaxed. I knew she could hear and understand the Word of God.

Even though it seemed Nellie had lost touch with the world, she had not lost touch with God, and the enemy was unable to emit his foul words through her lips. Her spirit lived on the words of God stored up in her heart.

About an hour before Nellie's death, a young nurse bathed her, and with her eyes still closed, she spoke to that nurse for the first time. She said, "Thank you, honey." People who deal with Alzheimer victims know how rare it is to get that kind of a response from a patient. With a stifled cry, the nurse fled from the room and wept for Nellie.

For our spirits to reflect God's beauty, it is necessary to watch what goes into our spirits, for those things will eventually come out of our mouths. "Let no corrupt word proceed out of your mouth, but what is good for necessary edification, that it may impart grace to the hearers. And do not grieve the Holy Spirit of God, by whom you were sealed for the day of redemption. Let all bitterness, wrath, anger, clamor, and evil speaking be put away from you, with all malice" (Ephesians 4:29–31).

God's Words Safeguard Soul and Spirit

In spite of the hardships that encumber our lives, with God's grace and His Word in our spirits, we can fight the good fight of faith and overcome the weariness of the journey.

Attending to the instructions in Proverbs 7:1–3 will help us receive and retain the Word in our spirits. "My son, keep my words, and treasure my commands within you. Keep my commands and live, and my law as the apple of your eye. Bind them on your fingers; write them on the tablet of your heart."

Nellie wrote God's Word on the tablet of her heart. Even though Satan was able to affect her mind and body, she kept control of her indomitable spirit that, through the Word of God, had been entrusted into the loving hands of her Father.

In 2 Timothy 1:12, we are assured of God's help, whatever the circumstances. "For this reason I also suffered these things; nevertheless I am not ashamed, for I know whom I have believed and am persuaded that He is able to keep what I have committed to Him until that Day." As Christians, we should look to God for wisdom and use His words in everyday conversation, always commanding our mouths to speak pleasant words to the listener.

Proverbs 15:23 tells us that controlling our tongues brings joy to our spirits instead of anger. "A man has joy by the answer of his mouth, and a word spoken in due season, how good it is!"

We often hear harsh statements answered with angry retorts until a full-blown argument ensues. We can stop an evil remark with a pleasant one. However, once we have listened to bad words, such as cursing, and allowed ourselves to meditate on them, they enter our spirits. Then, under pressure, those same words escape through our lips.

So it benefits us to pay attention to Proverbs 21:23, which says, "Whoever guards his mouth and tongue keeps his soul from troubles." Since we have an enemy who is looking for an open door into our lives, it is imperative we take control of our mouths.

Chapter 11

Canning Fruit for the Kingdom Of God

If you want to eat the good fruit of God's Word in the winters of your life, you have to can it during the summer.

After farmers have raised their crops for the year, they store food for the winter by canning their produce in the summer. Raising and canning are hard and tedious jobs, but the rewards are great, so the whole family gets involved in the process.

During the summer months on our farm, my family kept busy picking all the tomatoes, potatoes, and other vegetables we had grown. Then we shelled peas, snapped green beans, and shucked corn.

We picked wild gooseberries and blackberries. We were rewarded with eating all the sweet berries we wanted. The bad part was getting covered with chiggers and ticks—little insects that cling to the flesh.

We offset the drudgery of our chores by playing pranks on one another. My oldest brother enjoyed finding silkworms on the corn we shucked. He knew I hated worms. I couldn't even put a worm on a fishhook. The moment he found a silkworm, he started chasing me around the house, trying to get that thing on me. He also loved to catch garter snakes from the garden or blacksnakes from the chicken house and chase me with them. I unwittingly enhanced his fun because I always ran away instead of standing up to him.

PART ONE: NEGATIVE THINGS THAT COME AGAINST US

Discipline and Good Judgment

One summer my brother's fun got out of control. Mom sent me to the chicken house to get eggs for a cake she was baking. When I came out of the chicken house with the eggs, I saw my brother in the yard with a blacksnake circling his head like a rope. Mom called for me to hurry up with the eggs. After a long debate with myself, I finally got up enough courage to start for the house. As I ran past my brother, the snake slipped out of his hands, sailed through the air like a disk, and grazed the top of my hair. Everyone in the family, including my mother, had a good laugh at my expense.

While we were eating dinner, my dad heard the story. Instead of laughing, he became furious. He told the rest of the family that if the snake had gotten on me, fear could have made me physically or emotionally ill. Determining that my brother's teasing had gone too far, my father exercised his authority as head of our household and insisted it be stopped.

Our heavenly Father will also exercise His righteous control when He thinks Satan's fun with us has gotten out of hand. He allows Satan to go so far and no further, just as He did with Simon Peter. "And the Lord said, 'Simon, Simon! Indeed, Satan has asked for you, that he may sift you as wheat. But I have prayed for you, that your faith should not fail; and when you have returned to Me, strengthen your brethren'" (Luke 22:31–32).

God's judgments are righteous and His love is great. He will not let the enemy put on us more than we can bear. "No temptation has overtaken you except such as is common to man; but God is faithful, who will not allow you to be tempted beyond what you are able, but with the temptation will also make the way of escape, that you may be able to bear it" (1 Corinthians 10:13).

My earthly father recognized what a horror it would have been for me if that snake had curled around my neck. He was also aware that my brother enjoyed playing with snakes and did not fear them. We would have been spared trouble in the family if I could have conquered my childhood fears. And my brother would have lost pleasure in tormenting me.

Since Satan finds extreme pleasure in seeing us run from him, just as my brother enjoyed watching me run from worms and snakes, we must conquer every fear with the sword of the Spirit, which is the Word of God. This puts Satan on the defensive, so we are not as vulnerable to his mischief.

Variety of Nutrients

Jesus canned the Old Testament in His Spirit, and He was ready when Satan tempted Him in the wilderness. The health of our spirits will be determined by the amount of God's Word we consume.

Digesting God's food comes from meditation. God has prepared a wide variety of good food for us physically, and there is a plenty of spiritual food in the Old and New Testaments. All of the Word is necessary for a healthy, well-balanced spiritual diet.

I discovered an important truth in the process of canning. The kind of fruit we had in our cellar in the winter depended on what kind of fruit we canned in the summer. When we canned apples, we got apples. They didn't turn into peaches no matter how much I loved peaches.

Most people find it easier to can spiritual food from the New Testament than from the Old Testament. We can relate more easily to the New Testament. However, if we don't can fruit in the Old Testament, we will miss out on special nutritional sustenance for our spirits.

Dad bought bushels of apples and peaches for canning, so we weren't plagued with chiggers and ticks when we canned them, as we were when we scouted the countryside looking for wild gooseberries and blackberries. However, we wouldn't have had wonderful berry pies and cobblers as part of our diet without our perseverance and extra work.

Our physical bodies are healthier and stronger when we have well-balanced diets. Our spiritual bodies also need a balanced diet of God's Word to become strong and healthy. We must partake of all of His Word, not just pick and choose what we like. Then we will become strong Christian soldiers whom God can use in the harvest for His kingdom.

Understanding and Training

In the physical world we have to understand the proper way to prepare food: the right temperature for cooking, how and when to seal the food so it won't spoil, cooking for the right amount of time using the proper method. If you try to can without knowing all the problems you might face, you will end up with spoiled food before winter comes.

Mom was an expert at canning food, and her spoilage was minimal. She refused to buy canned food from certain neighbors who were known to have problems with spoilage.

If we can God's Word properly during the summers of our lives, we will be able to feed abundantly upon the fruit of the Spirit during the storms winter will bring. Galatians 5:22–23 tells us, "The fruit of the Spirit is love, joy, peace, longsuffering, kindness, goodness, faithfulness, gentleness, self-control. Against such there is no law." The fruit of the Spirit comes from meditating on God's Word. It takes a lot of prayer and discipline to prepare His good fruit in our spirits.

Just as we have to watch out for things that spoil the physical fruit we are canning, we also have to watch out for things that spoil the fruit of the Spirit. If we walk in the flesh, we will be storing spoiled fruit in our spirits. "Now the works of the flesh are evident, which are: adultery, fornication, uncleanness, lewdness, idolatry, sorcery, hatred, contentions, jealousies, outbursts of wrath, selfish ambitions, dissensions, heresies, envy, murders, drunkenness, revelries, and the like; of which I tell you beforehand, just as I also told you in time past, that those who practice such things will not inherit the kingdom of God" (Galatians 5:19–21).

Canning requires a great deal of training. When canning spiritual food, we must follow the instructions of the Holy Spirit. Then we will have a continual feast of healthy spiritual food. If we can from the flesh, which is the world, our fruit will be contaminated and spoiled.

Our senses are affronted when we open a jar of sour-smelling food because our bodies were not made to tolerate those kinds of impurities. Even the animal kingdom has been given wisdom to be wary of eating spoiled food.

Our spirits were not designed to partake of the unclean things of the flesh, either, so we should resist sin in the same way we reject unclean food. God meant for our spirits to feast on His goodness and His love, just as our bodies were meant to feast on His fresh fruits, vegetables, and wholesome foods, not foods that have become rotten from contamination.

A Storehouse of Treasure

When I lived on a farm, the cellar was our storehouse for food. During the winters, there was always a variety of good things to eat down there. What fun it was to come home from school on a cold winter night and smell a big pot of vegetable soup simmering on the stove. All the hard work of the summer shucking corn, snapping green beans, shelling peas, stewing tomatoes, and digging up potatoes from the garden had vanished from our minds. When Mom prepared a blackberry cobbler or gooseberry pie for dessert, the ticks and chiggers were long forgotten.

Psalm 119:162 says, "I rejoice at Your word as one who finds great treasure." We can fill our storehouse by canning God's Word in our spirits.

Jesus said, "A good man out of the good treasure of his heart brings forth good things, and an evil man out of the evil treasure brings forth evil things" (Matthew 12:35).

When winter sets in and the storms of life prevail, we can go to the storehouse of our spirits and bring out a feast of God's good spiritual food, such as peace, joy, love, long-suffering, kindness, forgiveness, patience, mercy, humility, meekness, self-control, wisdom, and perseverance.

God's Word Gives Light

The road we need to take is paved with God's Word, not the world's destructive words. We must heed what the psalmist tells us about the Word illuminating the way for us to walk. Psalm 119:105 says, "Your word is a lamp to my feet and a light to my path."

Wisdom and Knowledge

God's Word gives us the wisdom to make good choices, walk in love, and bear good fruit. Proverbs 16:21 tells us, "The wise in heart will be called prudent, and sweetness of the lips increases learning."

Proverbs 15:14 says, "The heart of him who has understanding seeks knowledge, but the mouth of fools feeds on foolishness." When Christians seek God's knowledge and wisdom, we help God prepare the world for Jesus' return.

Control the Tongue

Proverbs 16:1 says, "The preparations of the heart belong to man, but the answer of the tongue is from the Lord." As we become disciplined in God's Word, we will allow Him to have control over our tongues.

Proverbs 15:1 declares, "A soft answer turns away wrath, but a harsh word stirs up anger." Hell is stirred up with anger, and anger loves to escalate and produce evil. "Hell and Destruction are before the Lord; so how much more the hearts of the sons of men" (Proverbs 15:11). God knows the hearts of men as well as the evils of hell.

Proverbs 15:4 states, "A wholesome tongue is a tree of life, but perverseness in it breaks the spirit." Speaking wholesome words add to the length of our lives, but perverse words cause the spirit harm. That is why we are instructed, "Keep your tongue from evil, and your lips from speaking deceit" (Psalm 34:13).

Meditation on God's Word helps us to eliminate curses and receive blessings. We can increase our blessings by praying, "Set a guard, O Lord, over my mouth; keep watch over the door of my lips" (Psalm 141:3). When we guard our mouths we can produce good fruit for God's kingdom.

Father, we thank You for Your Word—the storehouse of treasure You have given us. We pray for wisdom as we can and store the good fruit of Your Spirit for the winters of our lives. Help us to stay set apart from the things of the flesh so that we will not pollute our spirits. We desire to walk in love and to pursue peace with all men. Amen.

Look to Thy God

God's words are precious as jewels to me,

And sweeter than honey from the bee.

For by His words He calms the sea,

And by His words He gives life to me.

Look, look, look to thy God.

Happy is he who looks to his God.

Put not thy trust in man,

But look, look to thy God.

Discipline #3: Negative Thoughts

It is Satan's aim to keep us in a negative mode.

When I was a child, I spoke as a child,
I understood as a child, I thought as a child;
but when I became a man, I put away childish things.
(1 Corinthians 13:11)

Chapter 12

Guard Your Thought Life

The Scripture says, "As he thinks in his heart so is he" (Proverbs 23:7). How and what a person thinks affects the physical, mental, and spiritual essence of his or her life. Our demeanor, personality, and character traits evolve from the myriad secret thoughts we meditate on during our lifetime.

This explains why some people are productive, healthy, and happy, even though life has dealt them severe blows. Others with similar or even lesser problems become angry, bitter, complaining people who constantly dwell on their misfortunes. Since each of us has a free will, we can determine how we will react to tragedy or misfortune. You can encourage yourself with positive thoughts, or you can concentrate on the negative aspects of your life. Our positive or negative thoughts affect our health, finances, and personal relationships.

Doctors warn us that too much sugar and fat are precursors for various diseases. Environmentalists caution us about chemicals that get into the fruits, vegetables, fish, and meats we eat. This pollution comes from many sources, such as manufacturers that discard harmful pollutants into lakes, rivers, and soil; ships dumping oil and refuse into the oceans; fertilizers used to enrich the soil; and pesticides sprayed on crops, trees, and plants. These chemicals contaminate wildlife, plant life, marine life, and human life.

Even people who are concerned about polluting the environment God created for us, because of greed for material things, ignore warnings concerning their mental and physical health.

God has three dimensions: Father, Son, and Holy Spirit. We are created in His image: body, soul, and spirit. If one part suffers, the other two parts are affected. Therefore, we must be cognizant of all the things that harm us, spiritually as well as physically. Negative thinking harms the person just as contaminated food does.

We are told in Ecclesiastes 12:7 that the body is temporal because it was created from the earth, but the spirit is eternal. "The dust will return to the earth as it was, and the spirit will return to God who gave it." However, as long as we are in charge of our bodies, God expects us to treat them properly.

Maintain a Clear Conscience

People often talk about the bad things God has allowed into their lives, or even caused to happen, apparently believing that He uses such things to discipline His children for some infraction of His rules. This idea has led many to develop a theory that God is directly involved in the misfortunes that befall us.

One day, as I was meditating on this problem, I asked the Holy Spirit how God does discipline people. He told me that He disciplines us through the conscience.

The conscience is part of our unique built-in warning system from God that sets us apart from the animal kingdom. It is the way God reaches the soul and spirit of a person. It is the small inner voice that can encourage or discourage us according to what God would have us do.

When our conscience is pricked, that's God's way of saying, "Listen! Wait! I am trying to tell you something for your benefit." Failure to listen to that inner voice short-circuits our connection to God, and then we end up in desperate straits—just as children who fail to listen to their parents' advice find themselves in distressing predicaments.

Ecclesiastes 11:9–10 warns us:

> Rejoice, O young man, in your youth, and let your heart cheer you in the days of your youth; walk in the ways of your heart, and in the sight of your eyes; but know that for all these God will bring you into judgment. Therefore remove sorrow from your heart, and put away evil from your flesh, for childhood and youth are vanity.

If a young man allows a rebellious spirit to take control over his actions, he will eventually become so hardened against God's voice he does not hear Him. His conscience becomes defiled and no longer works in his favor for protection or wisdom from God; instead, he becomes vulnerable to Satan's tactics.

In Titus we are told, "To the pure all things are pure, but to those who are defiled and unbelieving nothing is pure; but even their mind and conscience are defiled. They profess to know God, but in works they deny Him, being abominable, disobedient, and disqualified for every good work" (Titus 1:15–16). If our minds become defiled and impure, we can't hear the inner voice of the Holy Spirit when He gives advice from God's Word.

God's desire is to keep us from misfortune, not to cause it to come upon us. He has been trying to help man overcome evil since He created the first human being. However, Proverbs 15:26 tells us how He feels about the defiled conscience: "The thoughts of the wicked are an abomination to the Lord, but the words of the pure are pleasant."

As a child, I often heard the old adage, "You can't keep from thinking bad thoughts any more than you can keep birds from flying over your head. Yet you don't let birds nest in your hair, so why should you let bad thoughts lodge in your head?" Since we have a free will, we are able to choose the thoughts we allow ourselves to meditate on.

If we concentrate on hurtful, harmful, hindering, evil situations or problems, and allow our thoughts to dwell on them, we encourage Satan to enter into his favorite playground: the mind. It is hard for the Holy Spirit to counsel and impart wisdom to the Christian who keeps his mind in Satan's dominion.

Test the Spirits

When I began receiving revelation knowledge from the Lord many years ago, I knew enough to test the spirits. Yet I was an immature Christian, ignorant of the power in thoughts. Scripture tells us to beware of the spirits. "Beloved, do not believe every spirit, but test the spirits, whether they are of God; because many false prophets have gone out into the world" (1 John 4:1).

Therefore, I responded to information I was receiving in my spirit with questioning. "Is that You, Lord, or is that me?" Eventually, the Lord revealed to me, through both the written Word and a minister of the gospel, that I was indeed hearing from Him.

One day, as I did my usual questioning concerning revelation knowledge I was receiving in my spirit, I was startled and confused by a question from the Holy Spirit: *Is it a good thought?*

I meditated for a moment, then answered hesitantly, "I guess so."

Next came the question, *Does it matter?*

After another moment of hesitation, I weakly muttered, "I guess not."

After I received the message, I needed verification, so I searched for information and found Scripture that says, "He who keeps His commandments abides in Him, and He in him. And by this we know that He abides in us, by the Spirit whom He has given us" (1 John 3:24).

As I searched Scriptures on the topic of abiding, I came to acknowledge that He and I are one in the spirit and one in the flesh. If the Holy Spirit and I abide in the same body, I don't have to ask

Him if a thought is mine or His. I only have to heed the Scripture that says, "Satan himself transforms himself into an angel of light" (2 Corinthians 11:14). What we receive in the spirit has to line up with the Word of God.

Jesus says in John 10:27, "My sheep hear My voice, and I know them, and they follow Me." However, we have to always be careful of the wolf that is waiting to devour God's sheep.

Sometime later, while driving in my car, I was singing songs of praise to the Lord and making melody in my heart as we are instructed to do in Ephesians 5:19. Unexpectedly, these words came forth from my spirit: *Your blood is My blood, your breath is My breath, your heartbeat is My heartbeat, your hands are My hands. You are in Me and I am in you.*

My eyes gazed at my hands on the steering wheel. I have always considered my large, square, thin, bony hands on small wrists as ugly, but when I realized that my hands are an extension of His hands, they appeared beautiful to me for the first time. He uses our hands to glorify Him and His kingdom. The simplicity of service that hands perform gives them a special beauty as they adroitly attend to the physical body as well as the body of Christ.

We may think of our hands as having lowly positions because they are involved in a lot of menial tasks such as washing dishes, changing diapers, cooking, and cleaning. Yet we are inclined to dote on other parts of the body such as face, skin, hair, or physique. We dedicate hours to improving our appearances in these areas. However, 1 Corinthians 12:14–15 tells us, "The body is not one member but many. If the foot should say, 'Because I am not a hand, I am not of the body,' is it therefore not of the body?"

A malfunction in any part of the body makes the rest of the body uncomfortable. The Scripture reminds us that without the eye the body cannot see; without the ear the body cannot hear; everything works together to complete the physical body. A hand with four fingers is not as beautiful or useful as a hand with five fingers. That fifth finger is part of the hand, and it is needed to complete the hand.

Just as every part of the physical body is important and significant, so is every Christian essential and indispensable for the body of Christ. When Satan is allowed to harm one Christian, the whole body of Christ should be in empathy with his suffering, just like the entire physical body feels the pain if an eye is hurt or a leg is broken.

As I contemplated my hands being God's hands, I thought of my breath, my blood, and my heartbeat as being His too. The Scripture says, "Do you not know that you are the temple of God and that the Spirit of God dwells in you?" (1 Corinthians 3:16).

Wherever I am, whatever I do, the Spirit of God is with me. I can't get rid of His company any more than I can get rid of my own company, whether I like myself or not.

Though the Holy Spirit resides in Christians, He may not be allowed to do or say much. Each of us needs to provide an opening for Him to take part in our daily activities. This requires our spiritual antenna to be up and in working order, so that we may hear and receive the Holy Spirit's advice.

Unravel the Mystery

I continued to dwell on the revelation knowledge I had received on thoughts. One Sunday morning, while getting dressed for church, I heard in my spirit these words: *Your thoughts are not your own. You are constantly being influenced either by Satan or by the Holy Spirit.*

Although this was a mystifying revelation, I decided to evaluate the theory with various people.

I chose my husband as my first guinea pig. He told me in no uncertain terms that his thoughts were his own.

Undaunted, I then shared this tidbit of knowledge with my Bible study group. One dear lady was bold with her disagreement. "If I decided I wanted to go to the bathroom," she said, "that would be my thought." Of course everybody laughed. But I still believed what I had heard, even though I didn't understand it.

In spite of being ridiculed, I continued to meditate on the idea of our thoughts being influenced either by the Holy Spirit or by Satan.

The Lord helped me to better understand His statement when He revealed to me that there are three kinds of thoughts, each with a different function:

1. Thoughts relating to the body's mechanisms are conditioned responses to keep the body informed of its needs.

2. Thoughts concerning learning experiences come from the part of the brain used to increase mental growth.

3. Thoughts like daydreaming, reverie, or musing are influenced by positive or negative stimuli, proceeding from the Holy Spirit or Satan.

Scientists have spent centuries trying to understand the mechanisms of the human mind and body, but they have made far more progress with the body than with the mind.

As I shared my experiences with my daughter-in-law Elaine, who is a licensed counselor, she admitted that experts in her field do not know where negative and positive thoughts come from. They have never understood why some people stay positive in their thinking while others are constantly negative. Critical people are more inclined to need long-term counseling, since they have a difficult time recuperating from tragedy and don't deal well with the problems of life.

As a Christian, Elaine was able to accept the theory of two influences, good and evil; however, she was concerned about borderline thoughts. When she questioned the Holy Spirit about this, His answer to her was that she could tell by the fruit whether Satan or the Holy Spirit was influencing the thoughts.

Jesus said, "A good tree cannot bring forth evil fruit, neither can a corrupt tree bring forth good fruit. Every tree that bringeth not forth good fruit is hewn down, and cast into the fire. Wherefore by their fruits ye shall know them" (Matthew 7:18–20 KJV). Galatians 5:22–23 (KJV) says, "The fruit of the Spirit is love, joy, peace, longsuffering, gentleness, goodness, faith, meekness, temperance: against such there is no law." If our thoughts produce the fruit of anger, frustration, bitterness, envy, jealousy, hatred, contentions, or evil of any kind, they are being influenced by Satan (Galatians 5:19–21).

As I continued to research this concept, I discovered more things in the Word about thoughts. Proverbs 16:3 says, "Commit your works to the Lord, and your thoughts will be established." If we have committed our lives to God and are being disciplined by His Word, He directs our thinking. The more committed we are to fellowship with God, the more He is able to direct our thinking.

There is nothing to be gained by the world's influence. That is why the Scripture says, "Put not your trust in princes, nor in the son of man, in whom there is no help. His breath goeth forth, he returneth to his earth; in that very day his thoughts perish" (Psalm 146:3–4 KJV).

The Holy Spirit wants us to let Him influence our thinking. Influences from other people last only as long as they are here on earth. However, influences from the Holy Spirit are eternal and can help us achieve eternal rewards in heaven.

Renew the Mind

Another time, through meditation and prayer, I received these words in my spirit: *In the physical world man is insignificant, but in the spiritual world he ranks with God.* Since Satan is the god of this world, he has great influence, and he is a master at keeping our thoughts on the problems of the world. His goal is to keep us entangled by the worldliness octopus so he can stimulate our negative thinking.

The battle for the mind is fought in the spiritual world. Scripture says, "He who is in you is greater than he who is in the world" (1 John 4:4). Through the Holy Spirit, great power lies within us to overcome tribulation, persecution, distress, famine, peril, and sword. None of these things can separate us from the love of Christ (Romans 8:35).

Romans 8:37 tells us, "Yet in all these things we are more than conquerors through Him who loved us." A conqueror is someone who has been able to achieve control over people or a situation. However, many conquerors in history eventually lost what they conquered. For us to be more than conquerors, we must hold the conquered ground in all spiritual battles. However, we can short-circuit our connection to God, get into unbelief, and become as powerless as a burned-out light bulb, losing that which we thought we had conquered.

We are sons and daughters of the King. "I will be a Father to you, and you shall be My sons and daughters, says the Lord Almighty" (2 Corinthians 6:18). Romans 8:14 says, "For as many as are led by the Spirit of God, these are sons of God." We are told in Romans 8:16–17, "The Spirit Himself bears witness with our spirit that we are children of God, and if children, then heirs— heirs of God and joint heirs with Christ, if indeed we suffer with Him, that we may also be glorified together."

We rank alongside Jesus in the spiritual world if we have accepted Christ as our Savior. Our spiritual powers through the Holy Spirit achieve mighty victories for God—not fighting physical battles with other people, but fighting spiritual battles with unseen enemies.

Jesus died that we might have salvation, but also that we might have power through the Holy Spirit to enjoy our time here on earth. We are heirs of God and joint heirs with Jesus Christ. However, the mind of man is the battleground for spiritual battles. When we act as though we have no power over our thinking, we allow Satan to influence us, and we shame the Holy Spirit by nullifying His power. The Holy Spirit is powerless without our authority because God gave us free will, and we make the choice of who is directing our thoughts.

PART ONE: NEGATIVE THINGS THAT COME AGAINST US

Satan won his first victory in his battle for the mind after he convinced Adam and Eve they would be wise if they disobeyed God's commandment. However, all they gained was knowledge of evil. After their minds were open to the influence of evil, this knowledge resulted in wrong decisions. Yet, in His great mercy, God used the blood of Jesus, along with the sword of the Spirit (the Word of God), to help human beings overcome Satan's immoral ways.

Psalm 94:11 tells us that God is aware of our predicament concerning thoughts. "The Lord knows the thoughts of man, that they are futile."

Paul told the Ephesians that the problems of ignorance, hardening of the heart, and deceitful lusts alienate people from God and cause them to walk in the futility of their minds.

> This I say, therefore, and testify in the Lord, that you should no longer walk as the rest of the Gentiles walk, in the futility of their mind, having their understanding darkened, being alienated from the life of God, because of the ignorance that is in them, because of the blindness of their heart. (Ephesians 4:17–18)

A variety of thoughts fly around us continually, but we can distinguish God's thoughts from Satan's thoughts. God's Word tells us the kind of thoughts He has about us in Jeremiah 29:11: "For I know the thoughts I think toward you, says the Lord, thoughts of peace and not of evil, to give you a future and a hope."

When we think negative thoughts of despair or unbelief, anger or frustration, we are allowing Satan to influence us. Since Christians belong to God, He expects us to commit our works to Him so that He can renew our minds and establish our thinking (Ephesians 4:23).

We cannot give up the battleground to Satan. We have to fight for the control of our thinking, and it is a second-by-second, minute-

PART ONE: NEGATIVE THINGS THAT COME AGAINST US

by-minute, hour-by-hour, day-by-day, week-by-week, and year-by-year battle until death frees us from Satan's evil influence.

PART ONE: NEGATIVE THINGS THAT COME AGAINST US

Chapter 13

Create a Strong Defense

My grandson James was seven when His great-grandfather died. He questioned his mother on the subject of death, and she didn't want him to fear death, so she emphasized the glories of heaven. As he took in her teachings, James developed an overwhelming desire to live in a sin-free world.

One day James was lamenting about why he did things wrong even though he didn't want to get into trouble. His mom explained the story of Adam and Eve and how sin came into the world through their disobedience to God. James exclaimed, "That old Adam sure fixed our goat! If it hadn't been for him, we would be living in Paradise!"

Subtitle

A problem concerning Andy's dog, Buster, and my dog, Annie, forced me to explain old age and death to my granddaughter Ashley when she was a month short of four years old.

Annie was six months younger than Ashley. As soon as Ashley could walk, Annie followed her around the house with the leash on her head instead of her collar. When Ashley was old enough to put the leashes on both dogs properly, she took them for walks in our yard. After she grew tired, she'd hang their leashes on a doorknob until she wanted to play again.

Annie would sit patiently by the door, waiting for Ashley to return. But Buster, who was twelve years old, didn't like Ashley's energetic games. So he appealed to me for help by hiding behind me or between my legs. Ashley couldn't understand why Buster got so upset.

When I defended Buster by telling Ashley he was old, she asked, "What is old, Grandma?"

Without much forethought, I rambled on about the aging process, explaining that older people are unable to do things they did when they were younger. I tried to alleviate any fears she might have about getting old, but I entangled myself when I tried to explain death.

Hoping to keep Ashley from fearing death, I started talking about heaven. In my explanation, I told her about the salvation we receive through the death of Jesus. I mentioned the names of grandparents and other relatives who had asked Jesus to come into their hearts before they died. I told her they had been reunited with one another and now lived with Jesus in heaven.

As we continued our conversation about old age and death, I reminded her that her great-grandfather was ninety-three years old and he could still jump on the trampoline with her. I explained that many people, as well as animals, can live long lives, but others die young. I assured her that the most important thing for her to remember was that people need to ask Jesus to come live in their hearts so that when they die, they can be with Him and their loved ones in heaven.

After I finished my long-winded dissertation, a brief silence followed. A few seconds later, in a meek little voice, she asked, "Grandma, can I ask Jesus to live in my heart?"

I was elated. I gave her the words to pray, and she joyfully asked Jesus to live in her heart.

Helping Ashley receive Jesus strengthened our relationship in ways I couldn't have imagined. The old and the young became bound together with an unbreakable cord . . . all because a dog didn't like being pestered by a small child in his old age.

God can use any experience to draw our thoughts to Him.

Meditate on Virtue

Shortly after Ashley's fifth birthday, her mom and dad divorced. Since I lived in California and she lived in Missouri, we had daily conversations by telephone. With the help of the Holy Spirit, I tried to alleviate her sorrow and distress by getting her to concentrate on good thoughts.

I explained to her that God wants us to have a free will and not be like puppets on a string, so it would be our choice to please God, strive to walk in His ways, and accept Jesus as God's Son. I emphasized that living according to the ways Jesus teaches us keeps us from being influenced by evil demons that Satan sends to whisper bad thoughts into our ears. If we listen to the bad influence, we will be encouraged to get angry, resentful, and hurtful to others.

I assured her that everyone wants to be forgiven when they do something that harms other people or makes them sad. Therefore, God expects us to forgive people when they do malicious things to us. If we don't, He won't forgive us when we commit sins against others. I told her that she needed to forgive her mom and dad for making bad choices that grieved themselves and her.

Ashley always listened attentively to my lectures, but I was never sure how much she was able to comprehend until one day, as we were having our daily telephone conversation, she remarked, "Grandma, do you know what I do when those little demons bother me?"

"No, dear," I said. "What do you do?"

"I take a nap!"

She was still young enough to take daily naps and smart enough to know that when she slept the little demons couldn't influence her to think bad thoughts or to do things that got her into trouble.

Even though Ashley was only five years old, she recognized the virtuous thinking Paul referred to in Philippians when he wrote, "Finally, brethren, whatever things are true, whatever things are noble, whatever things are just, whatever things are pure, whatever things are lovely, whatever things are of good report, if there is any virtue and if there is anything praiseworthy—meditate on these things" (Philippians 4:8).

Take Thoughts Captive

It is easy to place God's values in the minds of children. Their hearts are open to spiritual things because they haven't become hardened and damaged by the world.

Adults tend to become pessimistic more easily than children when they have to deal with the tragedies of life. I think traumatized children are more inclined to relive their stress through nightmares or bad dreams.

Ashley had one recurring nightmare during her parents' divorce. She dreamed that she and her mom were in the street in front of their house, but the street had a high fence around it. Even if they could climb the fence, they had to contend with a big, black, monster-type figure between them and the safety of the house. Although her dad did not live there anymore, in her dream he was safely inside the house and they were trying to get to him.

As we discussed this dream, she was able to express the anguish she felt for herself and her mom. Even though she and her mother lived in the house, her dream put them in the street. She finally admitted her fear of not being safe without her dad, confessing that she had feelings of being abandoned.

Once she understood the cause of her dream, I made a concentrated effort to help her get rid of it. We discussed other people in her family and how much each one loved her, including her dad. We counted her blessings and refused to dwell on the negative aspects of the separation from her father. I used Scripture to assure her that her heavenly Father was always looking after her and her mom's welfare, and that He would never forsake them.

When Ashley was in the first grade, the Holy Spirit opened her spiritual eyes during a school performance. Ashley, accompanied by her mother on the piano, was assigned to sing two solos.

Rehearsals had been stressful. Ashley feared performing alone, and her mother had a problem hitting the right notes on the piano in one spot in a song.

The night before the performance, I received a tearful call from Ashley. We prayed about the situation and I assured her that Jesus would be with her. I asked her where she wanted Him to stand, beside her or in front of her. She was able to control her sobs by concentrating on Jesus. She wanted Him to stand beside her, and with that picture in her mind, she felt at peace and drifted off to sleep.

The next night, when I answered the phone, I heard a furtive little whisper. "Grandma, I saw an angel tonight! Out of the corner of my eye I saw Jesus beside me, but a big angel stood next to the piano while Mama played. When she got to the hard spot in the music he said, 'Now don't mess up,' and Mama didn't!"

She was elated that they both did well. However, she never shared that story with anyone but me.

Young children and teenagers who have trouble in school and issues with relationships usually blame their problems on divorced parents or unstable, unloving, seemingly uncaring parents. From their point of view, they have been rejected. They need a caring grandparent, teacher, or other adult to help prevent them from developing a reprobate mind.

Paul tells us in 2 Corinthians 10:4–6 that thoughts can develop strongholds in our minds, but we can take those thoughts captive and tear down the strongholds.

> For the weapons of our warfare are not carnal but mighty in God for pulling down strongholds, casting down arguments and every high thing that exalts itself against the knowledge of God, bringing every thought into captivity to the obedience of Christ, and being ready to punish all disobedience when your obedience is fulfilled.

Satan's strongholds are barriers that keep us from the blessings and peace God wants us to enjoy. When we take thoughts captive, and refuse to allow negative thoughts to run freely through our minds, we are using the free will God gave us for its intended purpose. Satan builds up strongholds with negative thoughts, but God's Word tears them down.

Develop Childlike Faith

Ashley and James both learned at an early age that evil thoughts and actions can affect their daily lives. I believe that if every small child can be taught *how* to think, not just told *what* to think, we would have teenagers and young people who could more easily overcome the worldliness and sin around them. They would learn how wonderful it is to think and talk like God, and how much easier life can be if they developed His personality traits. Living a moral life would be their choice, not something they felt compelled to do because of parents or teachers.

Most parents and Sunday school teachers have little training in how to think, since most churches emphasize *what* to think. When teenagers leave the security of home and church for college, many are lost for a while in the maze of worldliness that engulfs them. It is hard to defend beliefs that have not been arrived at from personal observations and conclusions earlier in life.

When children arrive at the conclusion that God's way of thinking is best for them, it becomes easier to stay away from worldly influences. After they enter high school and college, they aren't so easily drawn to the opinions of philosophers and professors who present mounds of evidence that confuse young students as they strive to live by the principles of Jesus.

Young people going into the workforce right out of high school are met with confusing ideas and are easily entangled by the many arms of the worldliness octopus. I believe this is why Jesus said, "Assuredly, I say to you, whoever does not receive the kingdom of God as a little child will by no means enter it" (Mark 10:15). The mind has to be free from the clutters of worldliness and sin before it can become childlike in its faith.

Once, while my grandson James was participating in sports competitions, he asked his mom to pray with him about winning medals. As she listened to his prayer, he asked God to help him win a medal, if it was all right with Him. If it wasn't, James said he would understand because he knew he couldn't win every competition. He already had one medal, but he said if God wanted to give him more than one medal that day, it would be all right with him.

His mom was amused by the sincerity of his prayer. But he won first place in many of the competitions that day.

Accept God's Wisdom

God wants us to become like little children and accept His discipline so that we might mature spiritually.

Many adult and teenage Christians make the mistake of thinking they don't need God's discipline and resist it mightily—sometimes to the point where they become sullen and disagreeable if someone mentions God's Word and encourages them to walk in His ways. They try to justify themselves and may think they are being criticized, condemned, or judged. Others will use the excuse "I'm only human" as their defense.

Christians will have a negative reaction to God's discipline if their minds have become hardened by the world's influence on them.

Determine God's Point of View

Often, you can't tell by a conversation with someone whether he or she is a Christian. Believers and unbelievers alike complain about events in their lives, and brood over negative incidents in the past that they have kept alive in their memories.

A group of critical-speaking people snapping and biting at one another can be likened to a pit of vipers. Entertainment on TV talk shows sometimes emulates the Christians being thrown into an arena full of lions. Still, there is no lack of people who want to appear on those shows to harass or criticize others, thinking it's fun.

Voicing a point of view can be healthy, but expecting others to share your point of view, and being a consistently critical person who reacts badly to opposition, is unhealthy for any individual.

One day, as I was meditating on disagreements some family members were having, the Lord presented a mental picture of a tree. He revealed that as each person looks at the tree, he sees only a portion of it. If he keeps moving around the tree, he can get a better idea of what it looks like, even though he can never see the entire tree, including its roots, the way God does. However, in arguments, each person is sure he has the entire picture of the tree; hence, they argue over what the tree looks like.

God never intended for us to see things the way He does. The Word tells us, "For now we see in a mirror, dimly, but then face to face. Now I know in part, but then I shall know just as I also am known" (1 Corinthians 13:12).

If we could know everything God does, we wouldn't need faith in Him. That is why God says, "My thoughts are not your thoughts, nor are your ways My ways" (Isaiah 55:8).

God wants us to strive to discern His point of view, using the wisdom He has so graciously given us in His Word, instead of choosing our own point of view and forcing others to agree with it. God has given each of us a piece of the truth. It's not the whole picture; however, it is enough for us to walk in His will.

Hear with Sensitivity

We hear negative speaking wherever we go. One day, as I was grocery shopping, an employee came up to the cashier and started talking about another employee. She vented her feelings of anger and justified her own judgments. I was forced to listen to the conversation before I could purchase my items.

This kind of talking and thinking is evident in our homes too. Satan enjoys pitting one family member against another because strife makes us vulnerable to his thoughts and his ways.

Jesus says, "Take heed what you hear. With the same measure you use, it will be measured to you; and to you who hear, more will be given" (Mark 4:24). He also tells us to be careful *how* we hear. "Therefore take heed how you hear. For whoever has, to him more will be given; and whoever does not have, even what he seems to have will be taken from him" (Luke 8:18).

Although we can't always control what we hear, we can control how we hear it. Meditation is the key to whatever enters our soul and spirit, good or bad. We must let the bad thoughts fly over our heads like birds so they will not take up residence in our spirits.

If we refuse to meditate on the goodness of God's Word, our faith will waiver. This causes us to fall prey to unbelief. Unbelief begets unbelief until we lose the faith we thought we had. That is why Jesus cautioned us to take control over what we hear and how we hear it.

Just as we are in control of what foods we allow to enter our bodies, we are in control of what thoughts we will meditate on. We can't be force fed with food. Try feeding an infant who doesn't want to eat—he blubbers and spits out food or just lets it roll out of his mouth. Neither can we be forced to think on certain things. We may have to hear many things we shouldn't hear. But we have the choice of letting thoughts fly away or harboring them in the mind.

Chapter 14

Eliminate Satan's Blame Game

We all have unpleasant things happen to us that are beyond our control. The usual strategy for dealing with problems is "the blame game."

I first learned about the blame game when I visited an institution for rebellious teenagers, alcoholics, and drug addicts. A retired army officer told these young people that the first thing they had to do before they could recover was to stop playing the blame game. Until they did that, their lives would continue to be messed up.

He encouraged them to concentrate on the day at hand and make plans for tomorrow. He told them they were each responsible for the success or failure of their lives, not their families or society. If they were drug addicts or alcoholics, that was their choice, and they could not blame their problems on others. He told those kids how dangerous the blame game is because it threatens any goal they might seek to achieve.

The blame game permeates our entire lives. This phenomenon begins as soon as a child is old enough to interact with other children or family members. It starts when Johnny grabs a toy from Susie's hand. Susie strikes back by punching Johnny in the face. He runs screaming to his mother and blames Susie for the problem. Susie defends her actions and blames Johnny for grabbing her toy.

These childlike incidents blossom into stronger and deadlier blame games as we become adults. We blame others for marital problems, financial problems, problems brought on by alcohol and drugs, health-related or work problems . . . the list goes on.

It is easy to develop the fine art of playing the blame game. When we focus on our discontentment, we can always find a scapegoat.

The word *scapegoat*, by the way, comes from Leviticus 16. Once a year, on the Day of Atonement, the Israelites took two equally fine goats. One was sacrificed to God. Aaron laid his hands on the other goat's head, confessed the sins of the people, and sent it away into the wilderness. When they transferred their sins to the scapegoat, they were cleansed from that year's sins.

Today, we might place the blame for our sins on our parents, spouses, children, friends, strangers, the government, or society in general. However, Jesus is our only true scapegoat. When we confess our sins, He carries them away. We don't need to blame others to be free from our personal or financial failures.

Uncover Hidden Traps

Satan has hidden traps lying in wait for us.

One hot, sunny day, as I headed out of the house for a swim class and then a doctor's appointment, I grabbed my purse and the bag that contained all my swim equipment. When I got in the car, I told my husband I'd forgotten to bring a long-sleeved jacket to cover my arms. Since I am allergic to the sun, I need to keep my body covered as much as possible. I explained that the reason I'd forgotten my jacket was that I was concentrating on what would keep me cool not protected.

Andy had been sitting in a hot car waiting for me, and he had grown restless. He suggested that when I had many things to do, I needed to get started on them earlier. That was his way of telling me he was tired of waiting for me. Time has always been a bone of contention with my husband, and he reprimanded me for making him wait so long in the car.

I went to my appointments without a jacket. But if I had thought of protection instead of heat before I left the house, it would only have taken a few seconds for me to grab a jacket.

PART ONE: NEGATIVE THINGS THAT COME AGAINST US

Andy and I could both have blamed each other for our discontentment. He could blame me for making him wait so long in a hot car, and I could blame him for not being concerned about my problem with the sun. But the Word says in Proverbs 17:14, "The beginning of strife is like releasing water; therefore stop contention before a quarrel starts." I let the subject drop and didn't pick up the ball to play the blame game, even though Satan tempted me to do so.

If we don't learn how to operate in the small confrontations in life, we will find ourselves playing the blame game on more dangerous levels. Stopping the game before it gets started is the only safe way to play. That means we have to avoid criticisms and insinuations in our conversations. If we try to justify our actions when we are criticized, we may set off a chain reaction of justification and condemnation.

There is no winner in the blame game because it's a satanic game that leads to hellish consequences.

Use Your Spiritual Trowel

If we constantly harbor thoughts of resentment against people, or become fretful with our daily problems, we will live unhappy lives.

Paul says, "Not that I speak in respect of want: for I have learned, in whatsoever state I am, therewith to be content. I know both how to be abased, and I know how to abound. . . . I can do all things through Christ which strengtheneth me" (Philippians 4:11–13 KJV).

Paul suffered much for serving Jesus. He spent many years of his life in prison for the sake of the gospel, and he died the death of a martyr. He knew how to play the blame game. Before he knew Christ, he blamed the Jews for following Jesus instead of remaining true to the Jewish traditions of worship. He was instrumental in the deaths of many Christians. But after his conversion to Christianity, he gave up the blame game and followed the teachings of Christ.

Jesus did not play the blame game, even while He was being crucified. He said, "Father, forgive them; for they know not what they do" (Luke 23:34 KJV).

When we allow seeds of discontentment to germinate and grow in our lives, they cause our thinking to focus on negative situations. This is harmful to the soul and it brings ill health to the body, not to mention the effect it has on the people around us. We have to guard ourselves daily against this weapon of Satan.

The seeds of discontentment choke spiritual growth like weeds choke the growth of a flower or vegetable garden. The only way to prevent discontentment from growing in the garden of the mind is to use our spiritual trowel—the Word of God—to keep digging them up.

Don't Pass the Buck

During the Depression in the 1930s, this country played the blame game with a frenzy. The stock market had failed. People stood in lines for food and jobs. It was a time of great despair. President Hoover was blamed for the Depression. Everyone blamed someone for something.

When Franklin Roosevelt became president, he instituted programs to get the country on its feet again. The people slowly recovered from their discontentment with one another and the government. The nation rallied around its positive-thinking leader, emerged from the Depression, and won the victory in World War II. Roosevelt became noted for his famous quote, "The buck stops here." That was the beginning of the healing the nation needed. The blame games stopped. Our country regained its dignity and honor.

Just as seeds of discontentment can radically change the morale of a nation, they can also radically change the nature of an individual. If the seeds of discontentment in a small child are allowed to grow until he becomes a teenager or adult, a rebellious spirit will develop. His rebellious spirit will cause him to lead an unproductive and unhappy life.

As soon as children are old enough to understand and communicate, they should be taught the principles that Jesus introduced. They should be taught that God desires them to do two things: (1) follow His rules and regulations so that they may enjoy their lives, and (2) produce much fruit for His kingdom.

Since we can't always know what our children are thinking, we must teach them how to think for themselves, and we must give them the Word of God to think about. It is crucial to their mental and physical health that they be reared in quiet, peaceful, loving homes, and taught how to settle disagreements without resorting to fights and outbursts of anger.

They need to be taught the golden rule: "Just as you want men to do to you, you also do to them likewise" (Luke 6:31). They have to be taught not to repay evil for evil, and to focus on positive rather than negative situations.

When parents become discontented, arguing in front of their children creates a tense atmosphere the children can feel. Anger begets anger. Arguments create more arguments.

On the other hand, peace and tranquility develop peaceful children, and love creates a loving spirit. Scripture tells us strife and confusion produce every evil work. "Where envy and self-seeking exist, confusion and every evil thing are there" (James 3:16).

Trash Bad Memories

All of us will experience some sort of discontentment in our lives. But a major catastrophe, such as death, can put a great strain on a person's ability to think properly.

My mind was in turmoil when I attended a retreat with the ladies of my church shortly after my husband Norman died. As I sat by myself on the shore of a small, man-made lake, I mentally sneered as I watched the other women having fun in the water with little rowboats. When my husband was in the military, oceans, ships, sailboats, large lakes, and motorboats had been the center of our recreation. I resented those ladies for enjoying themselves in what I considered childish, mundane ways. I was angry with them for stirring up memories of the festive activities I had enjoyed with my husband.

As I sat wallowing in my self-pity and feeling nothing but contempt for humanity, I thought of something that had been on the news for several days. A well-known doctor had been convicted of killing two of his four children for money. He had become an expert at hiding his evil thoughts, but those thoughts eventually influenced actions that led to murder.

I thought of the immense fear and grief those two remaining children and their mother must be enduring. I asked the Lord how people could overcome such tragedies and go on with their lives. He answered with three words: *Today is yesterday.*

As I meditated on this, I realized that each day that we climb out of bed we are given the opportunity to make a good yesterday. Our good yesterdays can outnumber our bad yesterdays. Concentrating on making happy memories will cause the sad memories to take their rightful place: in the sea of oblivion, not in the forefront of our minds.

That family had to overcome some very bad yesterdays, but with God's help I knew they could make it. (Many years later, I heard them tell their story on television, and they had learned to live happy lives again.)

While meditating on what God had revealed about today becoming yesterday, I realized I had to stop being angry with people who were enjoying life. My job was to find new ways to make good yesterdays. Anger and frustration would not make that possible. Good yesterdays happen when we use God's peace and love as motivators for our actions.

Develop Godly Love

Satan influences children and teenagers through their peers. They want to be popular, so they mimic the words, thoughts, music, activities, dress, and actions of their peers. The only thing that will keep them pure and their conscience undefiled is to teach them how to make wise decisions based on the Word of God. If parents do not walk in love—with each other as well as with others around them—they cannot teach their children to walk in love.

Jesus gave us just one commandment: "that you love one another as I have loved you" (John 15:12). "And this commandment we have from Him: that he who loves God must love his brother also" (1 John 4:21). Everything we learn in the New Testament is based on love—godly love.

In recent years, the media has reported several shootings in schools. The young adults who commit these crimes were involved in negative and destructive thoughts for years. Discontentment and resentment of authority, family, and peers created anger until it generated hate. That hate resulted in a monstrous display of emotions gone out of control.

The anger and hatred that lead to murder affect adults as well as children. After all, children only mimic what they see adults do.

When children who are not taught the things of God, they become vulnerable to satanic influences. These children's needs are not being met with godly love by those around them. Therefore, they find acceptance, and what they consider to be love, in ungodly places. The vultures in witchcraft and cults seek for prey among these unhappy children. They pretend to be benefactors and lavish special attention on them until they are pulled into the kingdom of darkness.

Witchcraft has always had Satan as its leader. Cults are led by men pretending to be godlike in nature, but they too fall under Satan's influence. Unless society exposes these fraudulent people as perpetrators from the kingdom of darkness, Satan will continue to have a field day with our children and society in general. His influence cannot be stopped until parents get back to the basics of God and His teachings.

Godly teaching has to start with parents. Church leaders, school teachers, and others who affect children will also be held accountable. However, I believe the Christian home can establish an environment that produces happy, well-adjusted children if the parents will discipline themselves in the Word of God and walk in God's love with their children and with others. Godly love will expel the ideas and situations that create prejudices in Christian homes. The children will feel good about themselves as they deal with the world, and they will be merciful and loving to all the people they will come in contact with.

Well-adjusted children from Christian homes and schools can make a difference in our environment. Thoughts influence actions—good or bad. By teaching our children how to think, we can control road rage, school shootings, alcoholism, drug addiction, divorce, sexual promiscuity, and other problems in society.

Chapter 15

Submit to God's Perfect Will

One day in Sunday school class, while we were discussing the problems in the church as well as those on the mission fields, I was surprised to learn that family relationship problems among missionaries outnumbered their concerns with health or finances. Issues such as divorce, infidelity, bankruptcy, and rebellious children are almost as prevalent in Christian homes as in non-Christian homes.

While in prayer one night, as I was considering the strife and confusion in Christian homes and the number of divorces among Christian families, I asked the Lord if these failures were because His people didn't love Him. The answer I heard in my spirit was: *It is not a matter of love but the surrendering of their will to Me.* He revealed to me that Christians surrender enough of their will to accept salvation but continue to embrace the ways of the world in their thinking, speaking, and actions.

In Romans, Paul addresses the dilemma that free will creates for men. "What I am doing, I do not understand. For what I will to do, that I do not practice; but what I hate, that I do. . . . But now, it is no longer I who do it, but sin that dwells in me. . . . For the good I will to do, I do not do; but the evil I will not to do, that I practice" (Romans 7:15–20).

As long as we live in a world where evil has a strong influence, we will be susceptible to Satan's influence. The higher the percentage of people surrendered to God, the smaller percentage of difficulties in our everyday lives.

PART ONE: NEGATIVE THINGS THAT COME AGAINST US

Most of us probably give about 50 percent of our will to God. The other half of our influence comes from the world. Those with a negative outlook on life are probably giving God less than 25 percent of their free will.

As long as we Christians continue to have an "I want to do it my way" attitude, the Holy Spirit will withdraw His influence and Satan will have a greater influence in our lives. Wisdom demands we take a daily inventory of our activities to determine when we are walking in our will instead of walking in the will of God.

If we start the day with a negative attitude that results in criticizing, complaining, and resentment, we allow anger or bitterness to nest in our minds.

We will be tested and tried every day, in many areas, while we live in the world. Nonetheless, God's will for us is to walk in the discipline of His Word with joyful hearts. Then we will prosper and be in good health, even as our soul prospers (3 John 2).

Repent

As I contemplated the inability of man to surrender his will to God, I thought of the problems Jonah had. If ever a man tried to get out of doing the will of God, it was Jonah. When he tried to run away from God and hide on a ship, a big storm came and nearly destroyed the boat. Since Jonah was the only stranger on board, the men figured he was responsible for their predicament. When he confessed that he was running from God, they decided to throw him overboard.

Even though we may not be prepared for the dilemmas we get ourselves into, God always is. In Jonah's case, God had a big whale standing by to swallow him. After he spent three days in the belly of that whale, in total darkness, away from God, Jonah finally repented. Then God did a miraculous thing: He had the whale spew Jonah out on dry land unharmed. Immediately, Jonah set off for Nineveh, willing to preach God's message of repentance to the evil city.

After Jonah preached to the people, they did what God wanted them to do. They repented, put on sackcloth, and declared a fast.

For some reason, Jonah didn't want God to use him to benefit the people. He was affronted when God, through his preaching, changed the people's hearts. He became angry with God. So he made a shelter and sat under it to pout about God's mercy and grace.

God caused a gourd to grow over Jonah to protect him from the heat of the sun for one day. That night God sent a worm to destroy the gourd. Jonah was more angry and bitter than ever because God destroyed the plant. But the Lord said, "You have had pity on the plant for which you have not labored, nor made it grow, which came up in a night and perished in a night. And should I not pity Nineveh, that great city, in which are more than one hundred and twenty thousand persons who cannot discern between their right hand and their left, and also much livestock?" (Jonah 4:10–11)

Jonah wanted to see the people persecuted because he had been forced to give them a message that commanded them to repent from their evil ways. He didn't understand that it was God's desire to save the people, not destroy them.

Christians are often like Jonah was. When God asks us to do things we really don't want to do, we procrastinate because we are unable to see the benefits derived from following His will. Even though, in our hearts, we know God wouldn't ask us to do anything that would harm us, we develop a rebellious spirit that leads us into unhappy situations because we are refusing to act upon the will of God.

This kind of thinking prevails when we are asked to change our way of reacting about certain people or past events. Have you been there? I have. Let's stop it! Our rebellious actions serve the enemy, not God.

PART ONE: NEGATIVE THINGS THAT COME AGAINST US

Reflect Jesus

Jesus came to earth to do the Father's will. He said, "I can of Myself do nothing. As I hear, I judge; and My judgment is righteous, because I do not seek My own will but the will of the Father who sent Me" (John 5:30).

Jesus constantly did His Father's will. He willingly allowed Himself to be crucified on the cross, then spent three days in Hades preaching to the spirits of the dead. He arose from the grave and spent some time on earth, where He was seen by various people, including the disciples, before He ascended to heaven to sit at His Father's right hand and intercede for us. Regardless of all the suffering Jesus endured here on earth, He continually reflected God's personality traits.

If we want to live happy, successful lives, we have to obey the will of God. Like Jesus and the apostles, it may mean doing things we aren't exactly thrilled to do. We don't want to imitate Jonah. His story shows us how ridiculous people can act when they run from God and refuse to do His will.

Many Christians exhibit Jonah's childlike behavior when they seem anxious to expose great men of God as fraudulent. Because many people have put such men upon pedestals, they desire to see God's wrath come down on them when they have publicly sinned and fallen short of God's glory.

Miniscule mercy is shown in the Christian community for those who fall. Why is that? I believe it is because many Christians are so worldly they are unable to reflect Jesus or the merciful and compassionate characteristics that comprise the personality of God. Love, honor, mercy, justice, understanding, kindness, gentleness, respect, long-suffering, joy, peace, wisdom, and forgiveness are just a few of His resplendent qualities, and they should be part of our own personality features as well.

However, our free will keeps us from exhibiting the true nature of God that we receive after we are born again spiritually. There are few Christians like Paul, who reflected Jesus as he poured himself out "as a drink offering on the sacrifice" to strengthen our faith (Philippians 2:17).

Many of us are so inundated with worldly thoughts and actions that it is hard for us to relinquish even a small portion of our will to God. Until we develop the desire to reflect Jesus by developing His personality traits, we will continue to walk in defeat in many areas of our lives. Yet God will continue to work in us "both to will and do for His good pleasure" (Philippians 2:13).

Seek God's Counsel

Regardless of the weapons Satan uses to sway our minds and our actions, if we listen to God, His counsel will give us the strength we need to defeat evil. Proverbs 19:21 says, "There are many plans in a man's heart, nevertheless the Lord's counsel—that will stand."

Proverbs 21:16 says, "A man who wanders from the way of understanding will rest in the congregation of the dead." Jesus said, "He is not the God of the dead but of the living, for all live to Him" (Luke 20:38). Without an understanding of God's wisdom, we open ourselves to all kinds of devilish things. Our spirits will no longer be connected to God and we will be spiritually dead as far as God is concerned.

Our reactions under tension reflect whether we have been wandering from God's way of understanding or have been meditating on His Word. What we meditate on enters into our spirits, and our thoughts influence our actions. If we put water into a jar, we can't expect to pour out milk. The same is true with thoughts. If the spirit is filled with ideas that come from negative thinking, God's Word will not flow out of our mouths in times of tribulation.

It is the Lord's desire that we sit down with Him, fellowship, and reason together, just as the ancient philosophers of Athens and Rome did when they met in courtyards and discussed the affairs of men. God said to the Israelites, "Wash you, make you clean; put away the evil of your doings from before mine eyes; cease to do evil; learn to do well; seek judgment, relieve the oppressed, judge the fatherless, plead for the widow" (Isaiah 1:16–17 KJV).

God laid out the plan of salvation and redemption for the Israelites and commanded them to walk according to His rules and regulations, follow His ways, and listen to His counsel. However, they failed to do that. And they have spent centuries suffering the consequences.

Ever since Jesus came to redeem man from sin, God has been asking Christians to walk in His counsel through the Word. However, we have failed most of the time because we covet our free will and refuse to allow God to control our thought life.

Recognize the Illusion

Scripture tells us God is speaking the same things to us today as He did to ancient Israel. "I am the Lord, I do not change; therefore you are not consumed, O sons of Jacob" (Malachi 3:6).

"His work is honorable and glorious, and His righteousness endures forever" (Psalm 111:3). God has always wanted His people to listen to His voice and follow His ways—not for His benefit, but for ours. Doing so gives us a healthy, happy, prosperous life.

So why do we ignore the Word of God? I believe we are looking for happiness but we don't understand what happiness is. We think it can be found in people or the things of the world.

During a time of prayer and meditation, I heard in my spirit: *Happiness as man knows it is an illusion.*

Happiness is like a butterfly: elusive, changing, and constantly fleeting. Nevertheless, we think if we run hard enough, we can catch it.

The water we see in the desert is only a mirage. Happiness as man knows it is also an illusion. It is not real.

However, we keep chasing that fleeting image, expecting to find something that will make us happy. We don't realize that happiness does not depend on people, things, wealth, or fame. True happiness for humankind lies in a relationship with God.

Each person is responsible for making himself or herself happy. Since it is an act of the will, we have to make a deliberate choice to be happy people. Proverbs 16:20 says, "He who heeds the word wisely will find good, and whoever trusts in the Lord, happy is he."

For our spirit to be happy, we must meditate on spiritual things: whatsoever is beautiful, pure, just, praiseworthy, and of good report (Philippians 4:8). The pleasures of worldliness create a facade of happiness, but harmony with God creates true happiness.

King Solomon chased the illusion of happiness. God gave Solomon his heart's desire: first wisdom, then power, wealth, fame, and a large family. Yet when Solomon spent too much time in worldly activities and too little time with God, everything became vanity and vexation of spirit to him.

Solomon made this observation about the spiritual and physical journey of life: "Let us hear the conclusion of the whole matter: Fear God and keep His commandments, for this is man's all. For God will bring every work into judgment, including every secret thing, whether good or evil" (Ecclesiastes 12:13–14).

Psalm 94:19 tells us that our thoughts of God will bring us the happiness we seek. "In the multitude of my anxieties within me, Your comforts delight my soul." The joy of the Lord does not come from circumstances, people, or material things. It comes through our relationship with God—His Spirit communicating with our spirit. We can be full of His joy even in the midst of our worst trials if those trials cause us to walk closer and draw nearer to our Creator.

Two Ways of Life

The mind is the battleground for the spirit of man. However, the mind has a free will, so each person is accountable for his or her own decisions. Even a child can be taught the difference between thinking bad thoughts that will make him sad or good thoughts that will make him happy. Regardless of age, our thoughts will ultimately influence our actions, and our way of life will reflect the thoughts we have chosen to meditate on.

The psalmist gives us a good description of a righteous man's life:

> Blessed is the man who walks not in the counsel of the ungodly, nor stands in the path of sinners, nor sits in the seat of the scornful; but his delight is in the law of the Lord, and in His law he meditates day and night. He shall be like a tree planted by the rivers of water, that brings forth its fruit in its season, whose leaf also shall not wither; and whatever he does shall prosper. (Psalm 1:1–3)

Although the Word assures us that a man who delights in the law of the Lord will prosper, that is not the case with the wicked. "The ungodly are not so, but are like the chaff which the wind drives away. Therefore the ungodly shall not stand in the judgment, nor sinners in the congregation of the righteous. For the Lord knows the way of the righteous, but the way of the ungodly shall perish" (Psalm 1:4–6).

The Choice Belongs to Us

Satan, our enemy, uses all his resources—including the pleasures and fortunes of this life—to entice human beings to follow his thoughts and his pattern of life. We have to choose whom we will serve. The final determination for the success or failure of our lives depends on the percentage of our free will that is willingly submitted to God.

"Blessed is the man whom You instruct, O Lord, and teach out of Your law. . . . For the Lord will not cast off His people, nor will He forsake His inheritance" (Psalm 94:12–14). God's plans are to prosper each person who walks in His will and His ways.

PART ONE: NEGATIVE THINGS THAT COME AGAINST US

Father, we thank You for Your Word, which teaches us how to think properly and focus on Your righteousness. Help us teach our children how to keep their thoughts free from the influence of Satan. Amen.

God's River

Let me drink from God's river

That flows from the throne above.

Let me drink of God's goodness,

Of His mercy and His love.

Oh, waters may be troubled;

Mountains may swell and shake.

But God has a peaceful river

That flows from His holy place.

PART TWO

NEGATIVE EMOTIOINS THAT COME AGAINST US

Negative emotions cause us to lose God's blessings.

Pride
Fear
Unforgiveness

No weapon formed against you shall prosper
and every tongue which rises against you
in judgment You shall condemn. This is the
heritage of the servants of the Lord, and
their righteousness is from Me, says the Lord.
(Isaiah 54:17)

Discipline #4: Pride

Pride keeps man centered on self instead of God.

By pride comes only contention,
but with the well-advised is wisdom.
(Proverbs 13:10)

Chapter 16

Pride Originates from Satan

Pride can be described as an overly high opinion of oneself, exaggerated self-esteem, and an excessive belief in one's own worth, which leads to conceit, haughtiness, or arrogance.

The sin of pride originated with Satan. If we acquire a depraved or debauched personality, we have degenerated in moral conduct to the point where we are as perverted in all of our thinking as Satan is.

In the beginning, Satan (originally called Lucifer) was beautiful, talented, and full of wisdom—until he let the sin of pride debase him. Pride changed the seal of perfection that God had placed on him and he became evil personified.

Ezekiel 28:14–16 says, "You were the anointed cherub who covers; I established you; you were on the holy mountain of God; you walked back and forth in the midst of fiery stones. You were perfect in your ways from the day you were created, till iniquity was found in you. . . . Therefore I cast you as a profane thing out of the mountains of God; and I destroyed you, O covering cherub, from the midst of the fiery stones."

Isaiah adds, "How you are fallen from heaven, O Lucifer, son of the morning! . . . For you have said in your heart: 'I will ascend into heaven, I will exalt my throne above the stars of God; . . . I will be like the Most High.' Yet you shall be brought down to Sheol, to the lowest depths of the Pit" (Isaiah 14:12–15).

Pride stimulates selfish ambitions and leads to moral decay. Satan entices us to concentrate on glorifying ourselves instead of seeking ways to glorify the God who created us.

Satan wheedled Adam and Eve into the sin of pride through coveting, because he knew from his own experience that God would banish them from the garden of Eden. After the seed of pride was planted in mankind, Satan was able to become the god of this world. This victory convinced him that he had outmaneuvered God.

Pride Is an Abomination

Proverbs 16:5 says, "Everyone who is proud in heart is an abomination to the Lord; though they join forces, none will go unpunished." God despises pride.

The twelve tribes of Israel joined forces with Satan when they decided to worship idols of clay instead of listening to God's prophets. They were punished for their pride and the abominable things it caused them to do. They lost their status as a nation and were exiled into foreign lands.

Satan still believes he can outfox God. Since he knows how much God loves people, he tries to make us reprehensible to God by getting us to imitate him instead of imitating our Creator.

Paul reminded the early Christians to align themselves with God. He said, "Be imitators of God as dear children. And walk in love, as Christ also has loved us and given Himself for us, an offering and a sacrifice to God for a sweet smelling-aroma" (Ephesians 5:1–2).

Though God created Satan to be highly intelligent, he couldn't visualize God's plan for humanity and how the blood from the crucifixion of Jesus would redeem mankind. God outfoxed Satan because he couldn't foresee the end results.

Christians have the capability to crush Satan's authority here on earth. But if we don't use the disciplines of God's Word, Satan can have his predominance over us.

Jesus went to hell and preached to the generations there who had died before He was crucified and rose from the dead. He is now seated at the right hand of God. Angels, authorities, and powers are subject to Him. (See 1 Peter 3:19–22.)

"They will give an account to Him who is ready to judge the living and the dead. For this reason the gospel was preached also to those who are dead, that they might be judged according to men in the flesh, but live according to God in the spirit" (1 Peter 4:5–6).

After Jesus returned to heaven He said, "I am He who lives, and was dead, and behold, I am alive forevermore. Amen. And I have the keys of Hades and of Death" (Revelation 1:18).

Pride Begets Negative Emotions

Negative emotions are from Satan, not God.

When I began studying negative emotions, the Holy Spirit informed me that all negative emotions could be summed up in three categories: pride, fear, and unforgiveness.

When I asked the Holy Spirit if a negative emotion could fit in more than one category, He brought to my mind a game I played when I was a small child. I would entwine my fingers in the palms of my hands and close my fists, leaving the two thumbs standing together outside, and say, "Here is the church-house (my fists); here is the steeple (two thumbs). Open the door and here are the people (fingers)." He said that these three negative emotions can be entwined like fingers.

In many cases, it is easy to distinguish whether a negative emotion is coming from pride, fear, or unforgiveness. However, pride can stem from fear, or fear can stem from pride. For instance, the person who has feelings of inferiority may be fearful of ridicule. Unforgiveness may stem from sensitivity and the pride involved in hurt feelings.

God created Satan, and Satan originated the sin of pride. All negative emotions stem from the original sin. Pride is like the trunk of a tree, and its branches consist of other negative emotions. The roots of the tree of pride are fed by Satan.

Adam and Eve did not experience a negative emotion until they disobeyed God. Satan was able to entice them to desire knowledge they didn't have. God did not want them to know about evil (Genesis 3:5–6). When they allowed the negative emotion of pride into their spirits, they received the negative emotion of fear. Their reaction to God was different because trust and love turned into distrust and fear.

After they had eaten the forbidden fruit and heard the sound of God walking in the garden, they hid. When the Lord God called to Adam, he said, "I heard Your voice in the garden, and I was afraid because I was naked; and I hid myself" (Genesis 3:10).

There was no sin in the garden of Eden until pride reared its ugly head. From that moment on we have had to fight against negative emotions that lead us into sin. (See Genesis 4.)

Pride affects all aspects of society, families, and nations.

The US Senate asked President Abraham Lincoln to proclaim a national day for prayer and fasting during the Civil War. He asked the people to abstain from secular activities on Thursday, April 30, 1863, to unite in their places of worship and fast and pray. In his proclamation he described man's sinful nature eloquently:

> We have been the recipients of the choicest bounties of Heaven. . . . We have forgotten the gracious hand which preserved us in peace . . . and we have vainly imagined, in the deceitfulness of our hearts, that all these blessings were produced by some superior wisdom and virtue of our own. Intoxicated with unbroken success . . . we have become . . . too proud to pray to the God that made us.[2]

Those same words could have been said about the Israelites after God took them to the Promised Land, but they were said

---

[2] Abraham Lincoln, "Proclamation Appointing a National Fast Day," in Roy P. Basler (ed.), *Collected Works of Abraham Lincoln*, Vol. 6 (New Brunswick, NJ: Rutgers University Press, 1953), 156.

about the United States of America in 1863. Today we are even more intoxicated with our self-sufficiency. Our government has been influenced to take prayer out of public schools, but that was just the beginning. Many political figures are trying to minimize our forefathers' dependency on the Christian principles our nation was founded on. Instead of looking to God for help, we are doing just as the Israelites did: trying to walk in our own counsel.

The Soul Is Pride's Domicile

The words *psychology* and *psychoanalysis* come from *psyche,* the Greek word for "soul." Pride is spawned in the mind and emotions and resides in the human soul. Psychologists teach that the mind is made up of the id, ego, and superego. The following explanations of these terms are based on Merriam-Webster's definitions.[3]

The id is completely unconscious and is the source of psychic energy derived from instinctual needs and desires. It is the reservoir of the libido, which consciously expresses that instinctive energy. The id is the driving force behind all human actions involving pleasure, sexual activity, and wishful thinking.

The ego is the self, the part we are aware of. It develops from the id and experiences the external world through the senses. It is the organized, conscious mediator between the person and reality. It controls the impulses of the id. All of our experiences are superimposed upon the ego. Egoism develops from focusing on self and one's own interests. That makes it easy for Satan to plant the seed of pride in the mind and emotions of a self-centered person. The extent to which the seed of pride is fertilized and allowed to ripen depends on the circumstances, experiences, and free will of each individual.

The superego is the part of the psyche that dominates the actions of the id at a partly conscious level. It represents the internalization of parental conscience and the rules of society. It rewards or

[3] *Merriam-Webster's Collegiate Dictionary*, 11th ed., (Springfield, Massachusetts: Merriam-Webster, Incorporated, 2007).

punishes through a system of moral attitudes, conscience, and a sense of guilt. Restraint of the id and ego by the superego helps us stay in balance.

God created these checks and balances of the mind, similar to the checks and balances in our government. The Supreme Court is an overruling power regarding decisions made by the president, House of Representatives, and Senate.

Our will is comparable to the Supreme Court. It is the final authority for the soul. Through the will, God allows us to make free choices. The will is an overriding power that determines how life's experiences are allowed to affect the psyche of a person.

Pride sneaks up on us at various stages. It subtly affects us every day. When we are puffed up with pride, we can fall into the same condemnation as the devil (1Timothy 3:6).

Chapter 17

Common Faces of Pride

Pride wears many faces. It is easy to recognize those associated with arrogance. But those that portray sensitivity may not even be recognized as a face of pride.

We have been led to believe that certain faces of pride are harmless. However, pride is a characteristic of Satan and we don't want our character influenced by any of his attributes. All faces of pride affect our behavior and keep us focused on self.

Aggressive Behavior

A person who develops a feeling of superiority often shows it in an excessively aggressive manner. He may be of super intelligence, multitalented, better educated than the average man. These qualities can make someone either egotistical or humble. The way we relate to our self-importance determines how our personality emerges.

People who seem to have a superiority complex can actually be bluffing their way through life because they feel inadequate. Their low self-esteem makes them feel defenseless, so they develop the bully syndrome, continually trying to prove that they have the superior qualities they see in others.

A person who acts superior due to an inferiority complex is fearful that someone will expose him. So he tries to hide his inferior feelings by boasting, swaggering, and criticizing others.

Destructive Behavior

Regardless of whether a person truly feels superior or if he is putting on a camouflage, the results can be the same. First John 2:16 says, "For all that is in the world—the lust of the flesh, the lust of the eyes, and the pride of life—is not of the Father but is of the world."

Proverbs 16:18 says, "Pride goes before destruction, and a haughty spirit before a fall." A prideful man will eventually cause his own destruction.

Satan could have gone about God's business, continuing to glorify God; instead, his contemptuous spirit got him thrown out of heaven. Jesus witnessed Satan's fall from grace. In Luke 10:18 He said, "I saw Satan fall like lightning from heaven."

Proverbs 14:3 says, "In the mouth of a fool is a rod of pride, but the lips of the wise will preserve them." The Word tells us that a prideful man is still a fool, even if he has been given wisdom from God. Satan allowed his beauty to pervert his wisdom when he challenged the authority of God.

During World War II, Adolf Hitler exhibited extreme feelings of superiority that were closely akin to Satan's. He not only felt superior himself, he enticed a whole nation to join him in his quest to prove that the Jewish people and other nationalities were inferior to the German people. He practiced genocide on Germans as well as the Jews.

Hitler was one of the most destructive men in history. It was his idea to develop a nation of super-intelligent people, physically and mentally perfect, all with blue eyes and fair skin. It didn't matter to him how much property was destroyed or how many people had to die to accomplish his fiendish whims.

At a Christian women's fellowship dinner I attended, a speaker gave us firsthand information on the horror she experienced and witnessed as a child in World War II. She mentioned one specific atrocity Hitler perpetrated on the German people. He took victims of epilepsy into supposedly protective confinement. After the war, when the families tried to locate them, they discovered they had been gassed.

Disparaging Remarks

This speaker also talked about the feelings she and other German children had in school. Along with pangs of hunger, they felt absolute terror from the bombings. However, the thing that affected them most was the spirit of cruelty that dominated the actions of teachers and parents.

The children were disciplined severely for the slightest infraction and were constantly told how worthless they were. They were seldom, if ever, shown loving, positive emotions from adults, and crying was considered a sign of weakness.

The German adults in World War II experienced stress from bombings, too, as well as freezing cold weather with no fuel, and insufficient food and clothing for their families. Striving to be strong while being subjected to barbaric treatment reinforced cruelty in the adults. This was part of Hitler's indoctrination program to make Germans feel superior to people from other nations.

Germany suffered a great defeat in World War I. The value of the German currency fell quickly and the citizens lost their confidence and self-respect. They experienced a condition similar to our Great Depression. The Nazis exploited this fear. They told the German people they were superior but that the Jews who were prominent in the banking industry had undermined their security. This led to persecution of the Jewish people, along with other ethnic groups.

In his book *Witnesses to War,* Michael Leapman tells how the Germans' problems with feelings of inferiority turned into feelings of superiority that allowed Hitler to succeed in murdering millions of people. Leapman presents eight true-life stories of Nazi persecution and tells how the children survived to become successful adults and live prosperous lives.

A few Jewish children who fit Hitler's superiority mold were adopted into German families who did not know they were Jewish. Most of these children were too young to remember their heritage, so they were never located and were presumed dead. But one girl who was adopted by a German couple had an older friend who remembered her and was instrumental in getting her returned to relatives after the war.[4]

The speaker I heard believed that if Germany had won the war, many blue-eyed German people, including her, might have been submitted to the carnage of Hitler's purge as well, because some children and adults wouldn't have measured up to his rigid standards.

In the United States, we heard reports that the Nazi military men were forbidden to marry girls who wore glasses. Hitler considered all congenital physical disorders, such as near-sightedness, as abhorrent as leprosy.

I was fifteen years old when World War II started. I was seventeen when I began wearing glasses for astigmatism. When I heard about Hitler forbidding his military men to marry girls who wore glasses, it gave me a feeling of inadequacy. Even in our society at that time, I heard remarks that men preferred to date girls who didn't wear glasses. In those days people were not given the option to cover weak eyes with contact lenses.

Fortunately, my popularity as a teenager began before I started wearing glasses. Pie suppers were held in my rural community to help raise money for the Red Cross during World War II. Bidding on pies made for a fun-filled evening, with the winner of the pretty-girl contest receiving a box of chocolates. This event raised community spirits during a time of tremendous stress. It also helped raise the morale of young teenagers like myself when we won.

---

[4] Michael Leapman, *Witnesses to War: Eight True-Life Stories of Nazi Persecution* (New York, NY: Scholastics, Inc., by arrangement with Penguin Putman, Inc., February 2000).

PART TWO: NEGATIVE EMOTIONS THAT COME AGAINST US

Young people strive to be popular with their peers. Any kind of teasing can represent cruelty to a sensitive person. I was teased and called "four eyes" when I started wearing glasses. A person with healthy eyes may experience a sense of superiority when he or she makes disparaging remarks about someone who wears glasses. Even this face of pride is an abomination to the Lord.

But God is faithful. Though it may take many years, His love can help us recover from inhumane treatment that society inflicts upon us as children or adults.

Contention

Parents should stop aggressive behavior in their children when they see it. In many cases, teachers and parents ignore the children who are tormentors and focus on helping the victims overcome their frailties.

We do a disservice to children when we allow them to ridicule others. They should be held accountable for their actions, because their pride will only get worse as they get older. It will leave them indefensible to Satan's traps.

A person with a superiority complex gets embroiled in situations that cause contention, hurt feelings, jealousy, and anger. Proverbs 29:23 says, "A man's pride will bring him low, but the humble in spirit will retain honor."

Adolph Hitler's superiority complex caused enough strife and discord to start World War II. Since pride can cause men to fall into the same condemnation as the devil, pride should be shunned in the same way we shun murder, stealing, and other sins.

Infallibility

Some people have a high percentage of being right in situations because they deliberate carefully before making decisions. They can develop an overwhelming desire to always be right. My dad was one of those people. He used to laugh at himself and remark, "I may not always be right, but I am never wrong."

People with feelings of infallibility are striving for perfection. Since they think and act methodically, they are positive that their decisions are best. Feelings of infallibility may keep them from admitting to an act of wrongdoing and instead try to justify themselves.

Such individuals are difficult to deal with. They tend to insist that the rest of the world march to the beat of their drums. They don't realize that they are imitating Satan.

Lucifer, a perfect specimen of God's creation, fell from God's grace because his feelings of superiority superseded his wisdom. At the end of the millennium, Satan will be allowed to lead a rebellion against the saints for a short time before God intervenes. Revelation 20:10 informs us of Satan's fate. "And the devil, who deceived them, was cast into the lake of fire and brimstone where the beast and the false prophet are. And they will be tormented day and night forever and ever."

When pride makes a person attempt to stand head and shoulders above the rest, his fall can be as great as Hitler's or Satan's. There has been only one perfect human being on earth: Jesus Christ, the Son of God.

Arrogance

After God led the Israelites to the Promised Land and helped them conquer their enemies, each tribe developed a feeling of infallibility that led to arrogance. Hosea 7:10 says, "The pride of Israel testifies to his face, but they do not return to the Lord their God, nor seek Him for all this."

When God fought for them, they were able to overthrow the giants and take the land that He had promised to the descendants of Abraham. Instead of being grateful to God and honoring Him, their arrogance caused them to disregard His ways. They walked in the lust of the flesh and worshipped idols.

The pride that spawned arrogance among the Israelites began when Esau's twin brother, Jacob, who was later called Israel, received his father's blessing instead of Esau. The curses of jealousy and hatred were passed on from generation to generation.

Esau was given the name Edom (which means "red") after he traded his birthright for red stew meat. God was furious at the nation of Edom because they delighted in the captivity of Israel and Judah. God warned of Edom's judgment when He said, "For violence against your brother Jacob, shame shall cover you, and you shall be cut off forever" (Obadiah 1:10).

The Edomites felt secure in their fortified cities because the land was a rocky, mountainous fortress, making it almost impossible for armies to penetrate into the region. However, the land they occupied became desolate and uninhabitable because the water in the area dried up. When God cursed the people, He also cursed the land. No survivor was left in the house of Esau because they continued to insult God with their arrogant behavior. (See Obadiah 1:15–18.)

Negative Sensitivity Is a Face of Pride

Some people get their feelings hurt easily and often. But hurt feelings also come from pride.

God wants us to be sensitive using the facets of His personality we inherit from Him: kindness, compassion, mercy, long-suffering, gentleness, meekness, humility, peace, and forgiveness. These emotions are positive. They help us grow spiritually and are good for our physical and mental health. They can reward us financially and socially.

But when we use our feelings of sensitivity in a negative way, they create friction, confusion, strife, and division. These negative emotions can be detrimental to our health as well as our finances. They harm relationships with spouses, children, coworkers, and other Christians. People with negative sensitivities find it hard to have a life of peace and joy because they are focused on defending themselves against nebulous attacks on their character.

Timidity

We are apt to confuse timidity with humbleness. But true humility comes from a person who is strong enough in the Word of God that no one can make him or her feel timid or insignificant, and humility does not propagate other negative emotions.

Those who are timid in their relationships are usually concerned about what people may say or think about them. Timid people do not consider themselves prideful, but timidity allows pride to rear its ugly head in many circumstances.

Timidity can affect us when we change jobs, schools, or churches, or whenever we have to deal with strangers. It can affect us in seeking employment, asking for raises, or getting promotions. Timidity can leave us feeling lonely and keep us from making friends easily.

Some people suffer timidity when they have to speak before a crowd. I have always been able to talk to strangers easily, but I dislike speaking in front of groups.

Timid people who hate to make speeches may worry about such things as how they look, whether their voice is pleasing, if their grammar is right, or how they can hold the attention of their audience. All of these negative reactions have the root of pride and the fruit of fear.

If you are a timid person, you need to stop thinking of yourself so much and ask God for favor in areas where you feel uncomfortable. Speaking in front of a crowd may seem like an enormous problem to overcome, but we should all glorify God with any talent He gives us. The Bible says that Jesus continued in favor with man and God (Luke 2:52).

God is our justifier, and those He justifies He also glorifies. If He is for us, it doesn't matter who is trying to come against us or put us down. If we know we have favor and justification with God, we should be able to overcome any problems we may have with timidity (Romans 8:30–31).

Anger and Criticism

One Sunday after attending a church service, Andy and I went to a local restaurant for lunch. A few other people came in after we ordered our meal. Their food arrived and they were half finished with their meals before our food came. After the waiter brought our lunch, he left to prepare drinks for a party of seven. We finished eating before our drinks arrived.

This was too much for my husband to tolerate, and he allowed pride's face of anger to surface. I was ashamed of his rude remarks, so my anger smoldered against him and the waiter who had treated us so shabbily.

The anger we were feeling stemmed from being treated unfairly. It made us succumb to the seed of pride that we had allowed to germinate in us. My demeanor was more composed than Andy's because I hate conflict in public. But God did not consider me any less abominable than my husband, because the sin of pride was being exposed in both of us. Instead of releasing patience in our spirits through the Word and prayer, we allowed anger and criticism to surface and ruin a good lunch.

If we listen to the voices around us in the workplace, in grocery stores, restaurants, homes, or wherever our day takes us, we will probably hear more angry, criticizing voices than happy voices giving good reports. When we are in full-blown anger, we become critical of everything and everyone around us.

The Word says, "Make no friendship with an angry man, and with a furious man do not go, lest you learn his ways and set a snare for your soul" (Proverbs 22:24–25). Anger causes us to fall into the traps set by Satan.

Television news depicts the results of uncontrolled anger every day. Anger is causing crime to increase at a high rate. It can become a bad habit in seemingly insignificant areas, then it explodes and creates catastrophes like murder or terrorism or war.

Christians usually try to justify anger when they have been maligned or have hurt feelings by saying Jesus got angry. But

Jesus' anger wasn't personal. His was a righteous anger against the people who defamed God's temple. He also spoke harshly to religious people who denied the power of the Holy Spirit. He never became angry with the common people, only the religious leaders who were ruling the people with prideful arrogance.

When Jesus was spit upon, beaten, ridiculed, and attacked, He never returned the insults. Just before He died, He asked His Father to forgive the people who had condemned Him to death. (See Luke 23:34.) We might occasionally have some righteous anger, but most of our anger is not righteous. And we don't fool God, only ourselves.

Offense

Whether we are offending others or being offended, we are involved in a face of pride. Our feelings of inadequacy around certain people or in particular circumstances may cause us to be overly sensitive. When we are made to feel incompetent, feelings of envy and resentfulness can emerge.

God's Word gives us wisdom to help us eliminate emotional outbursts. The psalmist shows us how he rose above offenses when he says, "Seven times a day I praise You, because of Your righteous judgments. Great peace have those who love Your law, and nothing causes them to stumble" (Psalm 119:164–165).

Praising God constantly, rejoicing in His Word daily, and standing in awe of God and His laws can bring the peace we need to rid us of our negative sensitivities. God desires that we not take offense at injustice or allow ourselves to offend others.

Paul admonished the Christians of Corinth because they had been in disputes about the new religion of Christianity. He said, "Give no offense, either to the Jews or to the Greeks or to the church of God, just as I also please all men in all things, not seeking my own profit, but the profit of many, that they may be saved" (1 Corinthians 10:32–33).

When Christians offend people, this detestable act is instigated by pride. If non-Christians see the face of pride in us, our sin might keep them from becoming believers.

Rudeness

Contemptuous actions receive little attention today because so many people are unmannerly and rude. We hear rudeness in conversations. Rudeness explodes into road rage. People push and shove to get ahead of one another in crowds, ignoring elderly people and small children.

Manners and diplomacy are part of our heritage from our forefathers. However, in the sixties, there was a gradual change referred to as "the me generation." It flaunted the established rules, was self-seeking, and disregarded the needs of others.

Even in our churches we find rude, insensitive people. Their actions create division and strife that stunt spiritual growth.

There was no place for rudeness in the heart of Jesus. And we represent Jesus to those around us. We can overcome rudeness with the help of the Holy Spirit.

Overcoming the Faces of Pride

Any face of pride keeps us from walking in love with the power and anointing that God desires. Instead of rejoicing in the Lord, we can let the stress of life lead to contention and jealousy, and keep us from receiving the peace of God that passes understanding. (See Philippians 4:5–7.) Without peace in our hearts we are unable to rise above the frailties represented in the negative sensitivities of our emotions.

Jesus said, "Come to Me, all you who labor and are heavy laden, and I will give you rest. Take My yoke upon you and learn from Me, for I am gentle and lowly in heart, and you will find rest for your souls. For My yoke is easy and My burden is light" (Matthew 11:28–30).

Pride in any form is a heavy yoke to bear. But Jesus said if we are yoked with Him, our burdens will be light. He does not carry the yoke of pride: feelings of superiority, infallibility, or negative sensitivities. Instead, He has a gentle spirit and a loving heart.

Chapter 18

Pride Manipulators Produce Vendettas

When pride rears its ugly head in personal confrontations between husband and wife, among children, within families, or in any relationship, it immediately seeks to justify itself. It begins plotting against its opponents in retaliation for perceived misdeeds. Pride's main desire is to divide and conquer, and its agenda is accomplished amazingly easily.

Each day on the news we hear of plots and counterplots going on in Israel between Muslims and Jews. These personal vendettas, raids, and terrorist attacks stem from centuries of war and hate. The quarreling started with Abraham and Lot, was passed down to Jacob and Esau and their descendants, and continued in the countries that God helped Israel overthrow when they left Egypt and entered the Promised Land.

God chose to work with Israel and Judah over all other nations because of Abraham's righteousness. However, Israel and Judah's pride caused them to be sent into captivity. Now that God has brought the nation of Israel back into their homeland, plots to overthrow them are as strong as ever. Unfortunately, the turmoil among the tribes of Abraham will continue until Jesus returns to set His kingdom in order.

Jealousy Produces Vendettas

Jealousy and pride caused continual threats against the lives of the kings of Israel and Judah. The plotting for David's life started when the prophet Samuel anointed him king over Israel to replace

Saul, Israel's first king. Saul did not follow God's commandments, so his sons could not inherit the throne of Israel.

God wanted Jesus to come through the seed of David. He knew David would never lose the faith he had developed as a child, and that he would always praise God and seek His face no matter what the situation entailed.

David says in Psalm 108:3, "I will praise You, O Lord, among the peoples, and I will sing praises to You among the nations."

As David was coming home after conquering the Philistines, "the women sang as they danced, and said: 'Saul has slain his thousands, and David his ten thousands'" (1 Samuel 18:7). This song put King Saul in a jealous rage, and David had to remain in hiding for many years to escape various plots against his life.

David was not to be officially made king until after Saul died. But because of his insane jealousy, Saul demanded David's death. Jonathan, the son of Saul, loved David like a brother, and he was a great asset to David during his years of oppression by Saul. David wept bitterly when Jonathan was killed.

Scheming Produces Vendettas

After David became king over Israel, he still had plots against his life. His son Absalom wanted to be king over Israel. But David was overwhelmed with grief when Absalom was killed.

Adonijah, Absalom's brother, tried to make himself king over Israel in David's old age. However, David stopped the plot by having Solomon sworn in as king in a special ceremony. Eventually, King Solomon had to put Adonijah to death because of his scheming and treacherous ways. (See 1 Kings 1–2.)

The psalms written by David show us that his life was full of physical suffering, sorrow, and grief. He spent a great deal of time trying to preserve his life because pride and greed caused men to scheme and war against him.

David says, "They devise iniquities: 'We have perfected a shrewd scheme.' Both the inward thought and the heart of man are deep" (Psalm 64:6). His psalms give us examples of how he received help from God. He presented his problems to God. He renewed his strength and courage during long ordeals of oppression and persecution by remembering God's blessings. And he put his trust in God while he waited for instructions and help.

David says to God in Psalm 63:6–7, "When I remember You on my bed, I meditate on You in the night watches. Because You have been my help, therefore in the shadow of Your wings I will rejoice."

The psalms David wrote inspire us, increase our faith, and encourage us to glorify God in times of tribulation. As we read about the kings of Israel, we can see that pride is a manipulator and that it pits man against man. (See 1 and 2 Samuel; 1 and 2 Kings.)

The same type of plots Satan used in the Old and New Testaments against God and His people are being used today to break up families. Children murder their parents for diverse reasons, including physical or mental abuse, or disagreements over money.

Christians, along with the rest of the world, engage in character assassination. The devil never changes a good strategy, and instigating prideful plots is one of his ways to keep God's people divided and in strife. It hinders us in our production of fruit for His kingdom.

Rebellion Produces Vendettas

Satan was delighted to coax Adam and Eve into the sin of pride. He knew it would cause the rest of mankind to inherit the curses that stem from rebellion.

However, because of Abraham's integrity and his love for God, his seed, Israel, although a small, insignificant nation, was chosen to show mankind God's way of life. God wanted Israel to honor Him and become a nation with His personality traits. Instead,

Israel imitated the pagan people around them and worshiped pagan gods.

God made good on his promise to Abraham to lead the Israelites from Egypt to the Promised Land. But He had to send them into exile because of their rebellious ways and for the sin of worshipping other gods. False prophets convinced the people that the prophecies of exile they were hearing from God's prophets would not be carried out.

In Ezekiel 12:16 God said, "I will spare a few of their men from the sword, from famine, and from the pestilence, that they may declare all their abominations among the Gentiles wherever they go. Then they shall know that I am the Lord."

When we aspire to think and act as we please, repudiating any authority over us, we are in rebellion. The Israelites openly resisted God's intervention in their lives after He rescued them from Egypt and after they entered the Promised Land.

When we openly resist any legitimate authority over us, we are emulating Satan's sin of pride. Adam and Eve's choice to eat of the forbidden fruit left us their legacy of rebellion. Since we are born in sin, the spirit of rebellion starts to develop in a small child and continues throughout adulthood. The greater the spirit of rebellion, the fewer blessings God is able to grant us.

The Word describes the effects of rebellion. Psalm 68:6 says, "God sets the solitary in families; He brings out those who are bound into prosperity; but the rebellious dwell in a dry land."

Dry land is a desolate place without water. There are no trees, green grass, fruits, or vegetables—everything that makes life pleasant and comfortable. When I went from Israel to Egypt on a tour, we crossed many miles of barren and desolate sand. If the rebellious spirit of a person resembles the desert, he or she will produce very little fruit for the kingdom of God.

In the past few years, our soldiers have had to survive the harsh desert life in Arabic countries as they fight against terrorism. These countries have been carrying on vendettas for centuries, and their attitudes of hate and revenge have dragged other nations into their conflicts. The rebellious philosophy that begets vendettas among the Arabic nations is in direct opposition to God's way of peace, joy, and love for neighbor as self.

"Love does no harm to a neighbor; therefore love is the fulfillment of the law" (Romans 13:10). Therefore, God will continue to leave the Arabs in a dry and desolate land. Before we can liberate ourselves from the sins of the flesh, we have to overcome the sin of rebellion.

Paul said to the Romans, "If you live according to the flesh you will die; but if by the Spirit you put to death the deeds of the body, you will live. For as many as are led by the Spirit of God, these are sons of God" (Romans 8:13–14).

The Holy Spirit gives us the power to love as Jesus loves. This love helps us to die to self, and it keeps us from being embroiled in the many faces of pride that confront us daily.

Chapter 19

Corrupting Features of Pride

Pride can corrupt. It can cause us to change from good to bad in our morals, manners, or actions. Webster's dictionary says corruption is an impairment of integrity, virtue, or moral principle; a departure from what is pure or correct; an inducement to wrong by improper or unlawful means.[5] Flattery, vanity, and slander are by-products of pride that propagate deceit and corruption.

Flattery

Flattery is excessive, untrue, insincere praise, exaggerated compliments, and false attention. People who flatter are trying to ingratiate themselves or receive favor from a person by trying to make that person feel honored. Flattery appeals to another's vanity, hoping for return favors.

Proverbs 29:5–6 says, "A man who flatters his neighbor spreads a net for his feet. By transgression an evil man is snared, but the righteous sings and rejoices."

Flattery is a snare that can entangle anyone. In order to keep from falling into the net, we need to examine our motives. If we are helping people for praise that strokes our vanity, if we have hidden agendas that require favors in return, or if we praise others in order to be noticed, we have fallen into the flattery trap.

The apostle Paul told the Romans to avoid those who cause division and strife about doctrine. "Those who are such do not serve our Lord Jesus Christ, but their own belly, and by smooth

[5] *Merriam-Webster's Collegiate Dictionary*, 11th ed., (Springfield, Massachusetts: Merriam-Webster, Incorporated, 2007).

words and flattering speech deceive the hearts of the simple. . . . I want you to be wise in what is good, and simple concerning evil" (Romans 16:18–19).

Proverbs 26:28 says, "A lying tongue hates those who are crushed by it, and a flattering mouth works ruin." Flattery is a form of lying.

A wise person will not flatter others or be deceived by flattery. A person who flatters is not trustworthy because he or she is self-seeking.

Vanity

King Solomon reviewed the aspects of life in Ecclesiastes. He pondered his and other men's achievements and said, "I have seen all the works that are done under the sun; and indeed, all is vanity and grasping for the wind" (Ecclesiastes 1:14).

When he considered wisdom and the pleasures of life, he said, "God gives wisdom and knowledge and joy to a man who is good in His sight; but to the sinner He gives the work of gathering and collecting, that he may give to him who is good before God. This also is vanity and grasping for the wind" (Ecclesiastes 2:26).

As he finalized his observations of life he said, "Vanity of vanities . . . all is vanity" (Ecclesiastes 12:8).

Solomon realized the uselessness of searching for pleasure, wisdom, fame, and fortune, and he observed that too much study is also wearisome to the flesh. In conclusion he said, "Fear God and keep His commandments, for this is man's all. For God will bring every work into judgment, including every secret thing, whether good or evil" (Ecclesiastes 12:13–14).

Searching for happiness in the vanities of life is like searching for the wind. The Holy Spirit once said to me, *Happiness as man knows it is an illusion.* We can have every need met and have our ego stroked daily, but that kind of happiness is unreal and does not touch the spirit. Until we attend to our spiritual needs by planting seeds of the Word in our spirit and allowing them to germinate into a personal relationship with God, this roller-coaster ride of life will become vanity and a vexation to the spirit.

Flattery, vanity, and deceit are strong motivators used to acquire fame and fortune. The insatiable desire to be considered a success in the world causes people to throw away caution and allow the winds of flattery and vanity to blow and scatter their seeds of deceit.

Slander

Those who engage in flattery are looking for vanity in others. If flattery doesn't work, they may change their tactics to slander.

Some politicians display vanity and deceit during elections years. A few may even turn to slander to weaken an opponent. As I listen to the daily news, I feel like weeping for people who seem a lot like those who caused the prophet Jeremiah to weep for them.

Jeremiah 9:3–5 says:

> "And like their bow they have bent their tongues for lies. They are not valiant for the truth on the earth. For they proceed from evil to evil, and they do not know Me," says the Lord. "Everyone take heed to his neighbor, and do not trust any brother; for every brother will utterly supplant, and every neighbor will walk with slanderers. Everyone will deceive his neighbor, and will not speak the truth; they have taught their tongue to speak lies; they weary themselves to commit iniquity."

The Israelites were a chosen people, set apart from the world to bring in Christianity. I believe the United States has been set apart by God for the important task of evangelizing. Even though our government has tried to be a nation for all people under God, it has failed miserably at times. The same root of pride and contempt for God and other people that caused Israel to blunder has brought our nation to the brink of disaster many times.

Romans 9:27 says, "Though the number of the children of Israel be as the sand of the sea, the remnant will be saved." I believe that God will continue to bless the United States as long as we are Israel's ally. Israel needs our prayers, but in order to help Israel we must keep our government out of the hands of men and women who do not speak the truth about God and who are quick to lie and slander others.

Scripture says, "Pray for the peace of Jerusalem: 'May they prosper who love you. Peace be within your walls, prosperity within your palaces'" (Psalm 122:6–7). God will prosper the countries who love Israel.

Chapter 20

Characteristics of Pride

It is so detrimental to man to covet what others have that God made a commandment against it, along with not committing idolatry (Exodus 20:2–5). They are both Satanic traps that people fall into easily.

Coveting

In Exodus 20:17 God says, "You shall not covet your neighbor's house; you shall not covet your neighbor's wife, nor his male servant, nor his female servant, nor his ox, nor his donkey, nor anything that is your neighbor's."

Coveting is the unquenchable appetite to have something that belongs to another, to crave the wealth that others have, or to envy someone else's abilities. A covetous person spends more time seeking materialistic things than seeking the kingdom of God. Jesus said, "Take heed and beware of covetousness, for one's life does not consist in the abundance of the things he possesses" (Luke 12:15).

The apostle Paul talked about covetousness to Timothy when he said, "Those who desire to be rich fall into temptation and a snare, and into many foolish and harmful lusts which drown men in destruction and perdition. For the love of money is a root of all kinds of evil, for which some have strayed from the faith in their greediness, and pierced themselves through with many sorrows" (1 Timothy 6:9–10).

The early Christians were warned about the evils of coveting. Since we have developed into a materialistic nation, Christians seldom hear sermons warning people against coveting. The standard of living in the United States is very high compared to many countries, and we are constantly seeking new gadgets to make life more comfortable. We have become accustomed to such a materialistic way of life that many are obsessed with "keeping up with the Joneses," an old saying for those who covet a neighbor's status for material possessions.

Some Christians may not be aware that coveting is idolatry. Paul made it clear when he told the Colossians, "Put to death your members which are on the earth: fornication, uncleanness, passion, evil desire, and covetousness, which is idolatry" (Colossians 3:5).

Idolatry

Writing to the Ephesians, Paul said, "No fornicator, unclean person, nor covetous man, who is an idolater, has any inheritance in the kingdom of Christ and God" (Ephesians 5:5).

We commit idolatry when we put money, family, work, or pleasure before our relationship with God. A covetous person is breaking two of the Ten Commandments: idolatry and coveting. His coveting causes him to concentrate on acquiring wealth and status in life until they become his idols and cause him to commit idolatry.

Jesus said, "No one can serve two masters; for either he will hate the one and love the other, or else he will be loyal to the one and despise the other. You cannot serve God and mammon" (Matthew 6:24). If a person's thoughts are constantly on how he can acquire more worldly fortune or fame, his heart is not on the spiritual things of God. This type of thinking is idolatry at work in a person's heart.

In Micah 5:14 the Lord said, "I will pluck your wooden images from your midst; thus I will destroy your cities."

Covetousness and idolatry feed off of each other. When God told man not to have other gods before Him, He meant not just statues made of gold, stone, or wood that the pagan people worshipped, but anything we put before Him that consumes our time and energy. God warns us that He is a jealous God, but He also shows mercy to those who love Him (Exodus 20:5–6).

Overspending

Overspending affects finances, health, and relationships. People who overspend are trying to cover up their feelings of inadequacy. Many people find themselves heavily in debt because they buy things they can't afford to pay cash for, so they use credit cards.

At one time credit cards were hard to obtain. You had to produce evidence of financial accountability. Today they are so easy to acquire that young families can overspend until they are forced into bankruptcy. Several organizations have reported that divorce over finances is becoming as prevalent as adultery.

Some companies will give college students credit without parental permission. This is harmful to the students because it plays into the hands of Satan, who is able to stir up covetous desires for things the wealthy students can afford. The poor or unpopular students need to feel accepted, and they do not realize that material possessions will not accomplish that. A vulnerable student overcome by debt and other problems may give in to thoughts of suicide.

Credit organizations and merchants are equally responsible for selling products to those who have no real means of repaying the loan. Greed causes them to prey on unsupervised students or young adults who have not been instructed about the dire misfortunes a credit card can incur.

Paul admonished the early Christians, "Let your conduct be without covetousness; be content with such things as you have.

For He Himself has said, 'I will never leave you nor forsake you'" (Hebrews 13:5).

If we keep our eyes on Jesus and not the things of this world, we can escape the snares Satan sets before us concerning material things, the lusts of life, and the pride that so easily besets us.

Selfishness

Coveting starts in small children. The desire to have what does not belong to us is noticeable even in babies. Selfishness makes them try to snatch toys or food from each other. As you watch young children play, you can distinguish between the passive and aggressive natures.

This face of pride needs to be seriously dealt with to keep children from becoming rebellious in their teenage years. If children's aggressive natures are not pointed in the right direction, they can become materialistic as they get older, putting them in the realm of Satan's dominion. Coveting and selfishness can cause financial collapse—not to mention the afflictions imposed upon their personal lives.

Young children can be taught that coveting is a sin and that giving and sharing bless others, and in return God will bless them. Scriptures relating to God's dislike of hoarding should be emphasized, and children should be discouraged from piling up toys in their rooms. Instead of showering children with gifts to show them how much they are loved, that love would be more meaningful if children are taught how to love others by giving of themselves and their possessions.

It is fine for a child to have some favorite toys, but the overflow can be given to others when he or she has tired of them. Children should be trained at an early age to take their toys to an organization that helps orphaned children or those whose parents are unable to buy toys. If it is the child's choice to share, he or she will develop a feeling of giving and sharing on his or her own, and natural selfish tendencies can be greatly reduced. The urge to own everything their peers have will diminish if children find more joy in giving than in receiving.

Proverbs 22:6 says, "Train up a child in the way he should go, and when he is old he will not depart from it." If we take the time to train our children, the Lord promises us that they will eventually walk in His ways.

Spoiled Children

Many years ago, when the Holy Spirit started teaching me about God's disciplines, He told me that children need to feel needed. He said God doesn't like spoiled children because they are vulnerable to Satan.

I knew immediately what He meant, because I am the second child and first daughter of a large family. I was aware that my mother needed my help with the younger children. However, I didn't realize until later in life how much I benefited from helping my mother. It gave me the feeling of being useful as well as a sense of security.

After I had children of my own, my mother commented that I was spoiling them by not insisting they be held accountable for specific chores. It wasn't until after the Lord told me that spoiled children are vulnerable to Satan that I understood what my mother was trying to teach me.

People who want their children to have more than they received as children are actually showing a face of pride by giving too much and expecting nothing in return. They are emphasizing materialistic things and not the value of service to other people.

Allowing children too much free time to play causes them to get bored easily and leaves them liberty to develop bad habits. Instead of being useful, they think of ways to entertain themselves. Centering too many things on children, whether activities or entertainment, leads them to expect a great deal more attention, and not enough time is spent teaching them how to serve others.

Jesus gave the example of helping His parents and serving others as the way to lead a happy life.

If we help children to become useful members in the family by doing chores, they develop a better self-image and an ability to serve others. This keeps them from being spoiled and concentrating on their own wants.

Evidence of these truths was seen during the Great Depression. Children helped support their families by earning extra money working at menial jobs for neighbors or by doing chores at home that allowed their parents to take on extra work. Every avenue was used to help the family survive.

When that generation found themselves in a world war, they served their country as faithfully as they had served their families. These unspoiled children grew up to save a nation.

Children today should be taught about the many debacles associated with greed and laziness. This will enable them to bear more fruit for God's kingdom and help them lead happy, well-adjusted lives.

I listened to a television talk show recently in which people were discussing the effects computers have on children and teenagers. Many hours spent on computers have taken the place of communicating with people face to face. Therefore, these young people are unable to relate to people with different personalities. The conclusion was that we are developing a generation of selfish people.

My grandson James was one of those children who worried his parents by spending many hours a day on his computer. However, at seventeen, he went to France for two weeks with his French class. Each student lived with a French family the first week. They spent their second week touring. James enjoyed learning about the culture of another country, and he was stimulated to socialize more.

Now he wants to travel more, learn about other cultures, and use his life to help others. Most of his time at the computer is spent on studies. All the teenage selfishness is disappearing.

The greatest change in James is that he enjoys going to church regularly. With the Lord's help, our teenagers can change. Instead of the pessimistic reports on television, we can have a new generation of intelligent and caring young people who will be an asset to God's kingdom.

Chapter 21

Overcoming Pride

The wisdom of God paves the road we must walk to overcome pride in ourselves and our children. Proverbs 16:16 says, "How much better to get wisdom than gold! And to get understanding is to be chosen rather than silver." We may have read the Bible many times, obtained degrees in theology, or received special revelation knowledge with the help of the Holy Spirit, yet our wisdom compared to God's wisdom is like a drop of water in an ocean. The Lord says, "As the heavens are higher than the earth, so are My ways higher than your ways, and My thoughts than your thoughts" (Isaiah 55:9).

After God allowed Satan to torment Job, his friends tried to impart their wisdom to him. They decided Job's sins were causing his affliction, but Job justified himself by saying that he had been a good person and concluded that he was as wise as any of them.

God took Job to task regarding his claim to be wiser than his friends. The Lord asked him who commanded the morning and caused the dawn to know its place; who made rain, snow, dew, and hail; who divided a channel for overflowing water and a path for the thunderbolt. Job realized that the wisdom of men is infinitesimal compared to God's wisdom. He felt foolish for talking about his own wisdom. (See Job 38–42.) Wisdom from the Lord is a gift not to be used in a prideful manner.

The psalmist says, "Incline my heart to Your testimonies, and not to covetousness. Turn away my eyes from looking at worthless things, and revive me in Your way. Establish Your word to Your servant, who is devoted to fearing You" (Psalm 119:36–38).

The psalmist cried out to God for revival and strength for his spirit. He insisted that God immerse Him in wisdom and understanding so that he might walk in God's ways. This should be the cry of Christians today.

Psalm 119:51 says, "The proud have me in great derision, yet I do not turn aside from Your law." God's law is His Word.

Meditate on God's Wisdom

Meditation requires concentrating on small portions of God's wisdom until the Word impregnates our spirit. We can inflate our spirits with the wisdom of God as we listen to the psalmists pour out their sorrows, aspirations, troubles, thanks, and praises to the Lord.

Solomon felt overwhelmed when he was anointed king over Israel, so when God asked him what he desired after he became king, Solomon asked for wisdom. This pleased God so much that he made him the wisest man on earth. Kings and queens traveled far to hear his wisdom.

The book of Proverbs is full of the wisdom that Solomon gleaned from God. Proverbs 3:13–18 gives us the knowledge that God's wisdom is profitable for man's wealth, health, happiness, peace, and joy, and a tree of life to those who take hold of her.

The book of Proverbs contains a wealth of wisdom for every trial and tribulation in life. We are taught about the evils pride brings. We are warned about lusting after the things of the world and told to be aware of the snares set for the wicked.

Proverbs 6:16–19 says, "These six things the Lord hates, yes, seven are an abomination to Him: a proud look, a lying tongue, hands that shed innocent blood, a heart that devises wicked plans, feet that are swift in running to evil, a false witness who speaks lies, and one who sows discord among brethren."

The seventh thing God considers an abomination is the discord sown among Christians. This friction comes from coveting, slandering, and other faces of pride. In order to win the battles that pride activates around us daily, we have to meditate on the wisdom of God's Word until it is steeped in our spirits.

In Proverbs 8:35–36 wisdom says, "Whoever finds me finds life, and obtains favor from the Lord; but he who sins against me wrongs his own soul; all those who hate me love death." When we refuse to listen to the wisdom of God, we are flirting with death.

Annihilate Pride

We use the word *pride* in so many of our daily conversations, we have dismantled its true characteristics. But pride is not a simple thing. It is a face of evil!

Pride brings devastation. It blights the human soul in the same way vandalism mars a building. Making light of pride is like ignoring the dangers from the aftershocks of an earthquake.

Once we have uncovered the many faces of pride, we are better able to deal with assaults from the enemy.

Take Joy in All Things

Most parents admonish their children to take pride in such things as their schoolwork, personal appearance, a clean room, and manners. However, the Holy Spirit informed me the appropriate word for this kind of encouragement is joy, not pride.

We are told in Colossians 3:23–24, "Whatever you do, do it heartily, as to the Lord and not to men, knowing that from the Lord you will receive the reward of the inheritance; for you serve the Lord Christ."

Trying to please other people is a lesson in futility and it kindles pride. If we do all things as unto the Lord, we will eliminate pride, because our service to God will be a personal endeavor and we will not be in prideful competition with anyone. Fellowshipping with God and serving Him keeps our joy replenished and becomes our strength in times of trial and tribulation.

When Ezra read the Book of the Law of Moses to the Israelites, they wept because they had not remembered the laws while they were in captivity. However, it was a time to renew and celebrate the rebuilding of the temple at Jerusalem. Ezra said, "This day is holy to our Lord. Do not sorrow, for the joy of the Lord is your strength" (Nehemiah 8:10).

Joy is like water—it evaporates. If a jar with water is exposed to the sun, it evaporates faster. Our joy can diminish quickly when our bodies, minds, and spirits are exposed to sorrows, stresses, and strife. The level of joy we maintain in our spirits will depend on the type of relationship we have developed with our heavenly Father.

The many faces of pride create openings in our spiritual houses through which Satan can enter like an impudent mouse. But we can seal up these crevices with the Word of God and the joy of the Lord.

Father, strip the hard shell of pride from us. Help us get to the point where no man can offend us. Teach us to be gracious with our talents, and stop us from being offensive to others. Show us how to take joy in all things, doing even the menial tasks we must perform daily as though we are doing them at Your request. Amen.

The Star of Jesus

There's a star shining bright in the window of my soul,

The star of Jesus, the star of Jesus.

It's a star shining bright through the sin and the strife,

The star of Jesus, the Light of Love.

May that light shine bright through the valleys of my life,

The star of Jesus, the star of Jesus,

O Star shining bright in the heavens tonight,

Shine Your love and joy on me.

Discipline #5: Fear

Satan uses fear to paralyze our faith.

The fear of man brings a snare,
but whoever trusts in the Lord shall be safe.
(Proverbs 29:25)

Chapter 22

Origin and Definition of Fear

As soon as Adam and Eve ate of the forbidden fruit, their eyes were opened to good and evil. They experienced their first feelings of fear: dread and anxiety. They understood they had disobeyed God, so their first reaction was to hide from Him.

What Is Fear?

Webster's dictionary says fear is a strong emotion caused by anticipation or awareness of danger. The stages of fear run the gamut from sheer terror to fright, panic, alarm, dread, and anxiety. Terror is so extreme that it can immobilize its victim. Fright is a sudden, startling aspect of fear. Panic is overmastering fear that causes hysterical action. Alarm suggests the presence of danger. Dread or anxiety produces extreme uneasiness about facing a situation.[6]

Satan hinders our faith by using all aspects of fear to keep us in doubt of our ability to succeed in what we are attempting. He enjoys watching us use the escape mechanism of flight instead of facing fear with faith.

Why Men Fear

Before Adam and Eve disobeyed God, they were full of peace and joy. After the sin of pride opened the door for Satan's negative emotions, fear walked in, violated peace and joy, then tied up faith.

---

[6] *Merriam-Webster's Collegiate Dictionary*, 11th edition (Springfield, Massachusetts: Merriam-Webster, Incorporated, 2007).

As people began to walk in the darkness of the world under the influence of Satan, the god of this world, fear became their constant companion. Fear, like pride, wears many faces, but any face of fear paralyzes faith in God. Anything that is paralyzed is immobile or unable to move. Satan's ability to use fear as bondage gives him the power to prostrate our faith, making it stationary and inoperable. He uses fear to bind our faith, but we can use faith to set us free from the bondage of fear.

Anytime we are not walking in faith, we are operating in some stage of fear. Faith and fear are as far apart as the east is from the west, and the two will never meet. However, when we apply the blood of Jesus and use the Word of God, we have the power to negate Satan's fear tactics. That is why God wants us to discipline ourselves to walk in His ways; it disrupts Satan's plans for evil against us.

What Men Fear

When Adam and Eve left the garden of Eden to face an unstable, cursed physical environment, fear followed them. God was no longer orchestrating His plans for their lives, days of peace and joy, as He had in the garden. Each moment was filled with apprehension and uncertainty as they painstakingly toiled for food, clothing, and shelter. They were no longer in the bubble of God's protection, strolling around the countryside free from worries. Instead, they lived in a cursed environment, continually afflicted with fear.

In the midst of Adam and Eve's struggle for survival, tragedy struck. Their son Abel brought the firstlings of his sheep and their fat to God, and his offering was accepted. When God refused Abel's brother Cain's offering of fruit from the ground, Cain grew angry. The inherited sin of pride had started its chain reaction of negative emotions in Cain. (See Genesis 4.)

God had to kill an animal to make physical coverings for Adam and Eve after they ate of the tree of good and evil. The blood that was sacrificed became a spiritual covering for sin, as well as a physical covering; thus, the blood sacrifice for sin began in the garden of Eden.

We aren't sure why God did not respect Cain's offering. He ignored the blood-sacrifice offering, and instead offered fruit from the ground. It apparently was not his first fruit and may not have been perfect fruit. Sin was involved somehow, and Cain's heart had already been hardened because of sibling rivalry.

Psalm 51:17 says, "The sacrifices of God are a broken spirit, a broken and a contrite heart—these, O God, You will not despise." God knew Cain didn't have a broken spirit or a contrite heart. Instead of learning to rule over sin, as God asked him to do, Cain followed the example of his parents and allowed sin to rule over him.

The fact that Cain would murder his brother because God blessed Abel's offering and wouldn't bless his own offering shows us that Satan had already begun to sway Cain's reasoning. Satan persisted in his endeavors until Cain's negative emotions led to murder.

After the murder of his brother, God put a curse on Cain and told him he would be a fugitive and vagabond on the earth. Cain became fearful for his life, so God set a mark on him that would keep him from being killed. He said, "Therefore, whoever kills Cain, vengeance shall be taken on him sevenfold" (Genesis 4:15).

Thus began Satan's triumphant enterprises of pitting man against man. History reveals his incalculable successes. From the time the first blood of humankind was mingled with the soil of the earth, both man and beast have fallen prey to a convoy of vultures waiting to escort them back to the dust. We have learned to fear other people, death, nature, animals, and all things related to our physical environment. Satan revels in his ample opportunities to

assist human beings in surrendering to fear instead of walking by
faith in the Word of God.

Chapter 23

Chimerical Fear

Chimera is defined as a fire-breathing she-monster of Greek mythology with a lion's head, a goat's body, and a serpent's tail; an imaginary monster compounded of incongruous parts; an illusion or fabrication of the mind.[7]

Chimerical or fabricated thoughts afflict us when we allow our imagination to run wild and unchecked. This kind of imagination is a playground for satanic fears. God gave us an imagination so we could be creative like Him, but we sometimes use it to engage in impractical or absurd reveries. This tendency to indulge in abstract phantasms makes it easy for Satan to communicate unrealistic fears to our minds. That is why we are told in the Word to bring all thoughts into captivity to Jesus, so He can establish our thinking for us (2 Corinthians 10:5).

Many years ago, the Holy Spirit showed me how Satan uses chimerical imagination to plant images in the mind and makes us think they are true. One night, after my mother-in-law had finished having dinner at our house, I took her back to her apartment. I always kept an extra set of her apartment keys in my purse to unlock her front door. When I returned home, a strong image of keys hanging in her front door kept flashing before me. I diligently searched my purse for her keys. When I didn't find them, I prepared to go back to her apartment, even though my mind and body were fraught with fatigue from the stresses of a long day. As I started out the door, the thought came to me: *The keys are in your purse.*

---

[7] *Merriam-Webster's Collegiate Dictionary*, 11th ed., (Springfield, Massachusetts: Merriam-Webster, Incorporated, 2007).

I looked in my purse a second time, but the only keys I found were a set that belonged to one of my children. So I jumped in the car. But as I was driving toward my mother-in-law's apartment, the message came again: *The keys are in your purse.*

I pulled into a nearby parking lot, parked under a street lamp, and hunted thoroughly in my purse, but the evasive keys were not to be found. So I hurried on, still driven by the strong image of my set of her keys hanging in her front door.

When I reached her apartment, no keys hung in her front door. Panic rose up within me. However, I composed myself with the thought that they must be on her kitchen table. When my mother-in-law opened the door, I started making incoherent statements about keys while I cased her apartment. I found no keys anywhere!

I figured someone must have taken them from the front door. I was unnerved by the thought of unsavory characters entering her apartment to rob or harm her.

I stifled the crescendo of fear rising within me because I didn't want to alarm my mother-in-law. Although ugly thoughts haunted me concerning her security and safety, I knew I had to return home. I approached the door to leave, then heard for the third time: *The keys are in your purse.*

I reached in my purse and took out the only keys there: mine. Against all reason, I inserted them in the lock. They worked!

The image of my extra set of keys hanging in her front door lock was so strong in my mind I could not believe that the keys I'd been looking at were hers. It wasn't until I acted on the information I was hearing in my spirit, and actually placed the "wrong" keys in the keyhole of her front door, that I was able to receive the truth.

Needless to say, I felt very foolish. However, on the way home, the Holy Spirit revealed that Satan operates by planting images of nonexistent problems in our minds. Satan badgered me when my logical thinking was stressed by physical exhaustion, and I became susceptible to the false image he planted in my mind. I clung to that image, even when truth was spoken to me and the evidence was in front of me.

Lies Promote Imaginary Fears

In the incident with the keys, I placed my faith in my own opinion rather than in the truth that was being spoken to me. I chose to believe an untruth.

Christians can be induced to believe that an opinion is truth when in reality it may be a lie. Satan's falsehoods are detrimental to our well-being and can wreak catastrophic damage in our lives. Satan's lies can cause Christians to walk in unbelief that will lead to a loss of blessings. His lies also cause unbelievers to lose their souls.

In Romans 4:17 we see that God calls things that do not exist as though they do exist. Abraham and Sarah believed that peculiar aspect of God, and Sarah delivered a child when she was past the childbearing years. Most of us are more apt to call negative things that do not exist as though they do exist in the physical world. We balk at the notion of calling spiritual things of God that do not exist as though they do.

Satan imitates God's precepts of calling good into existence with his counterfeit precepts of calling evil into existence. Many people predict dire catastrophes and call evil things that are not in existence as though they are. The world sees nothing wrong with this. But if a Christian is heard calling something good or positive into being, through faith in God's Word, he or she is considered weird or naïve.

Terrorists in the world today are accepting the most despicable lie Satan ever perpetrated on mankind. He has made them believe they will be martyrs with special favors in heaven, including a certain number of virgins at their disposal. This keeps them from desiring what normal people long for—a decent life with a family. They have no purpose or objective other than to die for the glory they believe awaits them in another life. The falsifications dictated to these brainwashed terrorists make them, as individuals, more dangerous to humanity than any nation has ever been.

Don't Encourage Imaginary Fears

My perception of Satan's craftiness increased immeasurably after my experience with the set of house keys. Satan will go to any length to plague us with imaginary fears by inventing fabrications. He receives great joy from watching us create mythical fiends as our fantasies run amok!

We help Satan to perpetuate this type of imagination and fear by telling ghost stories, wearing freakish costumes on Halloween, and watching horror movies in theatres and on television.

Although people use chimerical imagination in mischievously entertaining ways, Satan's intentions are more ominous. He uses Christians' fantasy fears to get them into unbelief or out of faith in the Word of God.

In Psalm 53:5, we are admonished about fearing where there is no fear. "There they are in great fear where no fear was, for God has scattered the bones of him who encamps against you; you have put them to shame, because God has despised them." The people feared something that God had already taken care of for them. When we are in great fear where there is nothing to be afraid of, we have succumbed to a satanic plot.

Many of us can recall, as children, playing outside at night when suddenly some noise or shadow created the feeling that we were about to be attacked by an imaginary monster. My husband Andy vividly remembers such a night as a child. He was coming home from a movie on a bright, cold, moonlit night, and as he walked, he observed the trees making grotesque shadows as they swayed in the wind.

He felt that something was pursuing him, so he started running. But when he looked back, he saw that only his shadow followed him. He kept his fearful experience a secret because pride made him ashamed to tell his parents or anyone else that he was frightened by his own shadow. However, he never forgot that moment of intense fear.

These kinds of fears start when we are children, but they are carried on in our imagination throughout our adult lives.

As parents, we spend a great deal of time and energy going through stages of imaginary fears. I was never able to sleep at night until all of my children were home in bed. My four active children forced me to survive on a few hours of nightly sleep for years. One daughter worked for an amusement park during the summer months and didn't arrive home until around 2:30 or 3:30 in the morning, but I never closed an eyelid until she was home and I listened to the accounts of her day.

Real Experiences Promote Chimerical Fears

Another incident involving my children kept me in a state of chimerical fear for a long time. I was on the telephone talking to a friend when an emergency call from a hospital interrupted our conversation. My son Mark had been in a motorcycle accident and needed surgery on a badly broken leg. After that, whenever the telephone rang, a formidable feeling of fear would engulf me. Even if my children and husband were at home, illusory accidents that might involve other family members popped into my mind.

It took a few years, but eventually, with the help of the Holy Spirit, I was able to release the pressure of panic that kept me wrestling with mythical fears. As I listened to His gentle reminders that God would hear my prayers and protect my family, He led me to pray Psalm 91:9–11, which says, "Because you have made the Lord, who is my refuge, even the Most High, your dwelling place, no evil shall befall you, nor shall any plague come near your dwelling; for He shall give His angels charge over you, to keep you in all your ways."

Since that time, I have been faithful to pray and believe that His angels are on duty at all times. Now I do not lie awake at night running sinister scenarios through my mind. If my imagination starts playing tricks on me, I listen to Bible tapes. Psalm 31:24 says, "Be of good courage, and He shall strengthen your heart, all you who hope in the Lord." The Word produces the courage and hope we need to walk in faith.

Faith Removes Fear

We have tornado warnings in St. Louis for several days during the month of May every year. Spring storms can cause people to lose a lot of sleep if they allow fear to rule them.

I had guests in the house one night when tornado warnings were sounded. My visitors were uneasy about the storm and wanted to stay in the basement for a few hours. I made them comfortable in beds there, but I decided to sleep upstairs in my room. My guests were concerned for me. However, I assured them I would be careful.

Andy stayed with my friends that night, and he was amazed that I could sleep through the storm. But I had been claiming the protection that says, "He will not allow your foot to be moved; He who keeps you will not slumber. Behold, He who keeps Israel shall neither slumber nor sleep. The Lord is your keeper. . . . The Lord shall preserve you from all evil; He shall preserve your soul" (Psalm 121:3–7). After hearing about other people using that psalm to conquer fear, I decided it would work for me, and it does.

I don't allow storms to interfere with my sleep. I believe that the Lord stays awake even while I am asleep.

In our chimerical fears, we can conjure up freakish accidents or extravagant incidents as good as any created in Greek mythology. To eliminate this type of thinking, we must apply the Word to any fear that is threatening our peace of mind. Hebrews 10:23 says, "Let us hold fast the confession of our hope without wavering, for He who promised is faithful."

We may not think imaginary fears are harmful, but an excess of such fears can lead to a neurotic personality and ultimately affect the body's general health. Fear also affects our spiritual progress with God because it keeps us from walking in faith. When any situation opens the door to fear, faith leaves. We are either walking in faith or without it.

Perfect Love Casts Out Fear

Scripture tells us that fear does not come from God. "For God has not given us a spirit of fear, but of power and of love and of a sound mind" (2 Timothy 1:7). After Satan gets us into stress through our imagination, we act foolishly instead of with the sound mind that is our heritage from Jesus Christ.

In 1 John 4:18 we are told, "There is no fear in love; but perfect love casts out fear, because fear involves torment. But he who fears has not been made perfect in love." Our struggle with fear can be related to the fact that we are not walking in love with one another or believing that God will protect us.

On September 11, 2001, four passenger planes were commandeered by terrorists. Two demolished the World Trade Center buildings in New York City, one struck the Pentagon in Washington DC, and the fourth was brought down by heroic passengers before it hit its target. After the attacks, many people expressed a desire to stay home and not venture out more than necessary. Some bought gas masks and tried to prepare for any kind of emergency.

There is no physical way to protect oneself from fear. But we do have spiritual protection. Isaiah 35:3-4 says, "Strengthen the weak hands, and make firm the feeble knees. Say to those who are fearful-hearted, 'Be strong, do not fear! Behold, your God will come with vengeance, with the recompense of God; He will come and save you.'"

Don't Fear the Unknown

The date of September 11, 2001, will be etched in our memories the way December 7, 1941, was when Pearl Harbor was bombed. President Roosevelt was able to calm the nation during World War II when he said, "The only thing we have to fear is fear itself."

President Bush urged the nation to do the only thing that will stem the tide of fear, and that is to pray. If we could get every church in the United States to pray for the nations, we could eliminate terrorism throughout the world. The terrorists are extremely dedicated to victory and death, but their achievements rest on human perseverance. Our successes will be a result of spiritual sources at our disposal through the power of the Holy Spirit.

When men are called into military service, their survival depends on the disciplined training the military gives them. God is just as interested in the well-being and success of His soldiers. He wants His soldiers disciplined in areas He deems critical for their survival.

We are now being put to the test in the area of fear. Even though our country is in great turmoil because of war, terrorism, and a failing economy, we can be at peace in our hearts—not walking in fear and trembling.

God told Isaiah not to walk in the ways of the people of Israel and Judah, and not to fear them even though he had to prophesy against them. They refused to listen to God's prophets and His word, so their fate was sealed. God said, "Do not say, 'A conspiracy,' concerning all that this people call a conspiracy, nor be afraid of their threats, nor be troubled. The Lord of hosts, Him you shall hallow; let Him be your fear, and let Him be your dread. He will be as a sanctuary" (Isaiah 8:12–14).

Even though God was speaking to Isaiah because he was prophesying against Israel and Judah, we can take this Scripture for ourselves as well and apply it to the conspiracy of the terrorists throughout the world. We are to relax while we wait for God to snare them in their own traps. He is our sanctuary and hiding place when we rest in Him. If we allow the Lord to absorb our fear and dread, we can walk in peace and the joy we receive from the Lord.

If we fail to keep our trust in Him during the days of peril that lie ahead, we'll be on the teeter-totter of faith and fear. It is imperative that we cling to His Word. The Lord said to the Israelites, "Fear not, for I am with you; I will bring your descendants from the east, and gather you from the west" (Isaiah 43:5). His Word is true, for the Israelites now have their own country.

When we believe in His Word and His promises, we can walk in faith and dislodge from our minds the chimerical fears that so easily beset us.

Chapter 24

Nebulous Fear

Although chimerical fears cause us to fear where no fear exists, nebulous fears afflict our lives as we make common, ordinary judgments in daily living. Nebulous fears are defined as cloudy, misty, vague or indistinct.[8]

Overcome Fear of Change and Decision Making

We often find ourselves dealing with nebulous, cloudy fears because life involves change, and change involves decisions. People who have trouble with change are afraid to seek new jobs, buy new homes, travel to unknown places, or move to strange cities away from family members. They work hard to keep change out of their lives and are content to live in a cocoon. They believe that they will remain in control of their lives if they stick with the old patterns, doing things the same way they have always been done. Some people prefer to stay in familiar ruts.

However, decisions have to be made in daily living whether they involve changing jobs, moving, or dealing with personal issues involving relationships, health, or financial problems. Some situations can be more stressful than others. Uncertainties confront all of us, and in many cases, they immobilize our faith more than when we come face-to-face with physical danger.

The common, ordinary events in our lives present a continuation of decision making that can cause us to be afflicted with nebulous fears such as anxiety, apprehension, worry, restlessness, concern,

[8] Me*rriam-Webster's Collegiate Dictionary*, 11th ed., (Springfield, Massachusetts: Merriam-Webster, Incorporated, 2007).

uneasiness, and misgivings. The uncertainty of the outcome is always at the forefront in our minds. Yet a disquieted, agitated spirit keeps us from relying on the Word of God and depending on Him to help us make good judgment calls. It is best never to make decisions when uneasiness prevails.

My family had nebulous fears for me when I married Andy and moved from Missouri to California. However, I knew it was the Lord's plan for my life. With the Lord's help I was able to start a new life far away from my family and friends.

Don't Fear Scare Tactics

Following the World Trade Center bombings, wrong decisions were made by many because nebulous fears overtook rational, intelligent, sound reasoning for some people, including Christians. The fear that other planes could attack any airport or plane at any time caused some people to quit flying.

After traces of anthrax were found in the postal system, people became afraid to open their mail. The anthrax scare caused many to rush to doctors for antibiotics even though they had not been exposed to the danger.

When fears that insufficient antibiotics would be available in case of an epidemic, many people went to Mexico to buy antibiotics without a prescription, not realizing that antibiotics have side effects that can be dangerous and should only be taken with a doctor's prescription. People who hoarded antibiotics didn't realize that after the expiration date passed, the antibiotics were useless. Pharmaceutical companies made huge sums of money as a result of a scare tactic.

It is impossible to listen to the news without feeling threatened by world events. We are constantly being warned about various epidemics, health problems, crimes, or terrorist attacks. Allowing scare tactics to override our common sense makes us easy targets for those who predict problems that cause nebulous fears to surface.

Move On after Making a Mistake

People who are afraid of failing or making mistakes miss the excitement of adventure. Some adventures are exhilarating and fun; others can be disappointing and painful. But life is a string of adventures—both good and bad.

One day on the way back to St. Louis from a visit to Springfield, Missouri, my husband and I had one of those not-so-good adventures. Andy and I stopped at a restaurant for lunch with our granddaughter Ashley. She decided to take her drink with her in the car. We had been on the highway about ten minutes when I heard a squealing noise from the backseat. Ashley had spilled her syrupy drink in her lap and her clothes were soaked. I told her we would stop at the next town, about forty-five minutes away, to find a bathroom where she could wash and change her clothes.

In the meantime, I made up a song about adventure. She joined in and we sang, "We're having an adventure, a cold, sticky adventure, not a very good adventure, but still an adventure." We proceeded down the road, and Ashley stayed in great spirits, making up fun stanzas to sing about her unpleasant experience. She never got to enjoy her drink, but instead of crying over her mistake, she sat in her sticky, wet clothes while we all laughed and enjoyed the ride to the next stop.

There are good and bad experiences in all adventures. Bad experiences can be tolerated, and may even be found amusing. Ashley's problem did not prevent her from deciding to take drinks in the car with her again, but since that time, she has never had an accident of that proportion.

At age seven Ashley learned that whatever mistake you make, you can adjust, laugh, overcome, and move on . . . even if you do have to sit awhile in your mess before you are able to clean it up. In the midst of her bad experience, she found a way to liven up the trip by making up impromptu adventure songs with her grandpa and grandma.

Whether we are learning to cope with small messes we have made as a child or bigger messes we make as adults, we often have to be patient until we can get them cleaned up.

Some decisions can lead to severe problems. Divorce, drug and alcoholic addictions, having illegitimate children or abortions, dropping out of school or wandering from job to job with no goals in mind for the future, getting deeply in debt . . . these are just some of the consequences of bad decisions. Nevertheless, if we hold fast to our faith in the blood of Jesus, we can be assured that there are no accidents, problems, or messes that God cannot help us clean up.

There is an old saying that when you fall off a horse, you've got to get back on and ride again. This eliminates fear. The same is true of driving cars, riding motorcycles, or anything else that might cause us to keep from moving forward in victory over fear. Many decisions we make will involve us in minor or major incidents. Decisions should be made using wisdom from God's Word, adding prudence, discretion, common sense, or foresight.

We can eliminate anxiety, apprehension, uneasiness, and dread through prayer. Most people who pray about decisions say they wait until they feel a sense of peace before they make a choice, especially about something important.

Conquer Nebulous Fears with a Fleece

Some people believe in putting out a fleece, as Gideon did. When the angel of the Lord came to where Gideon was threshing wheat in a winepress to hide it from the Midianites who were oppressing the Israelites, the angel said to Gideon, "The Lord is with you, you mighty man of valor!" (Judges 6:12). Gideon was not impressed with the eloquent compliment. He asked God why the Israelites were being so sorely taxed by the Midianites if the Lord truly was with them. The Lord said to him, "Go in this might of yours, and you shall save Israel from the hand of the Midianites. Have I not sent you?" (Judges 6:14).

Gideon was still not prepared to believe that he could save Israel. He continued to procrastinate. He told the Lord that his clan was the weakest in Manasseh and that he was the least in his father's house. Before he would proceed with the task the Lord wanted him to perform, Gideon asked for a sign. He put meat and unleavened bread on a rock. When the angel of the Lord touched the meat and bread with his rod, fire came out and consumed them both.

After Gideon was convinced he really was hearing from the Lord, he took ten men with him and broke down the altar of Baal. This created quite a ruckus, and the people wanted to kill the man who did the dastardly deed. That day his father, Joash, called him Jerubbaal because he contended against Baal. He told the people to let Baal defend himself if he was a god. (See Judges 6:31–32.)

Then Gideon said to God, "If You will save Israel by my hand as You have said—look, I shall put a fleece of wool on the threshing floor; if there is dew on the fleece only, and it is dry on all the ground, then I shall know that You will save Israel by my hand, as You have said" (Judges 6:36–37).

Sure enough, the next morning, Gideon was able to squeeze water out of the wool. That night he asked for another sign. This time he wanted God to let dew be on the ground and the fleece dry. God obliged Gideon again.

After that, Gideon fought to relieve the people from their oppression by the Midianites, but in each battle or task he performed, he asked for specific revelation knowledge. He would not budge until he was sure he was hearing from God. (See Judges 6–8.)

Refusing God's Counsel Stimulates Evil

We may try to bring our children up to follow the Lord, but we can fail just like Gideon (also called Jerubbaal) did. Abimelech, son of Jerubbaal, did evil in the sight of God and did not walk in the ways of the Lord. He reigned over Israel for three years until

God sent a spirit of ill will between him and the men of Shechem. They wanted to get rid of Abimelech because he had the seventy sons of Jerubbaal, his own brothers, killed so he could be ruler.

However, Abimelech pursued the men of Shechem and killed about a thousand of them. They hid in the stronghold in the temple of the god Berith, but Abimelech piled wood around the tower and set it on fire, and the men were burned to death. Yet Abimelech was not killed in a heroic battle, as military men tend to desire, but by a woman who was hiding in a tower in Thebez. She dropped a millstone on his head and crushed his skull. (See Judges 9.)

As we look at the differences between this father and son, we are reminded again of the power of the will of man. Gideon would not operate without signs from the Lord, and his son would not listen to good advice from anyone, including God. He walked in his own counsel and died at the hand of a woman when he was still a young man.

Prayer about Nebulous Fears

Our concern for our children or other family members can become nebulous fears that affect our faith. Job was a righteous man but he experienced nebulous fears. Scripture says he was "blameless and upright, and one who feared God and shunned evil" (Job 1:1). Job kept his eyes on his children and their activities at all times.

His sons enjoyed giving feasts. They always invited their three sisters as well as their friends to take part in the festivities. After these parties had run their course, Job regularly rose early the next morning and offered burnt offerings for all of those involved in the merriment. "For Job said, 'It may be that my sons have sinned and cursed God in their hearts'" (Job 1:5).

Job tried to keep his family free from sin, and his righteousness was a thorn in Satan's side. The devil's remarks about Job caused God to allow Satan to kill his children, destroy his possessions, and afflict him with a horrible disease. Job also had to listen to his friends tell him that he was responsible for everything that happened. Some Christians will blame anyone or anything for their problems instead of exposing the real culprit, Satan.

In spite of prayer and our efforts to make good decisions, we can anticipate Satan having predominance over us for short periods of time. It is his desire to rule over us through our sins. But Jesus is our High Priest. Through Him and the Word of God we are able to outmaneuver Satan. Job didn't have the blood of Jesus to intercede for him. Yet Job did not sin against God (Job 1:22).

We cannot give up either. God can restore and bless us the way He blessed Job after all of his afflictions. God healed Job and restored to him seven times more than he lost in personal wealth, then gave him seven sons and three daughters. (See Job 42:12–16.)

Trust God to Help Overcome Nebulous Fears

When I decided to go with a group to Israel and Egypt, I put out a fleece, as Gideon did. I waited as long as possible before making up my mind, then I asked the Lord to let there be no vacancy if I shouldn't go.

After I was able to get my ticket and join the group, I put out another fleece. I prayed that God would not let me lose luggage, passport, or other important papers or get lost in airports. I was so agitated with worry that one day, as I was praying, I heard in my spirit, *Visualize yourself getting over there and back.* As soon as I pictured myself home safely from the trip, fear left me. However, I was a little crestfallen because I'd lost some of the joy in anticipating the trip because of fear. But I felt prayed up and ready for my adventure.

Satan tested my frailties, so my prayers were essential.

One night, while my group was waiting in the lobby of a hotel for our rooms to be ready, I rummaged through my purse checking documents, and an important piece of paper was left on the couch. I had a dream that night of losing something. When I mentioned the dream to my roommate the next morning, we both wondered if I had lost something. I was sure I hadn't. However, when we went to breakfast, the leader on our bus told me someone had found a piece of paper that belonged to me. I couldn't have left Israel without it. That was my first blooper!

In Egypt, as we were preparing to go to London, I was instructed to check in at a gate with a couple to help keep the lines moving. After our check-in, I elected to remain behind the gates and wait on some friends who were still shopping. A few minutes later I saw the couple inside the guarded gate, waving at me. They were trying to return a paper to exit Egypt that was meant for me. The guards at the gate thought we were traveling together and had given my paper to the man by mistake. Satan was determined to cause me trouble!

My first anxiety about airports came when my daughter dropped me off in St. Louis. I felt like an abandoned child. The airport was extremely crowded, and I couldn't find a single unoccupied seat in the waiting area. But then a young lady removed the bag in the seat across from her. I eagerly took the only seat available in the area.

As I waited for my plane, vacillating between praying and fretting, the girl who'd moved the bag looked up from the Bible she had been reading and looked at me. She returned to her reading, but then peered up at me again.

She introduced herself and her mother, who was sitting next to her. She said they were from Arkansas. Then she told me that God had interrupted her concentration on her Bible reading and given her a message: "Speak to that lady sitting in front of you." She wondered what she was supposed to say. But when the message was repeated, she spoke up.

She noticed my tour pin and asked about my destination. We quickly learned that this girl and her mother and I were the only three people traveling from St. Louis to the Israeli airport in New

York. We knew it was no coincidence that an empty seat had been saved for me by my fellow traveler.

After our trip to Israel and Egypt was over, I started fretting again. My friends from Arkansas were going home from a different airport, and I had to change airports by taxi or bus. As we were retrieving luggage, I met a couple from the tour who lived in Colorado. They had to catch a plane from my airport, so we shared a taxi.

I was the only traveler from St. Louis who was on that tour. Yet I was never without the help and consolation of companionship.

Conquering Nebulous Fears Leads to New Beginnings

For me, the climax on that hectic trip was meeting the man who would be my new husband. If I hadn't conquered my fears about traveling alone, I would have missed the new life God had in store for me. Since I had no desire for a new life or a new husband, God had to help me overcome a lot of nebulous fears before and after I met the man I was to marry.

My children lived in St. Louis, Missouri, so I asked the Lord who would look after them if I moved to California. I was still dubious after He assured me that He would. But I replied, "Okay. I can't leave them in better hands."

Good Reports Conquer Nebulous Fears

In spite of the miracles God performed for the Israelites, they refused to believe His Word. They missed His greatest blessing. Because they did not conquer their nebulous fears, they were left to wander in the desert for forty years.

Moses sent twelve men, one from each tribe, to spy out the land God had promised for their homeland. Ten men brought back reports that the Israelites were like grasshoppers compared to the giants who lived in the land.

Caleb and Joshua told the people that the land was good. They said, "If the Lord delights in us, then He will bring us into this land and give it to us, 'a land which flows with milk and honey.'

Only do not rebel against the Lord, nor fear the people of the land, for they are our bread; their protection has departed from them, and the Lord is with us. Do not fear them" (Numbers 14:8–9). When the people tried to stone Caleb and Joshua, Moses had to plead for their lives. Their disobedience and disbelief angered God so much, He did not allow those who murmured to enter the Promised Land. Their nebulous fears caused them to die in the desert and miss the good life that God had promised them. We too can miss the blessings God has prepared for us if we don't conquer nebulous fears.

Chapter 25

Real Fear

Chimerical and nebulous fears extend over a period of time, and the imagination plays a part in producing them, but real fear is a direct, momentary confrontation. The way we react to real fear depends on our daily preparations in prayer and self-discipline in the study of the Word. Two excellent examples of facing real fear are given in the Old Testament when Shadrach, Meshach, and Abed-Nego were put into a fiery furnace and Daniel was thrown into a den of lions.

Stay Prayed Up

Daniel and his friends—Hananiah, Mishael, and Azariah—were youths of noble birth who were sent into exile when the tribe of Judah fell to the Babylonians under the reign of King Nebuchadnezzar. They were among a select group of young men and children who were good looking, without blemish, full of wisdom, and able to serve the king. They were offered special education and were given new names. Daniel's name was changed to Belteshazzar, Hananiah to Shadrach, Mishael to Meshach, and Azariah to Abed-Nego.

Daniel and his friends continued in prayer daily and purposed in their hearts not to defile themselves. So when they were told to eat of the king's delicacies and drink his wine, they convinced the steward they could remain healthy on their regular diet, which consisted of vegetables and water. After their three years of training were up, they were healthier and more intelligent than the other young men, so they were highly favored in Nebuchadnezzar's kingdom. (See Daniel 1.)

Godly Discipline Prostrates Real Fear

When Daniel interpreted one of the king's dreams, he was given a promotion: to sit at the king's gate. He intervened for Shadrach, Meshach, and Abed-Nego, and they were set over the affairs of the province of Babylon. Things went well for them . . . until King Nebuchadnezzar made an idol of gold and commanded all of the people to bow down and worship it when they heard the sound of horn, flute, harp, lyre, and psaltery. Those who did not fall down and worship would be thrown into a fiery furnace (Daniel 3:4–6).

When the people saw that the three Jews who had been set over them did not worship the idol, they reported the flagrant disobedience to the king. Shadrach, Meshach, and Abed-Nego were brought before the king and given one last chance to bow down before the idol. But they said to the king, "If that is the case, our God whom we serve is able to deliver us from the burning fiery furnace, and He will deliver us from your hand, O king. But if not, let it be known to you, O king, that we do not serve your gods, nor will we worship the gold image which you have set up" (Daniel 3:17–18).

After their refusal to obey the king, the three men were bound and cast into a fiery furnace. Shadrach, Meshack, and Abed-Nego had prepared themselves, through prayer and dedication to God, for the horror of being burned alive. When it came time to stand up to real fear, they went into the furnace willingly.

But when the king looked inside the furnace, he was surprised to see a fourth figure in there with them. And no fire touched them or their garments. "Nebuchadnezzar spoke, saying, 'Blessed be the God of Shadrach, Meshach, and Abed-Nego, who sent His Angel and delivered His servants who trusted in Him'" (Daniel 3:28).

The king made a decree that anyone who spoke erroneous things against the three Jews or their God would be cut into little pieces and made an ash heap (Daniel 3:29–30).

Many years later, when Babylon fell to the Persians and Medes, Darius became king. By that time Daniel was well established in the kingdom, having maintained favor with all the kings. This angered the governors and satraps, so they decided they must do something to usurp Daniel's position. They had the king make a decree that all who petitioned another god or man instead of the king for thirty days would be thrown into the lions' den.

Daniel, like his three friends, was prepared for the moment of real fear. It was his custom to kneel and pray three times a day in front of an open window. Even after he heard about the decree, he continued to give thanks to God and pray in front of the open window. His refusal to stop praying was reported to the king. Although the king was upset about his foolish decree, he knew he could not alter it.

After Daniel was thrown into the lions' den, the king said to him, "Your God, whom you serve continually, He will deliver you" (Daniel 6:16). The king didn't sleep all night. When morning came he rushed to the lions' den and in an anguished voice cried out, "Daniel, servant of the living God, has your God, whom you serve continually, been able to deliver you from the lions?" (Daniel 6:20).

Daniel said, "O king, live forever! My God sent His angel and shut the lions' mouths, so that they have not hurt me, because I was found innocent before Him; and also, O king, I have done no wrong before you" (Daniel 6:21–22).

Daniel and his friends lived in enemy territory, far from their homeland, among people who worshipped idols, yet they never forgot their spiritual training. They stayed focused on God's discipline.

If we are to be prepared to face sudden danger or real fear, we must stay focused on the training we receive from the Word of God.

Physical Training Helps Minimize Real Fear

I recently saw a young marine being interviewed on television about fear as he prepared to board a plane to fight in Afghanistan. His answer to the media was that the discipline he had received in military training and the dedication he had for serving his country would help him allay fear and stay focused in battle.

Training, discipline, and dedication are the three ingredients we need to overcome fear. If we train ourselves to become disciplined in God's Word and dedicate ourselves to serving Him, He will help us fight in the battlefields of life.

Real fear is not always as drastic as being put in a fiery furnace, thrown in a den of lions, or finding yourself in the heat of battle during times of war. There are many situations in which we face real fears. One notable example are the heroic stories of the men and women who evacuated the Trade Center buildings on September 11, 2001.

The evacuation took place in a calm, orderly manner. While firemen were going into the buildings, the people who worked there tried to rush down the stairways to the safety of the streets. Some took time to say prayers for the firefighters because they knew those men and women could be facing death as they helped evacuate people and put out the fires.

Police, fire, and other emergency personnel, who willingly put themselves in harm's way on a daily basis, are dedicated to serving others. They are disciplined and trained for their duties so in times of crisis they are not paralyzed by fear. Many of these people say that their spiritual training is just as important to them as physical training.

Spiritual Training Frees Us from Bondage of Fear

The more we trust in Jesus, the less we will fear death. Scripture says, "Inasmuch then as the children have partaken of flesh and blood, He Himself likewise shared in the same, that through death He might destroy him who had the power of death, that is, the devil, and release those who through fear of death were all their lifetime subject to bondage" (Hebrews 2:14–15).

For Christians, death has no sting or victory in the grave (1 Corinthians 15:54–55). When we are faced with deadly situations, we can expect the Lord to deliver us, as he did for Daniel and his three friends. But if He doesn't, we will not give in to fear. Our hope is in a glorious, eternal life, unlike life on earth, which passes quickly, like a vapor.

Satan lost his power over sickness, death, poverty, and sin when Jesus shed His blood on the cross for mankind, but he didn't lose his cunning ways. He continues to rob us, because fear plants images in our minds that convince us we cannot overcome in certain situations. When we walk in fear, our faith is paralyzed. When we are faced with the fear of death, faith in the promises of Scripture assures us that God will deliver those who love Him.

Psalm 91:3–6 says, "Surely He shall deliver you from the snare of the fowler and from the perilous pestilence. He shall cover you with His feathers, and under His wings you shall take refuge; His truth shall be your shield and buckler. You shall not be afraid of the terror by night, nor of the arrow that flies by day, nor of the pestilence that walks in darkness, nor of the destruction that lays waste at noonday."

Fight Fear with God's Righteousness

There are many ways we come face-to-face with real fear as we deal with the experiences of life. Our challenge is not to give in to that fear.

Peter tried to walk on the water to meet Jesus, but when he looked down, fear began to control him and he started to sink.

When he cried out to Jesus, He stretched out his arm to catch him, then said, "O you of little faith, why did you doubt?" (Matthew 14: 31). We doubt when we take our eyes off of Jesus and look at the circumstances.

Peter bragged that he would never deny that he knew Jesus. However, Peter denied knowing Jesus three times because he was afraid of the men who took Him hostage (Luke 22:54–62). Jesus told Peter that Satan wanted to sift him like wheat, but that He was praying for him, and when he did return to Jesus, he was to strengthen his brothers (Luke 22:31–32). Jesus knew that Peter would be a great apostle once he conquered fear.

We rejoice at the transformation in Peter as we read his two epistles. They remind us that with the help of the Holy Spirit, regardless of our circumstances or frailties, we can overcome fear and rise to any occasion.

Peter talks about rejoicing in the midst of trials when he says, "Beloved, do not think it strange concerning the fiery trial which is to try you, as though some strange thing happened to you; but rejoice to the extent that you partake of Christ's sufferings, that when His glory is revealed, you may also be glad with exceeding joy" (1 Peter 4:12–13). Peter admonishes believers that if they must suffer, let it be for righteousness and not as a result of sin.

As Peter traveled in various Roman provinces, spreading the gospel, he gradually lost his fear of men and circumstances. He instructed followers of Jesus Christ to be diligent and not to stumble over false teachings.

Peter no longer quaked with fear when he was under pressure. Even though he had been warned of his pending death, he focused on the Christians who would be left to struggle with the ungodliness of this world. He fulfilled Jesus' request to strengthen his brethren and became a man of great faith and valor.

He reminded the people of things they should do to walk in godliness. Then he said, "Moreover I will be careful to ensure that you always have a reminder of these things after my decease" (2 Peter 1:15).

While Jesus was with His disciples, He changed Simon's name to Peter, which means "rock." He knew that one day, after Peter had overcome his fears, he would become a rock in the Christian faith.

PART TWO: NEGATIVE EMOTIONS THAT COME AGAINST US

Chapter 26

Overcoming Fear

The mighty men of Israel were afraid to fight the giant Goliath, who had been baiting them for forty days. David, a mere youth, wanted to fight the giant and defend the honor of God. So he said, "What shall be done for the man who kills this Philistine and takes away the reproach from Israel? For who is this uncircumcised Philistine, that he should defy the armies of the living God?" (1 Samuel 17:26).

Speak to the Problem

After David's words were reported to King Saul, he was taken to the king. He told the king that he had fought a lion and a bear with his bare hands while he was tending sheep. The king decided to let David fight Goliath, and he insisted on arming David with a coat of mail, a sword, and a bronze helmet. David said the armor was too heavy for him and that he had not tested it. Therefore, he was allowed to challenge the giant with his slingshot and his shepherd's bag that held five stones.

When Goliath saw that David wore no armor, he felt humiliated that the armies of Israel would send a boy to fight him. He cursed David and uttered, "Am I a dog, that you come to me with sticks?" (1 Samuel 17:43).

David ignored the giant's curses and bravely replied, "Then all this assembly shall know that the Lord does not save with sword and spear; for the battle is the Lord's, and He will give you into our hands" (1 Samuel 17:47).

Before the giant could react, David drew his slingshot. With one stone he hit the giant in the center of his forehead and killed him. He used the giant's sword to cut off his head. The armies of Israel were galvanized into action. They pursued the fleeing Philistines and took spoils.

David was victorious in killing the giant because he had learned from his experiences that the battle is the Lord's. He spoke fearlessly to Goliath and told him in no uncertain terms what he intended to do. Even though David was a youth, he had already discovered that his victories did not lie in his own strength or in armor but in the hands of God.

The armies of Israel had been helped many times by the Lord, but they had not remained in close communication with God, as David had. Their lack of faith in God led them into unbelief, and unbelief opened the door to fear, which stupefied the armies for forty days while Goliath taunted and ridiculed them.

Prepare for the Mountains

The disciples also experienced a problem that entailed unbelief. They had been trained by Jesus to heal the sick and to cast out demons, but they were powerless in one case. When they asked Jesus why they couldn't cast that demon out, He answered, "Because of your unbelief; for assuredly, I say to you, if you have faith as a mustard seed, you will say to this mountain, 'Move from here to there,' and it will move; and nothing will be impossible for you. However, this kind does not go out except by prayer and fasting" (Matthew 17:20–21).

Although the disciples had fellowshipped with Jesus for a long time, they still didn't realize that some mountains don't move easily.

David didn't suddenly get the ability to kill a giant. He had spent years in preparation for such a moment by herding sheep.

Sheepherding is a lonely job. David spent his solitary time communicating with God. He developed a fearless nature because he knew he could rely on God for wisdom and strength. His faith was in God, not himself.

Unless we discipline ourselves daily in the Word of God, we will lack the wisdom, strength, and faith necessary for our moments of fiery trials. We need to be prepared. If we are not, we will merely react, as the armies of Israel did.

Stand Still Until Help Arrives

Sometimes action is imperative, but at other times, waiting on the Lord to move is required. Shortly after the Israelites left Egypt, Pharaoh's army started chasing them. When they approached the Red Sea, the Israelites felt trapped. They thought it would have been better for them to have remained slaves in Egypt than to be killed by the Egyptian armies.

Moses admonished them to stay calm and not panic. He soothed their fears by saying, "Do not be afraid. Stand still, and see the salvation of the Lord, which He will accomplish for you today. For the Egyptians whom you see today, you shall see again no more forever. The Lord will fight for you, and you shall hold your peace" (Exodus 14:13–14).

The Lord gave Moses instructions to stretch out his rod and divide the sea. A pillar of cloud behind them kept the Egyptians in darkness but gave light to the Israelites. The winds dried the water and the Israelites were able to cross the Red Sea by night on dry land. When morning came, the Egyptians started across, but God allowed the waters to rush forth and fill the Red Sea again.

As we read the story of how the Lord helped the Israelites escape from the Egyptians, we realize that sometimes, when we face fear, all we can do is stand still and wait to see what the Lord has in mind.

When the Israelites were told to stand still, they were also told to remain peaceful and not to fear. Faith brings peace. The Israelites could have stampeded and killed themselves like a herd of cattle if Moses had not been able to keep them calm.

Face Fear Head On

When we come face-to-face with fear, we may have to stand still until we can determine how best to react.

I remember a night in St. Louis, Missouri, when I faced a moment of sheer terror. It was the Fourth of July, and I was with my family, among about two hundred thousand other people, waiting for the fireworks show to begin.

Just after sundown, some of our group wanted to order food to eat during the fireworks. Elaine, my daughter-in-law, volunteered for the job, and I declared my intentions to go with her to help carry the food.

I followed her to some steps going down to the riverfront, where the food stands were. We had to squeeze between people who were sitting or standing on the steps, waiting for the fireworks. Elaine decided it would be easier to maneuver through the crowd by herself. She suggested I stay where I was until she returned with the food.

Daylight waned. Lights came on. People continued to mill around me, pushing and shoving. Claustrophobia threatened me. Fearing that Elaine wouldn't be able to find me, I decided to return to the family by myself.

I shoved myself through the jam-packed crowd and climbed back up the steps. When I broke through at the top, I gazed in confusion at the mass of people sitting on the dark hillside in front of me. I had been standing in a lighted area where the entertainment and food stands were and didn't realize that darkness had descended.

I was lost in a sea of thousands of people. I couldn't remember the name of the garage where we had parked the car. Visions of going to a police station and waiting to be claimed like a lost child unnerved me.

I had recently been studying Scriptures on fear, so in that moment of terror, I leaned against a tree and decided to wait until my fear subsided. I prayed for guidance and calmed myself with the knowledge that the Lord was with me. I recalled what Paul said to the Ephesians about overcoming fear: "Take up the whole armor of God, that you may be able to withstand in the evil day, and having done all, to stand" (Ephesians 6:13).

Peace and wisdom finally kicked in. When I finally had a clear head, I remembered the family being close to a small body of water. With that landmark in mind, I started in what I felt was the right direction.

I peered into the faces of strangers. An eternity seemed to pass until the dim outlines of familiar faces loomed before me in the darkness.

I was greatly relieved to be with my family but too embarrassed to tell them of my experience. My anxiety shifted to Elaine, who would certainly be looking for me. Fortunately, only a few moments passed before she appeared with all the food. She had been in the park all day and was familiar with the area, but she knew I wasn't. She'd started worrying about my welfare when she couldn't find me. But she refused to allow fear to overtake her. She relied on the Lord to take care of me.

God always makes a way if you let peace and wisdom guide you.

Master God's Word

It is critical for our well-being that we keep our spiritual weapons of warfare ready. Our daily battles are not against flesh and blood but against spiritual strongholds (2 Corinthians 10:3–4). We could have our waists girded with truth, and our feet shod with peace, we could be wearing our breastplates of righteousness, our shields of faith, and our helmets of salvation, but without the sword of the Spirit, which is the Word of God, our armor is not complete (Ephesians 6:14–17). Unlike the rest of the armor, the sword has to be polished daily or it will corrode.

Developing and maintaining a personal relationship with God by concentrating on what they had been taught led Daniel,

Shadrach, Meshach, and Abed-Nego—as well as Moses, David, and Gideon—to trust God. They knew they could not be victorious in battle in their own power or the power of other men.

David encouraged himself against fear, saying, "Whenever I am afraid, I will trust in You. In God (I will praise His word), in God I have put my trust; I will not fear. What can flesh do to me?" (Psalm 56:3–4).

David had many enemies to contend with before and after he became king of Israel and Judah. Many of his psalms deal with fear. He learned early in his youth to trust in God and not let fear defeat him. In Psalm 27:1 he says, "The Lord is my light and my salvation; whom shall I fear? The Lord is the strength of my life; of whom shall I be afraid?"

In Psalm 34:4 we see David wrestling with fear. "I sought the Lord, and He heard me, and delivered me from all my fears."

David thought of God as a Shepherd who watches over His sheep. He calmed himself by saying, "Yea, though I walk through the valley of the shadow of death, I will fear no evil; for You are with me; Your rod and Your staff, they comfort me" (Psalm 23:4).

Jesus tells us that we are His sheep. "Do not fear, little flock, for it is your Father's good pleasure to give you the kingdom" (Luke 12:32). Knowing that God is watching over us in the same way a shepherd watches over his sheep saturates us with peace.

Since we know that God is for us, we should not fear what man might do to us through Satan. We can be harmed in the body, but God is in charge of the spirit. The Holy Spirit gives us abundant joy for life here on earth and eternal joy in heaven.

Negative Fear

Satan assails us daily with fears pertaining to our environment, health, death, accidents, finances, and personal relationships. These fears can keep us from walking in faith with God. But we can neutralize fear with peace, joy, and the sound mind we have been given through Jesus Christ (2 Timothy 1:7). God wants to give us every good gift His kingdom possesses.

However, we have to learn to walk in His discipline and not in the ways of the world. Satan uses the age-old bondage of fear to control men's actions and thoughts. Fear paralyzes our faith, leaves us in unbelief, and counteracts God's power in our lives.

Godly Fear

A reverent fear of God is necessary before we can walk in His discipline. This beneficial fear is pertinent and essential for parent-child relationships as well as in walking with God. Children who obey godly parents are less apt to fall into Satan's bondage. Adults who fear God can more easily stay the course without falling into Satan's traps of unbelief.

Proverbs 1:7 tells us, "The fear of the Lord is the beginning of knowledge, but fools despise wisdom and instruction." The men of wisdom in Scripture knew the rewards of fearing God. Psalm 34:9–10 says, "Oh, fear the Lord, you His saints! There is no want to those who fear Him. The young lions lack and suffer hunger; but those who seek the Lord shall not lack any good thing."

Proverbs 14:26–27 says, "In the fear of the Lord there is strong confidence, and His children will have a place of refuge. The fear of the Lord is a fountain of life, to turn one away from the snares of death."

There are many reasons men should learn to have a reverent fear of God. Proverbs 19:23 says, "The fear of the Lord leads to life, and he who has it will abide in satisfaction; He will not be visited with evil." God wants the best for His children and He understands their frailties.

Psalm 103:13–14 says, "As a father pities his children, so the Lord pities those who fear Him. For He knows our frame; He remembers that we are dust."

Obedience is the key to His mercy and grace. "The mercy of the Lord is from everlasting to everlasting on those who fear Him, and His righteousness to children's children, to such as keep His covenant, and to those who remember His commandments to do them" (Psalm 103:17–18). Obedience gives us a reverent fear of God, and through obedience we receive His wisdom, knowledge, and power.

Satan delights in violating our faith with fear just as a mouse enjoys violating our houses with his refuse. But we can overcome Satan's tactics of fear with God's Word.

Father, we thank You for Your mercy and grace. We pray that we will develop the kind of godly fear that is necessary for us to follow Your commandments. Help us not to allow the negative fears of Satan to cause us to lose our peace and joy. Father, help us to walk in the perfect love that casts out fear. We know that we can overcome fear with Your help. Amen.

The God Kind of Love

O Spirit of Love, come into our hearts,

For God's love will mold us like clay.

What the world needs this day is love, love, love,

The Jesus, the God kind of love.

Cast out the spirit of fear with God's peace and love,

For perfect love will cast away all fears.

What the world needs this day is love, love, love,

The Jesus, the God kind of love.

Discipline #6: Unforgiveness

Unforgiveness causes harm to the body, soul, and spirit.

If You, Lord, should mark iniquities,
O Lord, who could stand?
But there is forgiveness with You,
That You may be feared.
(Psalm 130:3–4)

Chapter 27

To Forgive or Not to Forgive

The act of forgiveness comes with certain obligations, such as:

- overlooking an offense
- giving up the desire to punish
- eliminating anger
- canceling or remitting a debt
- giving up a claim to exact penalty
- absolving from wrongdoing (to *absolve* means to pronounce free from guilt or blame, exonerate, acquit, or pardon)
- releasing any resentment against the perpetrator

After meditating on the acts of forgiving and not forgiving, I received these words from the Lord: *To forgive is to forget.* I asked the Holy Spirit how a person could forget deep hurts. His answers came in the form of questions.

Do you remember everything you have ever read or heard? Do you remember everything people have said to you or about you?

Of course, I had to answer no to His questions.

The Holy Spirit asked why I remembered some things and not others. After puzzling over this, I responded, "I guess I remember things that are important to me." Suddenly, the light dawned, and I realized that if I am able to remember things I choose to remember, I am also able to forget things I want to forget.

Why Do We Remember Hurts?

Forgiveness is contingent upon an act of the will. Do we choose to forgive and forget, or do we choose to let an offense against us live on in our spirit, wrestling with it from time to time, and allowing old wounds to keep festering? It's an age-old dilemma coming from negative emotions that have plagued people since pride reared its grotesque head in the garden of Eden.

Receiving Forgiveness Requires Forgiving

Jesus said to His disciples, "Whenever you stand praying, if you have anything against anyone, forgive him, that your Father in heaven may also forgive you your trespasses. But if you do not forgive, neither will your Father in heaven forgive your trespasses" (Mark 11:25–26).

After meditating on this passage, I said to the Lord, "Okay, so if we don't forgive others, You won't forgive us." I was rebuked in my spirit: *You don't fully understand forgiveness because you don't understand unforgiveness.* The reprimand whetted my desire to delve deeper into the subject of forgiving or not forgiving.

Reasons to Forgive

Shortly after I began my research on unforgiveness, another message came: *Harboring unforgiving thoughts in the heart is like pressing a burning coal of fire to the bosom.*

Suddenly my senses were impregnated with thoughts of the indescribable pain and the awful smell that accompanies burning flesh. I recalled news reports of people setting themselves on fire in public places. They chose that way to die because it called attention to a perceived wrong in society that they wanted changed. Seeing someone set his or her body on fire is too grotesque to contemplate.

At the end of World War II, many Americans—including my husband Andy and my brother Leroy—had to endure the smell of hundreds of bodies burning when they liberated German concentration camps. My brother said the unforgettable smell lodged in his nostrils for days and seemed to excrete from the pores of his skin.

God tells us that refusing to forgive is like pressing a burning coal of fire to our bosoms. This is a powerful mental picture of how unforgiving acts smell in His nostrils. They are as appalling to Him as burning flesh is to us.

Kindling that Fuels the Flame

Holding a burning coal of fire to the body, even for a short time, would inflict excruciating pain, produce a terrible wound, and cause hideous scarring. It seems improbable that a person would willingly keep a coal of fire attached to his or her flesh, because it would torture or even kill the body. Yet people anchor unforgiving thoughts in their hearts for many years and do not realize they are tormenting the body, soul, and spirit.

Although we don't smell the burning flesh of people walking around with an unforgiving attitude, we can pick up on the unpleasant aura of someone who carries a "chip on the shoulder." It's offensive to be around a person who is quick to criticize, judge, and condemn, or people who spend their time in evil surmising while trying to second guess another's thoughts or actions.

Isaiah spoke to the Israelites about sin. "For wickedness burns as the fire; it shall devour the briers and thorns, and kindle in the thickets of the forest; they shall mount up like rising smoke. Through the wrath of the Lord of hosts the land is burned up, and the people shall be as a fuel for the fire; no man shall spare his brother" (Isaiah 9:18–19).

The result of sin in the land is presented as a consuming fire, and the people are the firewood that keeps it burning. A person with an unforgiving attitude fuels the flames of fire against himself and his brother or sister. God holds out His hands to us in forgiveness regardless of our sins, and He wants us to put out the fires of unforgiveness.

The Burden of Not Forgiving

Not even God wants to be handicapped with the cumbersome weight of unforgiveness. He says in Isaiah 43:25, "I, even I, am He who blots out your transgressions for My own sake; and I will not remember your sins." God spent centuries trying to teach the Israelites how to walk in His ways, but He was thwarted daily in His efforts to stop them from heinous sins that resulted in unforgiving attitudes among the people.

After the crucifixion of Jesus, God was reconciled to the world, and He no longer deals with sin as He did in the Old Testament. He now observes the sins of the world through the blood of Jesus and is no longer angry with mankind. Colossians 1:19–20 says, "It pleased the Father that in Him all the fullness should dwell, and by Him to reconcile all things to Himself, by Him, whether things on earth or things in heaven, having made peace through the blood of His cross." God waits patiently for the sons and daughters who will be His for eternity because they have accepted Jesus as their Savior.

Although our lives are full of unwanted experiences, most of those moments are blotted out of our minds. They go into the sea of oblivion, as though they never happened, because the memory does not recall them. That is what God wants us to do with memories that have caused us to develop an unforgiving spirit: forgive and forget. With the help of the Holy Spirit, bad memories can be blotted out through an act of the will.

Paul admonished the Corinthians by saying, "Now whom you forgive anything, I also forgive. For if indeed I have forgiven anything, I have forgiven that one for your sakes in the presence of Christ, lest Satan should take advantage of us; for we are not ignorant of his devices" (2 Corinthians 2:10–11).

The Word of God will penetrate into our spirits when we bring our thoughts into captivity to the obedience of Christ (2 Corinthians 10:5). His thoughts will help us blot out the transgressions that have been executed against us. But when we dwell on negative thoughts, we are controlled by bitterness and anger, which keep us in bondage to Satan. We can be free from the burden of unforgiveness when we cast our burdens on the Lord (Psalm 55:22).

Chapter 28

Acts that Cause Us Not to Forgive

The most widely spread abuse known to man generates from the tongue. We can create problems in another's heart when we speak out critical, judgmental comments or correct people in a condescending manner.

Perpetuation of Verbal Abuse

A child who has been overly criticized usually becomes a critical adult. His quickness to criticize will hamper him all the days of his life and will cause him to perpetrate on others the evils that were inflicted on him. Negative criticism hardens the heart, but positive criticism edifies and becomes a valuable teacher.

Unforgiveness comes without effort, but walking in love requires discipline. James gives us instructions on how to obey the Word and walk in love. "So then, my beloved brethren, let every man be swift to hear, slow to speak, slow to wrath; for the wrath of man does not produce the righteousness of God" (James 1:19–20).

Unrighteous Behavior

If we to listen to God's wisdom with a meek heart, we will be doers of His Word. We won't be goaded into the traps Satan sets that encourage self-righteousness, self-pity, anger, bitterness, and other negative emotions that keep us from walking in the righteousness of God and prevent us from forgiving people.

No one can take a lot of verbal abuse without anger smoldering in his or her heart, at least for short periods of time. The secret is to control the anger before it results in an unforgiving attitude.

Paul gives excellent counsel to the Ephesians on the subject of anger by saying, "'Be angry, and do not sin': do not let the sun go down on your wrath, nor give place to the devil" (Ephesians 4:26–27).

David said, "Be angry, and do not sin. Meditate within your heart on your bed, and be still. Selah. Offer the sacrifices of righteousness, and put your trust in the Lord" (Psalm 4:4–5). The festering spiritual wounds of anger develop into unforgiveness that reaps a whirlwind of disaster in many areas of our lives.

Abusive words wound us deeply. Yet, for the sake of our health and spiritual well-being, we must not allow them to keep us from walking in love with the offender. If we are not willing to forgive, we are yoked to Satan. Christians must be yoked with Jesus to enjoy His blessings of love, which produce peace and joy.

Religious Bondage

James says, "Pure and undefiled religion before God and the Father is this: to visit orphans and widows in their trouble, and to keep oneself unspotted from the world" (James 1:27).

Love promotes mercy and leads to favor with God. Religion induces bondage and finds favor with Satan. God wants us to study His Word and develop a personal, intimate relationship with Him. We are not to study the Word for the purpose of developing religious rituals or techniques that provoke division among the people, the way the Pharisees and Sadducees did.

James says, "So speak and so do as those who will be judged by the law of liberty. For judgment is without mercy to the one who has shown no mercy. Mercy triumphs over judgment" (James 2:12–13).

When Jesus paid the price for our sins, His mercy triumphed over any judgment brought against us. He spoke against religious bondage when He said, "Woe to you, scribes and Pharisees, hypocrites! For you are like whitewashed tombs which indeed appear beautiful outwardly, but inside are full of dead men's bones and all uncleanness. Even so you also outwardly appear righteous to men, but inside you are full of hypocrisy and lawlessness" (Matthew 23:27–28).

Paul warned Titus about judgmental teachers. He told him to avoid confrontations with them because there was nothing to gain from contentions (Titus 3:9).

We must not get caught up in man-made laws and the hypocrisy of religious men who are seeking their own agendas for gain. Many of our churches today have Pharisaic people who use religion as a weapon to condemn other Christians. They cultivate unforgiveness, hinder spiritual development, and impede the progress and growth of a church.

Cults in the United States and other parts of the world are reaping a bountiful harvest in religious bondage by using some of God's teachings. People who join these groups are brainwashed as they seek solace and acceptance from their perceived benefactors. When cult activities are exposed on the news, instead of being indignant Christians, we should be embarrassed. Jesus told Peter to tend His sheep and feed His lambs (John 21:15–17). We allow others to steal sheep away from the kingdom of God when we keep them in religious bondage.

The Heartbreak of Slander

Abusive word attacks sometimes expose the truth, at least in the opinion of the speaker. Slander, on the other hand, is a direct attack on a person's character using false accusations. Slander has malice behind it. False rumors are spread with the purpose of ruining a person's reputation.

Christians who take part in slander are walking outside of God's protection into Satan's territory, and the consequences can be calamitous.

Slander can ruin a person's life because it affects finances, health, and relationships. No matter how hard the slandered person strives to overcome the false allegations, many people will continue to believe the offenses he or she is accused of. The person being slandered will find forgiveness extremely difficult. If you find yourself in such a situation, your only hope is to let Jesus help you overcome the problems that slander imposes upon you.

Jesus dealt with vicious men, and He understands. After He healed the blind and mute man, the common people wondered if Jesus was the Son of David. But the Pharisees accused Him of casting out demons by Beelzebub, the ruler of the demons (Matthew 12:24). They were saying Jesus was a cohort of Satan!

Jesus knew their thoughts and told them that any kingdom, city, or house divided could not stand. Then He added, "If Satan casts out Satan, he is divided against himself. How then will his kingdom stand? And if I cast out demons by Beelzebub, by whom do your sons cast them out? Therefore, they shall be your judges" (Matthew 12:26–27).

No one has ever been slandered more than Jesus was when He was here on earth, yet He continued to walk in love. Even His own countrymen were offended by His teaching because they knew Him as Joseph's son, not the Son of God. He was unable to do any great works among them because a prophet is usually not honored among people who know him (Mark 6:4).

Jesus was slandered so much by the religious people of His day that even the common people believed the lies they heard and joined in the tumultuous cry for His crucifixion.

Now the kingdom of God lives in us through the Holy Spirit, who is our Counselor and Helper. Paul says, "As the sufferings of Christ abound in us, so our consolation also abounds through Christ" (2 Corinthians 1:5).

We cannot allow our feelings to be in charge of our wisdom. Jesus will console our emotional distress and heal every affliction that slander imposes on us. He can restore our honor when we walk in righteousness, but "a false witness will not go unpunished, and he who speaks lies will not escape" (Proverbs 19:5).

The slanderer will not escape punishment. But those who have been slandered can be so full of anger that they suffer punishment for unforgiveness. We must look to Jesus for healing, restoration, joy, and peace.

Paul gives this advice to Titus: "As for you, speak the things which are proper for sound doctrine: that the older men be sober, reverent, temperate, sound in faith, in love, in patience; the older women likewise, that they be reverent in behavior, not slanderers" (Titus 2:1–3). If we walk in God's love and wisdom, we can forgive the sin of slander.

Chapter 29

Not Forgiving Creates Disasters

In our society today, verbal abuse is prevalent. Like someone who is a drug addict or an alcoholic, a person who commits abuse with his tongue has to keep increasing his dosage to get the desired effect. When an abuser is not satisfied with angry words, he resorts to physical violence, sometimes even leading to murder.

Physical Abuse

Physical abuse between parents and children is accelerating at an alarming rate, and this involves Christians as well as the secular world. Some parents are unable to control themselves, even when a child is small. They torture, maim, and even kill their own children. The nightly news frequently reports mothers abandoning newborn babies in trash barrels or in public places, and fathers killing their children in fits of rage.

Domestic abuse is not limited to poverty-stricken families. It used to be a common belief that if we could rid society of poverty we could eradicate crime. But that is not the case, because crime is on the rise even in affluent families.

This horrific epidemic has led to the growth of gangs among teenagers. Abusive parenting instills a desire in young people to have a group of peers to vent with. When they are no longer satisfied with abusive language, they resort to bloodshed. Their activities stem from the unforgiving attitude they hold against one another, their parents, and society in general.

I believe this kind of behavior is the forerunner of Satan's end-time strategies. He is employing all of his forces to disrupt family life because society depends on children for the next generation. Before Satan can bring more people into his kingdom of darkness, he has to undermine the organization of families. He is attacking at the core of God's creation because God created families for His kingdom.

Satan started out by attempting to destroy the family of Adam and Eve. He successfully promoted the first family murder when he enticed Cain to slay his brother Abel. Today, he still incites parents to kill their children, and children to kill their parents, and siblings to kill one another.

The crimes committed today are so heinous that no one but Satan could mastermind such diabolical acts. Unless today's parents return to the disciplines of God, and teach those disciplines to their children, we can expect Satan to increase his daily carnage of human flesh throughout the world.

Sexual Abuse

Sexual abuse is on the rise today among children as well as adults. When my daughter-in-law Elaine first started working as a professional counselor, she was shocked at the number of patients who reported a family history of incest.

Incest is found even in the Old Testament. In David's family, unforgiveness instigated a diabolical plot that ended in murder. David's son Amnon raped his half-sister Tamar. When Absalom, Tamar's brother, heard of the rape, he took Tamar to live with him. Absalom pretended to forgive Amnon, but for three years his rage heightened.

Absalom's inability to forgive inflamed a passion that desired revenge. So he planned a party for all of King David's sons, including Amnon. At the party, Absalom ordered his servant to kill Amnon when he got drunk with wine.

When King David received the report of murder, he thought all of his sons were dead. Though he grieved over the murder of Amnon, He was relieved when the rest of his sons returned home.

David allowed Absalom to flee but banished him from his homeland. Later David was persuaded to allow Absalom to return home, but he refused to be in contact with him, so Absalom began plotting to overthrow David's kingdom.

Absalom was an extremely handsome young man with great talents. Some of David's subjects listened to his advice and willingly followed him into battles against David's army. Eventually, Absalom was killed. His death caused David to grieve uncontrollably, because he loved Absalom dearly. (See 2 Samuel 13.)

Hatred and an unforgiving spirit kept Absalom from establishing a good relationship with his father and his other brothers. Absalom had good reason to be angry because of the dastardly deed of rape committed against his sister, but that anger generated an unforgiving attitude and caused his early death. Absalom gave up a happy, carefree life as a king's son, because he wouldn't forgive a trespass against his sister.

People who have been victims of incest or rape are still sons and daughters of the King. Instead of being like Absalom, who chose death instead of forgiveness, they are able to enjoy the privilege of His kingdom.

Revenge

When we read the Old Testament stories, with their eye-for-an-eye philosophy, we must remember that the Israelites did not know Jesus. Yet they had no excuse for seeking revenge, because the covenant God made with Noah included the sacredness of human life. In addition, God spoke against murder when He gave Moses the Ten Commandments. The Israelites had plenty of knowledge concerning evil acts of revenge.

Proverbs 25:21–22 emphasizes God's way: "If your enemy is hungry, give him bread to eat; and if he is thirsty, give him water to drink; for so you will heap coals of fire on his head, and the Lord will reward you."

Jesus reminded His disciples that the first commandment was to love God, and then to love our neighbors as we love ourselves (Mark 12:30–31).

As Christians we are sanctified and made holy by the blood of Jesus, and the Holy Spirit dwells within us to give us His wisdom and revelation knowledge. But if we allow it, the devil can entice us to walk in his evil ways.

Since unforgiving thoughts burn the soul like a hot coal burns the body, we should return good for the evil that is done to us. Then coals of fire will be heaped on our perpetrators instead of us carrying around coals of fire in our bosoms. Instead of harboring evil thoughts in our minds that will backfire against us, we will be free to walk in peace and sing songs of rejoicing.

Chapter 30

Not Forgiving Affects Finances

Stealing is disobeying one of the Ten Commandments. It is a barbaric act because it takes away someone's security. It is traumatic for the victim emotionally as well as financially. The act of stealing, defrauding, or not paying a debt can cause physical problems as well as financial ruin. Therefore, it is easy for someone who has suffered such a loss to develop an unforgiving attitude against the offender.

However, when Peter asked the Lord if he should forgive his brother seven times, Jesus said, "I do not say to you, up to seven times, but up to seventy times seven" (Matthew 18:22).

Then he told Peter about a servant who was going to be sold with his family to pay a debt he owed to his master. When the servant begged for more time to pay, the master forgave his debt. Yet that same servant went to a fellow servant who owed him money, caught him by the throat, and demanded that he pay his debt. When the fellow servant asked for more time to pay what he owed, the first servant showed no pity and had him thrown into prison until the full amount was paid. (See Matthew 18:23–30.)

The other servants told the master what the dishonorable servant had done, and the master was so angry that he reversed his decision of forgiveness. Instead, he had the unforgiving servant thrown into prison and delivered to his tormentors until he could pay all of his debt.

Then Jesus said, "So My heavenly Father also will do to you if each of you, from his heart, does not forgive his brother his trespasses" (Matthew 18:35).

If we want to be protected from evil, we have to follow the instructions Jesus gave the disciples concerning forgiveness (Matthew 6:12–15).

Labor Disputes

From the day Adam and Eve were cast out of the garden of Eden, men have struggled fiercely against both environmental elements and one another for power and financial success. When a man thinks he has been unjustly treated, he falls into the unforgiving trap. But in a parable about laborers, Jesus tells us the world sees things differently than God sees them.

A landowner contracted to pay the first laborers a denarius, but at the last hour of the day he hired other workers. When it came time to pay them, he gave a denarius to the last workers. The first workers thought they would get paid more and were angry when they too got paid a denarius. But the landowner said it was lawful for him to spend his money for good. (See Matthew 20:15.)

Today if a businessman attempted such a fete, not only would the people be bitter and unforgiving, they would have union leaders attempting to overthrow the decision with lawsuits. However, in the parable, there was no financial abuse because the workers hired in the first part of the day had agreed to work all day for a denarius.

The parable of the laborers reminds us that although Christians live in the world, we are workers in the kingdom of God. Even though we may have concerns about our finances, God knows our needs, and we are not to worry about food or clothing. Jesus said in Matthew 6:34, "Do not worry about tomorrow, for tomorrow will worry about its own things. Sufficient for the day is its own trouble."

We do not have to follow the ways of the world to be successful or powerful. Jesus tells us that the lilies of the field are more beautiful than Solomon was in all of his glory. He reminds us how well God clothes the lilies, takes care of the grass of the fields that withers and dies, and feeds the birds of the air. Then He assures us that we are more valuable to God than they are. (See Matthew 6:26–30.)

When we are being abused financially, Jesus expects us to forgive our offenders, because when we are in right standing with God, we can expect His help. "The righteous cry out, and the Lord hears, and delivers them out of all their troubles. The Lord is near to those who have a broken heart, and saves such as have a contrite spirit" (Psalm 34:17–18).

Chapter 31

Spiritual Effects of Not Forgiving

When we contrast one individual who has a sweet, loving spirit with another who has a bitter, critical spirit, it is like comparing a good apple to a rotten apple. A good apple is firm and sweet, and a rotten apple is mushy and sour.

Salt Preserves—Bitterness Pollutes

The old saying that one rotten apple can spoil a whole barrel is correct. Nature has not given vegetation a way to preserve itself. Only God can do that. However, God gave the earth one great preservative: salt. It seasons as well as preserves foods, especially meat. Jesus said to His followers, "You are the salt of the earth; but if the salt loses its flavor, how shall it be seasoned? It is then good for nothing but to be thrown out and trampled underfoot by men" (Matthew 5:13). Christians are God's preservative on the earth if they stay salty.

Vegetables or fruits contaminate one another because they have no defense. We, on the other hand, have a choice of whether we will contaminate others with our bitter, unforgiving spirit or if we will allow God's grace to preserve His nature in us.

A root of bitterness defiles the soul, just as a piece of rot will defile an apple. Paul warned the people against developing a bitter spirit in Hebrews 12:14–15 when he said, "Pursue peace with all people, and holiness, without which no one will see the Lord: looking carefully lest anyone fall short of the grace of God; lest any root of bitterness springing up cause trouble, and by this many become defiled."

Psalm 37:8 says, "Cease from anger, and forsake wrath; do not fret—it only causes harm." The kingdom of darkness brings into the world every amoral and disastrous situation that men will submit to. The depravity of these pressures on people has its roots in pride, the beginning of evil. Pride promotes anger, and if anger is allowed to smolder too long, it flames into bitter and unforgiving acts that lead to backbiting, discord, division, and fighting—prerequisites for dysfunctional families and corrupt governments.

A bitter spirit can procreate despair in individuals to the point where they develop unhealthy, unhappy, degenerating qualities that lead to promiscuous sexual affairs, an inability to develop good personal relationships, financial mismanagement, difficulty holding down a job, or becoming an alcoholic or drug addict. Since all of these things require money, stealing, pimping, and prostitution may be added to the inventory of a bitter spirit.

Bitterness can result in a finely tuned hatred, which many times develops into malice, a forerunner of murder. The atrocities from anger, bitterness, and unforgiving acts have been played out on the stages of life since Cain murdered his brother Abel. The earth is exhausted from the hellish inferno kindled by the spirit of bitterness, fueled by the eternal fire of unforgiving people.

Legalistic Attitudes

Since the beginning of Christianity, legalism has divided the church. Holy wars were fought over legalistic attitudes in the early church. Legalism is still bandied around today among the various denominations of Christians.

Paul warns us against becoming stumbling blocks to our brothers and sisters in Christ when he says, "Let us not judge one another anymore, but rather resolve this, not to put a stumbling block or a cause to fall in our brother's way." (Romans 14:13).

Unforgiving spirits are ignited by judgmental attitudes. The Pharisees continually questioned Jesus, trying to find fault with His teachings in order to denounce His ministry. One of their complaints was that Jesus and His disciples did not wash their hands and utensils in the religious fashion of the Pharisees. They accused Him of defiling Himself and allowing the disciples to defile themselves. Jesus in turn accused them of holding to the traditions of men and rejecting the commandment of God (Mark 7:8–9).

When Jesus was asked to dine with a Pharisee, He did not follow the hand-washing ritual. All the religious leaders attending the dinner were offended, so He took them to task for their hardness of heart and hypocrisy (Luke 11:42).

Another time when Jesus was invited to eat with a group of Pharisees, a woman came in and anointed His head with precious oil, kissed His feet, then wiped His feet with her tears and hair. The Pharisees were horrified because she was a woman of the streets. However, Jesus spoke kindly to the woman and told her to go in peace, assuring her that her sins were forgiven because her faith had saved her (Luke 7:36–38).

Turning to the Pharisees, He reminded them that they had not washed His feet or anointed Him with fragrant oil. Then He rebuked them, saying, "Therefore I say to you, her sins, which are many, are forgiven, for she loved much. But to whom little is forgiven, the same loves little" (Luke 7:47).

Since the Pharisees had legalistic mind-sets, they were positive their actions did not require forgiveness. The woman they despised knew she was carrying a heavy burden of sin, so love gushed out of her like water from a broken dam when she was freed from her burdens.

Jesus knows that murderers, prostitutes, alcoholics, drug addicts, swindlers, and others who have led a degrading kind of life will love Him intensely and will work hard to accomplish things for His kingdom after they receive Him as Savior. They understand forgiveness and are as capable of great love as they were capable of great sin.

When these people turn their lives over to God, they willingly work with despicable kinds of human beings, the ones the average Christian does not associate with. They can do this because they identify with the plight of the deceived, and they know the redeeming value and great depth of God's love.

Even though we don't know the people God wants to redeem, we do know that He asks us to forgive everyone. He has been instrumental in helping hardened criminals obtain release from prison. Some have committed atrocious deeds against humanity, but they are restored by the blood of Jesus. Some develop prison ministries after they are released.

Jesus told us that when we minister to the prisoner, we minister to Him, but if we refuse to help a prisoner, we are refusing to help Him (Matthew 25:36–39). When I was convicted by this admonition from Jesus, I started giving offerings in support of The International Prison Ministry started by Chaplain Ray many years ago. I have read several books about the conversions of prisoners he has ministered to. Chaplain Ray spent his life working with prisoners, and today his son carries on his ministry. The person who refuses to forgive a criminal or help a prisoner is kindling a fire that promises to fill his life with ashes instead of beauty.

God wants "to console those who mourn in Zion, to give them beauty for ashes, the oil of joy for mourning, the garment of praise for the spirit of heaviness; that they may be called trees of righteousness, the planting of the Lord, that He may be glorified" (Isaiah 61:3). Our purpose in life is to glorify God, and forgiveness is the catalyst.

Hypocrisy

A hypocrite is one who spouts his religious ideas and refuses to associate with the common sinner. Jesus knew how the religious people of His day thought, so He voiced a warning to His disciples.

"Beware of the leaven of the Pharisees, which is hypocrisy. For there is nothing covered that will not be revealed, nor hidden that will not be known" (Luke 12:1–2).

After Jesus raised Lazarus from the dead, many of the Jews believed in Him and wanted to follow His teachings. The Pharisees and other leaders became so fearful of His influence over the people, they began to plot His death. (See John 11–12.)

In His Sermon on the Mount, Jesus made a statement to the multitude of listeners that all Christians should heed: "For I say to you, that unless your righteousness exceeds the righteousness of the scribes and Pharisees, you will by no means enter into the kingdom of heaven" (Matthew 5:20).

Jesus came to set the captives free from the legalistic cords of man-made traditions. God requires that we walk in His disciplines to keep us from falling into the pits of darkness prepared by the enemy. We do this by walking in love and not judging others. Jesus spoke harshly against the Pharisees because they considered themselves righteous, trusted in their judgments, and despised others who did not think as they did.

Many people were prevented from being converted to the teachings of Jesus because they were fearful of the religious leaders. Even the disciples were caught up in religious doctrine after Jesus was crucified. Through the anointing of the Holy Spirit, and with the help of Paul's teachings, they were finally freed from man-made doctrine and were able to teach what they had learned from the disciplines of Jesus.

Churches today all have their own rules and regulations. These doctrines have been agreed upon and set forth by a group of people representing a particular denomination. However, in following any church doctrine, we must be careful not to be led into the hypocrisy and unforgiveness found in legalism the way the Jewish nation was led by the group of men who represented the Jewish doctrine of their day.

Jesus warned people against being judgmental by saying:

Why do you look at the speck in your brother's eye, but do not perceive the plank in your own eye? Or how can you say to your brother, "Brother, let me remove the speck that is in your eye," when you yourself do not see the plank that is in your own eye? Hypocrite! First remove the plank from your own eye, and then you will see clearly to remove the speck that is in your brother's eye. (Luke 6:41–42)

Paul knew only too well how easy it is to have the judgmental spirit of a Pharisee because he was born a Pharisee. He enjoyed seeing Christians persecuted and killed before he accepted Jesus as the Son of God and his Savior. So he attempted to prevent followers of Christ from being judgmental over small things, such as what they were allowed to eat or drink or how they observed certain days. In Romans 14:4 he says, "Who are you to judge another's servant? To his own master he stands or falls. Indeed, he will be made to stand, for God is able to make him stand." God is our Judge as well as our Redeemer.

Blaming Others

An ungrateful heart is the by-product of an unforgiving temperament. Complaints, criticism, condemnation, and bitterness are its fruit. The years of enslavement and persecution the Israelites suffered under the Egyptians are a good example of how mistreatment can cause people to develop unforgiving dispositions.

When God helped them escape from Egypt, He made sure they were able to take all kinds of material possessions with them, although as slaves they owned nothing. Nevertheless, when they reached the Red Sea and the Egyptians were approaching, they became afraid and cried out to Moses that it would have been better for them to stay in Egypt than to die in the wilderness. They lost their faith in God very quickly (Exodus 14:11–12).

Moses was told to use his rod to split the Red Sea, and the people were able to cross over on dry ground. When the Egyptians tried to follow them, the sea closed in and they were drowned. The people of God rejoiced and praised Him for that miracle. Yet when they reached the next impasse—hunger—complaining started again. Instead of praising God and expecting another miracle, they grumbled against Moses for rescuing them from the Egyptians. God came to their rescue again and sent manna, food from heaven, to feed them. They were satisfied for a while; then they wanted meat, so God sent quail (Exodus 16:3–4).

Their contentment was always short-lived. God kept listening to their complaints and miraculously solved them all, until they made a golden calf and worshipped it. Then He threatened to destroy the people and start over with just the family of Moses, but Moses pleaded for their lives. Despite all that God did for them, no amount of miracles could change their demeanor. As slaves they had murmured and complained so long against their masters in Egypt that unforgiveness permeated their thinking.

Blaming God

If people are not blaming others for their misfortunes, they blame God. It seems to be the curse of men to play the blame game. Adam said the woman God gave him as a helpmate encouraged him to eat the fruit that God had commanded him not to eat (Genesis 3:12).

When the Israelites were sent to spy out the land for their inheritance, the spies came back with glowing reports of a land flowing with milk and honey. It wasn't a dry land like Egypt. It was a land that had plenty of water all year around, and the Lord's eyes were always upon the land (Deuteronomy 11:9–12). Regardless of the good reports from Joshua and Caleb, the people were petrified of some giants that inhabited the land. They kept complaining to Moses that they wanted to go back to Egypt (Numbers 14:3–4).

Their murmuring finally caused God to leave them in the wilderness for forty years, one year for each of the forty days the men spied out the land. He said, "The carcasses of you who have complained against Me shall fall in this wilderness, all of you who were numbered, according to your entire number, from twenty years old and above. . . . But your little ones, whom you said would be victims, I will bring in, and they shall know the land which you have despised" (Numbers 14:29–31).

The Israelites had developed such bitter and unforgiving spirits that God's miracles could not change their attitudes. Christians develop unforgiving hearts, too, even though God performed His ultimate miracle for us: the sacrifice of His Son on the cross for the sins of the world. Still, when disaster and trouble strike, we hear people say, "Why did God allow this to happen?" Blaming God for catastrophes is the act of an unforgiving spirit—one that has not been perfected in godly love.

The Israelites did not trust or love God the way Job did. Although Job lost his family, fortune, and health, and didn't understand why, he still refused to curse God. Job was a righteous man who had developed a thankful heart, so he could say of God, "Though He slay me, yet will I trust Him. Even so, I will defend my own ways before Him" (Job 13:15).

Whether we are trying to forgive some horrendous crime that someone has committed against us, or striving to overcome constant criticism, we must trust God to help us choose to forgive and forget.

God wants us to prosper and be in good health, but we have an enemy who wants to steal everything God has given to us. Jesus reveals this to us in John 10:10, where He says, "The thief does not come except to steal, and to kill, and to destroy. I have come that they may have life, and that they may have it more abundantly." Instead of blaming God when things go wrong, we must look to the source of our trouble. Satan desires to capture our will, and he is looking for loopholes that will allow him to perform his dastardly deeds of destruction and chaos in our lives.

Our God is a God of love, mercy, and grace, not a dictator; otherwise, we would not have been given a free will. Psalm 84:11

reminds us, "The Lord God is a sun and shield; the Lord will give grace and glory; no good thing will He withhold from those who walk uprightly."

From the time they are toddlers, we teach our children how to be safe in order to keep them free from accidents. Yet if a child runs out into the street or walks behind a car that is backing up, and he or she gets hurt or killed, we don't blame the parents. So why should we blame God? We teach our teenagers not to drink alcohol, take drugs, get involved in criminal activities, or become sexually promiscuous. But if a young person gets pregnant outside of marriage, or becomes an alcoholic or drug addict, we can't blame the parents or God, because we have all been given a free will.

Romans 8:28 says, "We know that all things work together for good to those who love God, to those who are the called according to His purpose." God can take whatever mess we make in any area and cause it to work for our good if we will give Him time to come to our rescue and not develop an unforgiving attitude toward man or God.

God says, "Behold, I am the Lord, the God of all flesh. Is there anything too hard for Me?" (Jeremiah 32:27).

Chapter 32

Putting Out the Fires of Unforgiveness

It is easy to develop a critical or unforgiving spirit when we are constantly being condemned. But edifying others instead of looking at their mistakes will help us to overcome an onslaught of criticism against us. The world's way leads to arguments, misunderstandings, and other negative emotions that come from people tearing each other down.

Edify Others

Edifying means reinforcing and building up the strengths of another person. We can build people up spiritually in the same way we reinforce a building. To repair an old building, we would look at its weaknesses, tear it down, and replace the previous material with material that will support the building and make it useful again. We choose paint that will enhance its beauty. When we edify people, we reinforce their strengths and help them overcome their weaknesses. We strive to help them express their inward beauty.

Paul told the Romans to seek peace and edify one another (Romans 14:19). Later he admonished them, saying, "We then who are strong ought to bear with the scruples of the weak, and not to please ourselves. Let each of us please his neighbor for his good, leading to edification" (Romans 15:1–2).

Paul told the Thessalonians, "God did not appoint us to wrath, but to obtain salvation through our Lord Jesus Christ, who died for us, that whether we wake or sleep, we should live together with Him. Therefore comfort each other and edify one another, just as you also are doing" (1 Thessalonians 5:9–11).

Paul tells us we grieve the Holy Spirit when we allow negative emotions such as anger and jealousy to lead to quarreling and evil speaking. Bitterness that germinates from unforgiveness will keep us from edifying others. Paul instructs us to be tenderhearted and kind and to forgive one another as we are forgiven by Jesus Christ (Ephesians 4:30–32).

Teach the Truths of God

Paul encourages us to speak God's truth in love instead of using truth to criticize or condemn. He urges Timothy to remain in Ephesus and stop the teaching of wrong doctrine concerning the law. He told Timothy that the law is good, but when used wrongly, it causes disputes and ceases to build up the body of Christ.

Paul says, "The purpose of the commandment is love from a pure heart, from a good conscience, and from sincere faith, from which some, having strayed, have turned aside to idle talk, desiring to be teachers of the law, understanding neither what they say nor the things which they affirm" (1 Timothy 1:5–7).

If we are constantly finding fault with little things that others do, or are murmuring and complaining, we are not pursuing peace, comforting, striving to please, or walking in the love that leads to edification for an individual or the body of Christ.

First Corinthians 8:2 tells us that knowledge makes us full of pride but love edifies. Knowledge can cause us to focus on self. But when we edify others we edify ourselves. Instead of concentrating on differences of opinions that lead to strife, confusion, and discord, we must strive to develop the attributes of God.

When Nehemiah read from the Book of the Law, he reminded the people how they had hardened their hearts, walking in sin and rebellion against God, regardless of the wonderful things He had done for them. He also reminded them that God was merciful and ready to pardon if they would return to Him. God would never abandon them (Nehemiah 9:17).

Paul said, "There is one God and one Mediator between God and men, the Man Christ Jesus, who gave Himself a ransom for all, to be testified in due time" (1 Timothy 2:5–6).

Promote Peace

Jesus spent His time of ministry on earth continually edifying people by teaching God's Word. He showed them how to bear good fruit and helped them restore their confidence in God. In John 16:33, He said, "These things I have spoken to you, that in Me you may have peace. In the world you will have tribulation; but be of good cheer, I have overcome the world."

In John 14:21 He says, "He who has My commandments and keeps them, it is he who loves Me. And he who loves Me will be loved by My Father, and I will love him and manifest Myself to him."

An unforgiving spirit alienates us from God and results in an unhappy, unproductive life. We will be inundated with criticism throughout our lifetime. But if we allow it to offend us, bitterness will follow. The old adage of "What goes around comes around" is true. When we walk in anger and bitterness, we do not receive peace and joy. Before we can live in peace we must become peaceful people, focusing not on the wrongs done to us but on forgiving and edifying others.

Die to Self

Martyr living is the only way we can accomplish the goals of discipline that God requires of us. Many people throughout history have given up their lives so that others may live. This is the greatest sacrifice a human being can perform. We applaud these people as heroes, sing their praises, and compose ballads about them. They give us hope for a better tomorrow, and they strengthen our spirits.

However, no martyrs have died so that people's sins could be forgiven. That is why Jesus Christ is the greatest martyr of them all. Romans 5:8 says, "God demonstrates His own love toward us, in that while we were still sinners, Christ died for us."

God sent Christ to live among people so that He might understand what it is like to live in a world influenced by evil. Christ did not come to teach us how to die as martyrs. His goal was to teach us that living martyrs die to self. Jesus said in John 12:24, "Most assuredly, I say to you, unless a grain of wheat falls into the ground and dies, it remains alone; but if it dies, it produces much grain."

Just as the wheat seed dies and produces much wheat, when we die to self, we can produce a greater harvest of souls for God's kingdom. Christians have been freed from sin and raised from the dead to live according to the Word of God. A dead martyr has found a cause to die for outside of himself. A living martyr must find a cause to live for greater than his life. This kind of ongoing sacrifice entails giving up selfish desires daily, concentrating on things that are pleasing to God, and walking in love with our fellow human beings.

Prevail with Kindness

When God allowed Satan to afflict Job, He knew that Job would overcome Satan's attacks on him because Job knew about martyr living. His friends, however, forgot all about the righteousness of Job's life. After observing his plight, they were sure he had committed some great sin. Instead of attempting to edify or comfort him, they spent hours criticizing and condemning him.

Job admonished his friends, saying, "To him who is afflicted, kindness should be shown by his friend, even though he forsakes the fear of the Almighty. My brothers have dealt deceitfully like a brook, like the streams of the brooks that pass away" (Job 6:14–15).

Instead of being like Job's friends, we need to let kindness be our watchdog. The Word says, "Let us consider one another in order to stir up love and good works . . . exhorting one another, and so much the more as you see the Day approaching" (Hebrews 10:24–25). Before we can accomplish these things, we must adopt the nature of our Savior and become gentle, humble, and kind. Because God forgives us our trespasses, we can forgive others and in turn bear more fruit for His kingdom.

The Tumbleweed of Sin

An unforgiving person picks up the excessive baggage of sin the way a tumbleweed rolls into a bigger ball. The pressure of erosion from wind may uproot a little bush the size of a basketball, but as the wind keeps rolling it around, it picks up other weeds until it becomes large enough to damage a car. Winds of adversity may cause enough stress in an individual that his anger grows into bitterness. The person defiled by bitterness will keep latching on to offenses until he accumulates the destructive force of an unforgiving nature that makes him capable of all kinds of sin, including murder.

We are to refrain from anger because it leads to an unforgiving attitude and bitterness. Proverbs 22:24–25 says, "Make no friendship with an angry man, and with a furious man do not go, lest you learn his ways and set a snare for your soul."

Paul says, "Let all bitterness, wrath, anger, clamor, and evil speaking be put away from you, with all malice. And be kind to one another, tenderhearted, forgiving one another, even as God in Christ forgave you" (Ephesians 4:31–32). As we concentrate on kindness and forgiveness, we will smother the fire of unforgiveness and cease to be entrapped by satanic snares that make small sins amass like the tumbleweed.

Forgive and Forget

Regardless of the dastardly deeds perpetrated on us, we have the unrelenting tasks of forgiving and forgetting. Edifying others is an act of the will, a choice we can make.

The Word exhorts us to please, comfort, and love others. It doesn't tell us to please ourselves first, and please others when we feel like it. Nor does it instruct us to comfort only those we think deserve comforting. Romans 15:1 says, "We then who are strong ought to bear with the scruples of the weak, and not to please ourselves."

Jesus did not command us to love the lovable and ignore the unlovable. For us to accomplish our goal to walk in love, we have to avoid the critical and judgmental attitudes of the Pharisees and build up the body of Christ through restoration and edification.

God will protect us from the snares set by Satan if we follow His instruction to edify and bless one another and not walk in unforgiveness. This will help us to keep the mouse from creeping in and defiling our bodies, the temple of the Holy Spirit.

Father, we thank You for the power in Your Word. Help us to be quick to forgive those who trespass against us so that we will not allow the burning coal of unforgiveness to damage our souls. We pray that we will strive to imitate Jesus by becoming kindhearted and gentle in spirit. Help us to die to self and edify others. Amen.

Precious Blood

When our dear Lord was crucified,

He was crucified with thieves.

His name was among the transgressors

And they nailed His hands and feet.

But He murmured, "Father forgive them,

For they know not what they do."

And it was written over Him,

This is the King of the Jews.

PART THREE

BATTLEFIELDS OF LIFE

God's disciplines help us fight the battles
in the crucial areas of our lives.

Finances
Health
Prayer

*If you keep My commandments, you will abide in
My love, just as I have kept My Father's
commandments and abide in His love.
(John 15:10)*

Discipline #7: Finances

God's Word teaches us how to have our finances blessed instead of cursed.

Incline my heart to Your testimonies,
and not to covetousness.
(Psalm 119:36)

Chapter 33

God's Blessings and Curses

In the battlefields of life we struggle with problems concerning our finances because Adam and Eve's sin caused us to inherit a cursed environment. However, God's Word teaches us how to overcome those curses. If we are looking for financial blessings, we have to be aware of what causes financial curses.

In Genesis 1, we read that God created the earth; then He created everything the earth would need to sustain it and help it reproduce. After God created all living things—birds, beasts, creeping things, cattle, and sea creatures—He blessed them and told them to multiply. He planted every green herb and every tree that yielded fruit for them to eat.

In Genesis 2, we are told that the earth was dry until God caused a mist to come upon the earth to keep things watered. There was no one to tend the earth, so He formed man from the dust and planted the garden of Eden, and every tree was good for food.

Later, He prepared a special river with four riverheads to water the garden. The first river, Piton, encompassed the land of Havilah, which contained gold, bdelium, and onyx stone. The second river, Gishon, encompassed the land of Cush. The third river, Hiddekel, ran east toward Assyria, and the fourth river was the Euphrates. (See Genesis 2:10–14.) So God put man in a beautiful garden, blessed the land, and surrounded it with special rivers.

When God decided Adam needed a helpmate, He took a rib from Adam and created the woman. Adam named her Eve. God told them everything in the garden was theirs to enjoy except the fruit from the tree of knowledge in the midst of the garden.

Adam and Eve disobeyed God and ate the forbidden fruit. They realized they were naked and tried to cover their bodies with fig leaves. In the evening, when they heard God walking in the garden and calling their names, they hid from Him among the trees. When God questioned why they were hiding, they told Him they were naked and afraid of Him. God killed an animal and made tunics of skin for their clothes. Then God cursed everything He had created and blessed, including man and the earth. (See Genesis 3.)

God had already told Adam that he could eat of every tree, "but of the tree of the knowledge of good and evil you shall not eat, for in the day that you eat of it you shall surely die" (Genesis 2:17). This meant that man's body, soul (mind, emotions, and will), and spirit would die because of sin. Man was no longer in a state of grace—the sinless spiritual relationship he had known with God before he willingly became involved with Satan. The slaying of an animal set a precedent as an offering to God in atonement for sin. The shedding of animal blood led to Jesus and His blood sacrifice for man.

The Curse of Rebellion Brings Poverty

After Adam and Eve left the garden, they had children, including two sons: Cain and Abel. As adults, Cain and Abel took their offerings to the Lord. Abel was a keeper of sheep and brought the firstlings of his flock and their fat to the Lord. Cain brought an offering of the fruit of the ground to the Lord (Genesis 4:3). God did not respect Cain's offering. Cain apparently did not give of his first fruit from the ground, and he refused to acknowledge the sinful nature he had inherited from his parents that required a blood sacrifice to atone for sin.

When God realized Cain had developed a spirit of rebellion, He tried to reason with him about his sin, but Cain wouldn't listen, and he became angry when God refused to bless his offering. So

God said, "If you do well, will you not be accepted? And if you do not do well, sin lies at the door. And its desire is for you, but you should rule over it" (Genesis 4:7).

After God blessed Abel's offering, Cain's anger turned into jealousy against his brother. Then hatred overcame him, and he slew Abel. Cain's sin of murder forced God to put a curse of poverty upon him. At that point, God said, "When you till the ground, it shall no longer yield its strength to you. A fugitive and a vagabond you shall be on the earth" (Genesis 4:12). However, when Cain feared for his life, God set a mark on him and said, "Whoever kills Cain, vengeance shall be taken on him sevenfold" (Genesis 4:15).

From Cain's experience, we learn that sin against man and God can lead to curses that affect our prosperity. The curse of poverty God put on Cain caused him to become a vagabond—a drifter. This type of person wanders from place to place; he has no fixed abode; he lives an unsettled, irresponsible life with no visible means of income. He may become a person of ill repute or poor character, which renders him unable to be blessed financially.

Curses from Evil Bring Destruction

As time passed, God blessed Adam and Eve with another son, Seth, who became the father of Enosh. Even though men began to call upon the name of the Lord, evil slowly conquered the earth, so God decided to destroy man and the earth. (See Genesis 4:26.).

However, God found one righteous man, Noah, who came through the generations of Seth. Noah's father, Lamech, said of Noah, "This one will comfort us concerning our work and the toil of our hands, because of the ground which the Lord has cursed" (Genesis 5:29).

Since Noah found favor in God's eyes, the earth was saved from complete destruction. Noah's family, and the animals he chose, went into the ark. Then God covered the earth with water to wipe the stench of sin out of His nostrils.

After the flood, Noah planted a vineyard. When he got drunk on wine, his son Ham saw his nakedness and told his brothers. Noah said of Ham's son, "Cursed be Canaan; a servant of servants he shall be to his brethren" (Genesis 9:25). The cities of Sodom and Gomorrah were established by the descendents of Canaan, and their citizens became so corrupt God destroyed them with fire.

Evil continued to multiply upon the earth through Ham's descendants. His son Cush became the father of Nimrod, who began his kingdom in Babel. There God confounded the language of the people and scattered them (Genesis 11:7).

Although evil was establishing a stronghold in the world again, God no longer wanted to destroy the earth, so He found a righteous man called Abram, who was a descendent of Noah's son Shem. Through the faith of Abram, later called Abraham, blessings were established for people of faith so they could overcome evil and prosper in a cursed environment.

Righteousness of Faith Reverses Curses

God asked Abraham to use his son Isaac as a burnt sacrifice. Abraham knew God would restore him to life, so he prepared his son for death. At the crucial moment, God sent Abraham a ram to put on the altar instead of demanding Isaac for the sacrifice. He blessed Abraham because of his faith, and the blessings of Abraham were passed through the Seed (Christ) to the generations (Jews and Gentiles).

"The Scripture, foreseeing that God would justify the Gentiles by faith, preached the gospel to Abraham beforehand, saying, 'In you all the nations shall be blessed.' So then those who are of faith are blessed with believing Abraham" (Galatians 3:8–9).

God worked with Isaac and his son Jacob to establish a nation that would be taught God's ways. After Jacob's sons, the twelve tribes of Israel, ended up as slaves in Egypt, God elected Moses to take the Israelites out of their slavery to the land He had given to Abraham. Since the people were full of rebellion and sinned against God, He kept them in the desert for forty years. During that time He instructed Moses to teach the people His commandments, rules, regulations, and laws.

Law Establishes Curses and Blessings

God listed the blessings that would come from obeying His commandments, and the curses that would follow, if His people refused to obey Him. Moses reminded them before they entered the Promised Land that they were a chosen people, a holy people, and God was keeping His oath that He had sworn to their fathers to take them out of the land of Egypt and deliver them from bondage. (See Deuteronomy 7:6–8.)

During the time Moses was helping God to establish Israel as a special nation, he continually challenged the Israelites concerning their sinful and corrupt ways.

Since the Israelites provoked Moses and Aaron to anger, they lost the blessing of being allowed to take the people into the Promised Land. After living on manna, and spending forty years in the desert with a murmuring, complaining people, Moses and Aaron would have been delighted with the prosperity of a land that flowed with milk and honey (Deuteronomy 11:9). However, they died an early death like the people who murmured in the desert.

Curses Follow Disobedience

God proclaimed the blessings for obedience, and the curses for disobedience, that Moses was to teach the Israelites. After they crossed over the river Jordan, He instructed Moses to have the people erect an altar of stones. They were to whitewash the stones, write plainly all the words of the Law on them, follow the laws, and teach them to their children.

Joshua and the people followed God's commandments when they entered into the Promised Land. After Joshua's death, God appointed judges to rule over the people. Shortly after Joshua's death, the Israelites began to vacillate in their allegiance and obedience to God. As they associated with the people of ungodly nations, some started worshipping pagan gods and following pagan practices. The Israelites demanded that God appoint a king over them because the pagan nations had kings.

God warned them about the problems of having a king rule over them instead of Him—it would affect their prosperity because they would have to support a king and a kingdom. But the Israelites persisted with their demands until God anointed Saul to be their king.

In a few centuries the rebellious and corrupt kings brought disaster to their people. Israel was no longer a blessed nation. It was split into two kingdoms: Judah and Israel. Both nations were overpowered by other nations, and the people were sent into exile. Some of the ten tribes of Israel stepped back into slavery; most became lost among the pagan nations.

Eventually, people from the tribes of Benjamin and Judah, along with a few stragglers, went back to Jerusalem, rebuilt the temple, and established a relationship with God again. However, Israel was not a blessed nation, because the people would not obey God's rules and regulation.

Curses Continue without the Blood

The Israelites received the Ten Commandments and the other laws that God wanted them to obey until Jesus came to fulfill the law and reverse the curses. God made a faith covenant with Abraham and his Seed, who is Christ, 430 years before He gave the covenant of laws to the Israelites. He chose Moses to teach the people how to live by His rules and regulations until Christ became the Mediator between man and God. Moses pleaded with the people to choose the blessings instead of the curses, but they chose the curses.

After World War II, Israel became a sovereign nation again. Nevertheless, they still refuse to accept the blood of Jesus for their salvation and justification, so they are subject to the laws and curses that were given to their forefathers.

For as many as are of the works of the law are under the curse; for it is written, "Cursed is everyone who does not continue in all things which are written in the book of the law, to do them." But that no one is justified by the law in the sight of God is evident, for "the just shall live by faith." Yet the law is not of faith, but "the man who does them shall live by them." (Galatians 3:10–12)

Accepting the Blood of Jesus Reverses the Curse

Jesus broke the curse for mankind. Galatians 3:13–14 says, "Christ has redeemed us from the curse of the law, having became a curse for us (for it is written, 'Cursed is everyone who hangs on a tree'), that the blessing of Abraham might come upon the Gentiles in Christ Jesus, that we might receive the promise of the Spirit through faith."

Chapter 34

That Which Leads to Poverty

There are many things that cause poverty, so it is up to each individual Christian to be aware of pitfalls that will affect his or her prosperity. Psalms, Proverbs, and the teachings of Jesus help us spot those traps.

Lack of Resourcefulness

Proverbs 6:6–8 admonishes, "Go to the ant, you sluggard! Consider her ways and be wise, which, having no captain, overseer or ruler, provides her supplies in the summer, and gathers her food in the harvest." As you study the ways of an ant, you realize its ingenuity is phenomenal.

My home in California seems to be built on an anthill. Until my husband and I started an exterminating program, ants entered our house in every conceivable way: through the attic, walls, windows, doors, light fixtures, plumbing . . . constantly scouting in every room, including closets and bathrooms. When a single ant discovers food, he quickly assembles relatives to help him escort his findings back to the nest.

Many years ago, when I was teaching homebound students, I had one student read about ants and write an essay from the ant's point of view. She chose to concentrate on the efforts of a worker ant, whose job was to bring in food for the colony. She gave her ant a name and wrote her story based on his struggles and hardships for one day. The climax of the story came when the ant discovered a family picnic with a table full of food that would feed his army of brothers and sisters.

This ant was not familiar with the perils of a picnic. He had to fight for his life during a flood of Kool-Aid. He managed to climb up on a pickle, and from his advantage on the pickle raft he watched the red river rage around him until it receded. Even though he lost his food, resourcefulness preserved his life, and he gleaned wisdom to be used in future activities.

My student discovered that ants have a complex society with servants, workers, and warriors all working for the good of the colony. The perils involved in surviving do not keep them from working at their self-appointed tasks. Each ant has a unique place in his colony and each one is dedicated to his duty; consequently, he is never rejected nor made to feel worthless by his fellow ants.

After my student finished her essay, she came to the conclusion that observing the ways of the ants would benefit people of all cultures. We need to realize there is joy in being resourceful and useful. Serving others and receiving God's blessings bring satisfaction and joy to us when we realize how important we are to family, community, and country.

Slothfulness

There is no such thing as a slothful ant, but there is an abundance of slothful people in all cultures. Lazy individuals cannot receive God's blessings, because Proverbs 13:4 tells us they are reserved for diligent men and women, who will be made rich through their industrious labors.

Our society needs to emphasize the benefits of working instead of glorifying retirement. Some young people today seem to think of nothing but getting ready to retire because entertainment has become a panacea for this life.

We are warned in Proverbs 10:4–5, "He who has a slack hand becomes poor, but the hand of the diligent makes rich. He who gathers in summer is a wise son; he who sleeps in harvest is a son who causes shame."

The best wisdom we can impart to our children is that God honors those who are diligent in their labor. If they do not learn how to make their own living, they will become a shame to their parents and a burden to society. Laziness does not lead to a fruitful or happy life.

Proverbs 15:19 informs us, "The way of the lazy man is like a hedge of thorns, but the way of the upright is a highway." A lazy man might think he is traveling an easy path by not working, but instead of blessings preparing and smoothing the road before him, curses of poverty put a hedge of thorns in front of him.

The slothful man will not make preparations to be blessed because he refuses to get ready for the harvest and will end up having to beg for food (Proverbs 20:4).

Farmers are highly disciplined workers. They know there is a time to prepare the soil, a time to plant, and a time to expect a harvest. Proverbs tells us of a man who looked at the field of someone who had refused to abide by the rules of planting and reaping. In the field of the slothful man, he found broken stone walls and overgrowth of thorns and nettles. After considering the situation, he concluded, "A little sleep, a little slumber, a little folding of the hands to rest; so shall your poverty come like a prowler, and your need like an armed man" (Proverbs 24:33–34).

Proverbs lists some foolish things a slothful man does: He is afraid to go outside because he might see a lion in the road. He turns in his bed like a door swinging on its hinges. He gets weary putting his hands in a bowl of food and taking it to his mouth. Yet he considers himself wiser than seven sensible men. In other words, he is bored with life but doesn't know what is causing his problems (Proverbs 26:13–16).

Economic Failure in Government

Regardless of how diligent a man is, if the government has money problems, so do its people. The United States was built on the premise established by the Pilgrims, who knew the Word of God. The people were told that those who didn't work couldn't eat (2 Thessalonians 3:10).

The bank failures of 1929 caused the Great Depression. Until then our young country believed that working at any kind of job was considered honorable and necessary for survival and growth for our democracy. During the 1930s, millions of people, both the educated and the uneducated, couldn't find any kind of employment. A professor in the college I attended told us he helped dig the swimming pool for our college and that he was delighted to have the job.

Then welfare programs were instituted to give employment, and soup lines were formed to feed the hungry. Many people refused to accept free meals because Americans felt charity for able-bodied working men was a disgrace. Those who refused the soup lines ate whatever food they had on hand. If they had a little flour and milk, they ate bread and gravy; those who had corn lived on cornbread or corn mush and corn gravy.

A salesman who lived in a nearby town once stopped by our house and told my mother he had eaten nothing but pumpkin for three weeks. He had managed to raise a few pumpkins in a small yard, and since he couldn't buy food because his sales were scarce, he and his family ate pumpkin baked, fried, and stewed.

Since we lived on a farm, our food consisted of whatever we could grow to eat. Money was scarce, but Mom took her hard-earned "egg money" and bought a bottle of her favorite vanilla extract from the salesman, along with a couple of other cooking necessities.

Though we were a poor family with several children, Mom always had something to feed the men we called hobos when they stopped at our house. Through those turbulent years, many stopped for food and a place to rest. Some men were looking for work to support their families; others were aimlessly wandering.

I've often wondered whether Mom may have fed an angel or two unaware, as Paul implied in Hebrews 13:1–2 when he said, "Let brotherly love continue. Do not forget to entertain strangers, for by so doing some have unwittingly entertained angels." Even with all of her children to feed, Mom considered it a commonplace occurrence to feed a hungry man.

The Word tells us to cast our bread upon the water and we will find it after many days (Ecclesiastes 11:1). We never had many things during the Depression years, but we always had a variety of food because Dad insisted on renting a farm where we could raise enough food for the table and Mom shared the food we had with destitute men. Today, however, with fast foods and a fast-paced lifestyle, it is rare to find people sharing what little food they have with strangers.

Slow Cash Flow

When I was seven years old, I broke my wrist swinging on handlebars at school. My teacher rushed me to the doctor to get it set, then took me home to Mom and a newborn baby. Dad was still at work. We made several trips to the doctor because the bone slipped in the cast; it had to be re-broken, reset, and recast. Somehow Dad had money for that episode.

Then Mom had another baby, and a few months later, I broke my elbow riding my pet calf. By this time, Mom and I had depleted Dad of his cash. We had no medical insurance, and we didn't have any money to pay the doctor. So Dad gave him a beef cow that would feed a family of six for a year.

When my elbow came out of the cast, it was bent wrong. Since we couldn't afford therapy, the doctor told Dad he must invent something to straighten my arm, which had been in a sling for three months. Dad's method of putting weight on my arm was to have me carry an empty milk bucket; he gradually increased the weight with more milk. Each day, he used his big hands to manipulate my arm to loosen up at the elbow. Within a year, my arm was straight, and the elbow bent perfectly.

During those troubled times, many farmers poured milk out on the ground when the market overflowed with milk products. Although people were starving, distribution of products cost money, and since few people could afford to buy farm products, they were wasted. During the Depression years some people reverted to the way of life our forefathers started with: bartering.

Welfare Programs

The welfare programs instituted by the government were meant to be short-term solutions for the benefit of the homeless, hungry people during the Depression years. However, the inactivity for those who couldn't find work resulted in passivity for some people. Those who developed a passive disposition never regained the ingenuity necessary to become productive members of society again. The money and food given to those who didn't work encouraged dependency on welfare. Like all dependencies, welfare helped form bad attitudes and lazy work habits.

Eventually, our government realized welfare programs had produced generations of sluggards who created a tax burden for the rest of our society. The welfare system started the erosion of an American idea based on God's Word that hard work helps develop good character. Receiving charity is necessary at times, and it is God's way when people need help. But I believe God would prefer people and churches, not government, to aid the poor.

Anything that takes away initiative and the God-given talents of a man encourages listlessness and loss of interest in his work. Communism was instituted to help poor people, but it is not of God, and it cannot be profitable as a government because it too takes away people's desire to use their talents as their hearts dictate. Under Communism the sluggard receives the same amount as the diligent, and the Word tells us that is not God's way.

The economic system of Communism in Russia and Europe failed because the countries fell apart. Buildings, roads, and farm equipment fell into decay when people lost interest in keeping things up for the government. Lethargy and inertia brought down the Berlin Wall and the demise of Communism in that part of the world. Though the capitalistic form of government has its own evils, it advocates initiative and discourages idleness.

Poor Judgment

Judgment is the ability to understand a situation before an opinion is issued, an act is attempted, or a problem is solved. Refusing instruction on financial matters through the wisdom of man and God, or spurning the wisdom that has been taught, leads a person down the road to poverty and ruin.

Lack of education or training in how to handle what one has received is another reason people find themselves in poverty. Many people work hard but do not know how to manage their assets.

Proverbs 13:23 says, "Much food is in the fallow ground [uncultivated land] of the poor, and for lack of justice there is waste." This proverb indicates that a poor man who has some assets but doesn't make proper use of them will spend money foolishly and end up in poverty.

Proverbs 21:20 speaks of how some people make good judgment calls and others do not. "There is desirable treasure, and oil in the dwelling of the wise, but a foolish man squanders it." This proverb describes the prodigal son Jesus spoke of. He wanted his inheritance before his father died. He got it, spent it extravagantly, and returned to his father penniless. Fortunately, his father loved him enough to help him get on his feet again.

Lack of Wisdom

Proverbs 23:12 says, "Apply your heart to instruction, and your ears to words of knowledge." A man lacking in understanding does not realize that his assets are his capital, or that he needs his capital to make more money. Any businessman will tell you that spending your capital along with your profits will lead to bankruptcy. My dad was not involved in the corporate business world, but he knew the importance of putting his money back into the farm for machinery and the upkeep of his farm.

When my dad owned his first farm and worked it as a full-time farmer, he knew his assets lay in his equipment, cattle, and land. Those things were necessary for his survival, so his assets exceeded his liabilities. He spent a certain portion of his profits, and kept improving his assets. Most successful business people experience some lean years, but if they keep their assets and liabilities under control, they can eventually be financially solid.

My husband Andy learned about the business world after World War II, when he owned and ran a variety store. He and his first wife, Ila, pinched their pennies for many years as they struggled to raise three daughters, but eventually their experiences paid off and they prospered in the business world.

Andy started working on a golf course when he was ten years old. He learned the benefits and disadvantages in having money to spend. When he was sixteen, he left home and hopped a freight train from Nebraska to California to live with his sister. Yet he always desired to have his own business. With a lot of hard work and sacrifice, he was able to start and run a successful money-order business.

When Andy decided to retire, he sold his business. The man who bought it went bankrupt because he disregarded Andy's experience and instructions and never learned anything about the business he was purchasing.

The man already owned several businesses, but Andy's involved the government. When the man tried to take money from one business to put in another, the government found out. The man lost that business as well as his other businesses. He was like the man in Proverbs 21:20 who went from millionaire to pauper by squandering his money foolishly.

Lack of Training

Most people know little about handling money. We would have a lot more financially successful people in the United States if children were taught the principles of handling money wisely. A lot of men and women who become successful in the business world had dealings with money as children.

As soon as a child is old enough to earn a little money for chores, it would be wise to teach him or her the two principles Jesus taught in Matthew 22:21: "Render therefore to Caesar the things that are Caesar's, and to God the things that are God's."

Children need to learn how to divide their money into four piles. One pile is used to pay Caesar, or the government. Since a child's parents provide certain benefits for him, like the government provides for adults, he could consider paying them "taxes" for those benefits. He should pay 10 percent for taxes, give another 10 percent for a tithe to God, and save 10 percent for investments. His parents should teach him how to spend wisely the remaining 70 percent.

Once a child has literally seen his money divided into portions, it will be natural for him to live his life by those guidelines. Under this type of discipline, he will develop a passion to give to the poor instead of piling up debts. He will be rewarded and honored for his faithfulness if he has been taught that "poverty and shame will come to him who disdains correction, but he who regards reproof will be honored" (Proverbs 13:18).

His goal will not be earthly success or materialism, but a desire to store up treasure in heaven. He will not mind giving his portion to Caesar because he will understand the important role the government plays in his life; therefore, he won't be tempted to cheat on his taxes. He will know his worth by his close walk with God. As a result, his life will be full of peace, joy, love, and prosperity.

Credits Cards

Advertising is a big business in the United States and it encourages people to squander money. Credit cards enable lustful spending. Adults as well as children want things they see advertised on television. When credit cards are used to make purchases, people tend to spend money haphazardly. Spoiled and pampered children usually follow in their parents' footsteps in their desire to acquire "things."

When people use credit cards to indulge in their fantasies, they have forgotten the warning of our forefathers to "save for a rainy day." The high interest rate on credit cards keeps many people hopelessly in debt, and they live from paycheck to paycheck until the day of reckoning takes them into bankruptcy.

It is hard to live without credit cards today, but my mother and father never had one. My first husband, Norman, and I started our marriage as college students after World War II. Like many young people in those days, we divided our cash and put it into designated envelopes for necessary expenses.

Since we were children during the Great Depression, we understood the value of money. Norman worked at odd jobs from the time he was twelve years old, so he knew how to handle money. Necessity became an excellent teacher.

Many people today do not know what necessity means. They see what they want and buy it because they have a card to pay for products instead of money. However, Proverbs 27:20 testifies, "Hell and Destruction are never full; so the eyes of man are never satisfied." People overspend, lose homes, and go into bankruptcy because Satan stimulates materialism.

Regardless of how people earn their living, they must give proper care to the money God gives them for their labor.

Norman and I lived without a credit card for the first thirty years of our marriage. Finally, he decided to obtain a credit card for practical purposes, but he never paid interest on it.

Christians who have obtained large liabilities with credit cards should tear them up and start living on cash until they can adjust their spending habits. Though some ministries have been trying to get Christians to live within their means and spend cash instead of using credit cards, few have heeded the warnings.

Today our nation is in the worst economic crisis since the Great Depression. This condition has come about mainly as a result of problems caused by credit. People have bought homes they couldn't afford, companies are going out of business because of overspending, and loans have been made to people who were not financially stable.

All of this has led to financial chaos in the world. Wealthy men are being imprisoned for defrauding the public. For the first time in the history of the United States, our government is lending billions of dollars to companies and financial institutions to keep them from going bankrupt. However, many people are concerned that the government itself could go bankrupt. The present money crisis proves that love of money produces all kinds of evil (1 Timothy 6:10).

Proverbs 28:22 says, "A man with an evil eye hastens after riches, and does not consider that poverty will come upon him." The wealthy men sitting in prison who have defrauded a nation are reaping the judgment of God's Word.

Lack of Use

In Matthew 25, Jesus talks of a master giving money to different servants, each one according to his ability. One servant was given five talents, one was given two talents, and the last servant got one talent. The servants who received five talents and two talents doubled their money. The servant with one talent was fearful of his master, so he saved his talent by hiding it.

The master was angry because the servant made no effort to use his talent. He told him he should have taken his talent to the bank and received interest, at least. His talent was taken from him, and he was left with nothing because he hoarded his money. The other two servants received more talents to invest.

Jesus is telling us in this parable that God gives us talents according to our abilities, but He expects every man to manage his talents wisely.

In times of financial crisis, people tend to hoard their money instead of investing it. Hoarding saves but it doesn't increase. Instead, we should learn how to invest our money. Besides interest in a bank, options include stocks, bonds, land, houses, equipment, or business investments.

When we meditate on the parable of using talents, we are reminded of the old adage "Use it or lose it." My mother-in-law, Nellie, worked in a bakery when she was a young woman; consequently, she excelled in baking. However, as she grew older, her baking became minimal. After many years, remembering her wonderful baked goods, I encouraged her to make pies for us when she visited at Thanksgiving. I was disappointed with the results. I had increased and she had decreased in her baking abilities.

My husband Andy and I are at the age where our abilities in certain areas have diminished too. Some days he feels capable of running his own business again; other days he admits he would be bankrupt in a week.

Recently I made the same mistake in baking brownies that I made when I baked my first cake at age ten. I read the three teaspoons of baking powder as nine teaspoons in the cake, and the one-third cup of water as one and a third cups in the brownies. Mom had laughed when she saw the cake bubbling in the oven, so I managed a weak smile when I threw out the spongy brownies.

God understands the frailties of people at certain ages. Nonetheless, He wants us to be faithful with the talents He gives us and use them to the best of our abilities, not hoard or misuse them.

Not Counting the Cost

When Esau came home hungry and thirsty after a day of hunting, he found Jacob had cooked a pot of stew. He begged Jacob to give him food and drink, but before Jacob would let him eat, he insisted Esau sell him his birthright because the firstborn always got a double blessing from the father.

To momentarily appease his stomach, Esau made a rash decision. He spurned his inheritance and swore to Jacob that he could have the birthright. After he ate the bread and the stew Jacob gave him, he went about his business, ignoring what he had just sworn to do. He didn't believe that he would really lose his father's blessing. (See Genesis 27.)

Proverbs 28:21 tells us how easy it is for people to sin when material blessings are involved. "To show partiality is not good, because for a piece of bread a man will transgress." Once a person transgresses in one situation, it becomes easier to make wrong judgments in other areas.

Esau did not repent, even though he wanted to receive his blessing. (See Hebrews 12:16–17.) Therefore, Jacob received Isaac's blessing.

When Esau became angry with Jacob for taking his blessing away from him, he did not realize his behavior toward his brother would start family feuds that would pass through generations of his descendants, the Edomites. God became angry with the people of Edom when they gloated over Judah as the Babylonians led Judah into captivity. God told them they should not have entered the gates of His people, nor gazed on their affliction, nor laid hands on their substance in the day of their calamity. Neither should they have stood at the crossroads to help the Babylonians capture those who were trying to escape. God said, "For violence against your brother Jacob, shame shall cover you, and you shall be cut off forever" (Obadiah 1:10).

Esau did not know that his gluttony for a bowl of soup would eventually lead his nation into oblivion. It wasn't hunger for a bowl of soup that led to the demise of a nation, but the idea of doing something on the spur of the moment without counting the cost. His entire life, Esau failed to count the cost before he made decisions. The patterns he lived by were passed on from generation to generation.

Jesus talked about counting the cost when we are being His disciples and when we are working for ourselves (Luke 14:27–30). If we don't count the cost beforehand, we can fail to succeed in the task before us.

Ignoring the Poor

In Proverbs 17:5, we are told, "He who mocks the poor reproaches his Maker; he who is glad at calamity will not go unpunished." Esau's descendants did not go unpunished when they laughed at their brothers who went into slavery.

Proverbs 21:13 says, "Whoever shuts his ears to the cry of the poor will also cry himself and not be heard." Proverbs 22:22–23 further states God's concern for the poor: "Do not rob the poor because he is poor, nor oppress the afflicted at the gate; for the Lord will plead their cause, and plunder the soul of those who plunder them."

God remembered the poor when He was making His laws. "The poor will never cease from the land; therefore I command you, saying, 'You shall open your hand wide to your brother, to your poor and your needy, in your land'" (Deuteronomy 15:11).

Moses reminded the people of God's law when he said, "You shall not show partiality in judgment . . . for the judgment is God's" (Deuteronomy 1:17). If we take advantage of the poor because they do not understand how to handle finances, God will allow Satan to rob us of what we accumulated at their expense.

We hear a lot about what happens to a rich man who takes advantage of a poor man, but Proverbs 28:3 says, "A poor man who oppresses the poor is like a driving rain which leaves no food." Nobody prospers when the poor oppress one another.

In Matthew 18 we read the story of a servant whose debt was forgiven by his master, but he refused to forgive another servant who owed him money. The master found out about the deed and sent the servant to prison until he could pay his debt. The poor man who oppresses the poor reaps judgment from God the same as the rich man. "He who does wrong will be repaid for what he has done, and there is no partiality" (Colossians 3:25).

Leviticus 19:15 says, "You shall do no injustice in judgment. You shall not be partial to the poor, nor honor the person of the mighty. But in righteousness you shall judge your neighbor." There is no partiality with God, whether we are rich or poor (Ephesians 6:8–9).

Rash Conduct

Our conduct determines whether we are blessed or cursed. Saul, the first king of Israel, did not anticipate that his rash conduct would cause him to lose his kingdom and keep his children from inheriting their rightful places as sons of a king.

When Samuel the priest was delayed in coming to Saul and his men who were getting ready to do battle, Saul felt compelled to make the burnt-offering sacrifice to the Lord himself. He knew only priests were sanctified by God to make sacrifices for the people. The pride of being Israel's first king enticed Saul to think he could assume the duties of a priest without experiencing the wrath of God.

Saul paid dearly for his impulsive decision. When Samuel saw what Saul had done, he said to him, "But now your kingdom shall not continue. The Lord has sought for Himself a man after His own heart, and the Lord has commanded him to be commander over His people, because you have not kept what the Lord commanded you" (1 Samuel 13:14).

David, the second king, was a man after God's own heart, and Christ came from his seed. His son Solomon was the third king, and God anointed him with great wisdom. After his death the people didn't get along, so the kingdom was divided into two kingdoms: Israel and Judah. Future kings continued to make ungodly decisions until God allowed both kingdoms to be taken by their enemies and their people carried into foreign lands.

Proverbs 11:29 warns, "He who troubles his own house will inherit the wind, and the fool will be servant to the wise of heart." Israel and Judah troubled their houses and inherited a whirlwind of disaster when their people were taken captive by pagan nations.

As Christians, we too can inherit the wind that will blow away blessings, leaving our children and ourselves with curses if we do not walk in God's rules and regulations. We can trouble our own houses with rash decisions in business dealings, inappropriate relationships with others, and dealing rashly with the health of our bodies by what we eat and drink.

Lack of Integrity

Proverbs 22:1–2 says, "A good name is to be chosen rather than great riches, loving favor rather than silver and gold. The rich and the poor have this in common, the Lord is the maker of them all." When I was young, I was impressed with the phrase "His word is his bond." If a person had a good name, a handshake could be his surety on any business deal.

Though my grandfather was a poor man, his word was his bond. He was a county constable at one time, and his asset of integrity was so well known that his word could secure a loan from our local bank. Even as a child, I was aware that few people had that asset, but many in my grandfather's generation were concerned about their good names.

Unfortunately, in this day and time, the appetite for riches often diminishes the craving for a good name. God is our Creator, and He desires to bless us, yet He warns us against seeking wealth instead of His righteousness.

God does not want us to be lazy or use poor judgment in handling our finances; neither does He want us to focus on acquiring wealth instead of righteous living. When a man seeks wealth for the wrong reasons, his mind is not on the kingdom of God; therefore, he usually handles money deceitfully.

Today many large companies are causing stockholders to lose invested savings because their money was handled deceitfully. Some of the men and women responsible have been sent to prison. Lack of integrity in lending and borrowing practices has resulted in bankruptcy and a credit crunch that affects our economy.

The same undisciplined practices in handling money deceitfully resulted in the crash of 1929 and the worldwide money crisis in 2008. Proverbs 13:11 says, "Wealth gained by dishonesty will be diminished, but he who gathers by labor will increase."

Only God knows how the United States will recover from the deceitful money practices of individuals and companies.

Lust for Wealth

We are warned against lusting for wealth in Proverbs 23:4–5: "Do not overwork to be rich; because of your own understanding, cease! Will you set your eyes on that which is not? For riches certainly make themselves wings; they fly away like an eagle toward heaven."

Wealth is a fickle companion. Just when we are indulging ourselves in luxury and enjoying "the good life," wealth can disappear and leave us at the mercy of poverty, as it did for many people in the years of the Great Depression and in the money crisis of 2008. Wealthy men lose fortunes, and the small savings and retirement funds of ordinary people are affected when the banks fail, the stock market plunges, and businesses go into bankruptcy.

After Communism fell, the evil side of capitalism emerged in the form of the Russian mafia. Immoral ways of making money caused corruption in the government as well as with individuals. When Christianity is not a number-one priority, people have no idea that wealth can bring curses as well as blessings.

Proverbs 28:22 warns, "A man with an evil eye hasten after riches, and does not consider that poverty will come upon him." The evil man does not realize that God will give his riches to the righteous man in due time.

Proverbs 13:22 verifies that the wealth of a sinner is stored up for the righteous. "A good man leaves an inheritance to his children's children, but the wealth of the sinner is stored up for the righteous."

Proverbs 28:20 says, "A faithful man will abound with blessings, but he who hastens to be rich will not go unpunished." God desires to bless righteous, faithful people as He blessed faithful Abraham. Even though He allows the sun to shine on both good and evil, the Word plainly states He is against the evil person.

Riotous Living

The prodigal son asked his father for an early inheritance. After he received it, he went on a partying and spending binge instead of seeking ways to invest his inheritance. He ended up tending to pigs and eating slop from their troughs. Proverbs 21:17 says, "He who loves pleasure will be a poor man; he who loves wine and oil will not be rich."

Proverbs 14:23–24 also tells us that poverty awaits the person who fritters away his time. "In all labor there is profit, but idle chatter leads only to poverty. The crown of the wise is their riches, but the foolishness of fools is folly." Some people brag about what they are capable of doing or the deals they are going to make, yet because of their frivolous ways, time produces nothing but poverty for them.

The frivolous party seeker should be aware of the wisdom in Proverbs 12:11, which states, "He who tills his land will be satisfied with bread, but he who follows frivolity is devoid of understanding." A person devoid of understanding is not walking in God's wisdom, so his foolishness causes him to fall into Satan's traps of poverty.

Riotous living seems to be at an all-time high with today's young people, mainly because they have lived in a society that emphasizes pleasure instead of hard work. This attitude got its start in our country after World War II, when the economy was good and the older generation wanted things for their children that they didn't have when they were young.

Just as the father enabled his prodigal son to take an early inheritance and spend it foolishly, older generations have enabled their children to desire a higher living standard than they can earn themselves; hence, the piling up of debts on credit cards.

Just like the prodigal son, those who are led astray through riotous living can return to the Father, repent, and seek wisdom that will enable them to develop proper attitudes and eliminate wasteful spending.

Excess Food and Drink

Proverbs 20:1 states, "Wine is a mocker, strong drink is a brawler, and whoever is led astray by it is not wise." Those who indulge in excess with strong drink find themselves in all kinds of troubles that eventually lead to poverty.

Psalm 75:8 tells us that fools and wicked men receive the dregs from God's cup of life. "For in the hand of the Lord there is a cup, and the wine is red; it is fully mixed, and He pours it out; surely its dregs shall all the wicked of the earth drain and drink down." Dregs are the dark, dirty residue or grains at the bottom of a liquid and are considered worthless.

Just as wine has dregs in the bottom of a cup, so does coffee. Most of us know how terrible the dregs of coffee taste, and if we had nothing but the dregs to drink, the demand for coffee would cease. Scripture is telling us that foolish and wicked men can be assured that their cups will always be full of dregs; in other words, their days will be filled with the worthlessness that brings curses instead of blessings.

In Proverbs 23:19–21 we are counseled that excess wine encourages overeating, laziness, and many other sins that lead to poverty. The business world seems to believe that social drinking and eating are necessary for increasing business opportunities, so many employers encourage their employees to eat and drink with clients for sales and business prospects. Even though big business is borrowing billions of dollars from the government, they are spending millions of taxpayers' dollars for their employees to have business meetings that include a lot of parties and drinking.

When these social behaviors are taken to excess, alcoholism can develop. Heavy drinking negatively affects finances and can leave a family destitute or on welfare. Overeating is a precursor of debilitating diseases that can keep a person from working, thereby affecting his prosperity in the same way alcoholism does.

Sexual Immorality

Adulterous relationships affect health and prosperity. Proverbs warns about the seductress woman: "Remove your way far from her, and do not go near the door of her house, lest you give your honor to others, and your years to the cruel one; lest aliens be filled with your wealth, and your labors go to the house of a foreigner; and you mourn at last, when your flesh and your body are consumed" (Proverbs 5:8–11).

Another warning involving a prostitute or an adulterous woman says, "By means of a harlot a man is reduced to a crust of bread; and an adulteress will prey upon his precious life" (Proverbs 6:26). "Playing around" can cause a man or woman to lose everything. He or she will be lucky to end up with a crust of bread and be able to eat it.

Men and woman have always dabbled in illicit sex. Through the ages even kings and queens have suffered from this sin, as King David did.

Apparently, the world enjoys seeing a man or woman fall from grace, because the news media loves to report on sexual immorality among those who are in high positions in government. Mayors, senators, governors, and even presidents have been caught in such sins. Illicit sexual activities can affect finances, and many families have ended in divorce as a result.

Chapter 35

Taking Back the Dominion

After Jesus Christ died on the cross for our sins, humankind received authority through His name to regain all of God's blessings and take back the dominion of the earth. However, we can't regain our blessings or establish an intimate, personal relationship with God without abiding in the Word of God and acknowledging the blood of Jesus as our authority.

Jesus is the Word made flesh, and when we abide in the Word, we are in Him just as He resides in the Father. We are an integral part of Him just as He is an integral part of the Father. The Word binds us together and makes us whole—essential parts of each other. Jesus is the vine and we are the branches (John 15:5–6).

When Jesus was praying to the Father and asking Him to keep the disciples from the evil one, He said, "I do not pray for these alone, but also for those who will believe in Me through their word; that they may all be one, as You, Father, are in Me, and I in You; that they also may be one in Us, that the world may believe that You sent Me" (John 17:20–21).

We can't receive God's blessings without abiding in His Word. Abiding in the Word means that as we bring our thoughts into captivity to Jesus, we will hear, speak, and act on nothing but the Word of God.

Jesus said to those Jews who believed Him, "If you abide in My word, you are My disciples indeed. And you shall know the truth, and the truth shall make you free'" (John 8:31–32). The truth in God's Word makes us free from the curses of the law, free to receive God's blessings.

Glean for God's Wisdom

People want to receive God's blessings, but many don't understand that developing a personal relationship with God is a highly disciplined way of life. God's blessings don't fall off of trees like ripe fruit. They have to be gleaned, and gleaning is hard work. Those who clean up the fields after the harvest know a lot of ground has to be covered in order to gather a small amount of grain. Gleaning takes time because gleaners pick up small pieces.

Boaz, Naomi's kinsman, allowed Naomi and her daughter-in-law Ruth to glean in his fields, picking up pieces of grain left in the fields by the reapers. Since Ruth and Naomi had been left widows, they were delighted to have the opportunity to glean and gather enough grain to support their household.

As we glean God's wisdom from the field of the Word, we gradually pick up bits and pieces of useful information that are necessary for the spiritual survival of our households against Satan. This bit-by-bit gleaning of wisdom enables us to seek first the kingdom of God and His righteousness. Then our heavenly Father will give us the things we need to survive in this world. (See Matthew 6:19–34.)

Proverbs 8:20–21 says, "I traverse the way of righteousness, in the midst of the paths of justice, that I may cause those who love me to inherit wealth, that I may fill their treasuries."

Proverbs 24:3–4 promises, "Through wisdom a house is built, and by understanding it is established; by knowledge the rooms are filled with all precious and pleasant riches." The wisdom of the Word enables us to have the prosperity that God has prepared for us.

Chapter 36

God's Law of Reciprocity

Reciprocity is reflected in the golden rule of doing unto others as we would have them do unto us (Luke 6:31).

Proverbs 21:15 says, "It is a joy for the just to do justice, but destruction will come to the workers of iniquity." There is joy in being a just person, but the unjust person will experience destruction instead of blessings.

In Luke 6:38 we find that God's law of reciprocity can be used for good or evil. "Give, and it will be given to you: good measure, pressed down, shaken together, and running over will be put into your bosom. For with the same measure that you use, it will be measured back to you."

If we shortchange people in money, labor, or merchandise, these measures will come back to us in financial losses. If we give others encouragement, we will receive an overflow of blessings. However, if we give criticism or judgment, we are promised the same in return. That is why God desires that we walk in love with one another.

Sowing and Reaping

We are admonished in Galatians 6:7–9 that we cannot fool God into prospering us, because He knows the intent of man's heart. What a man sows he will reap.

We find God's principle for giving in 2 Corinthians 9:6–7. "But this I say: He who sows sparingly will also reap sparingly, and he who sows bountifully will also reap bountifully. So let each one give as he purposes in his heart, not grudgingly or of necessity; for God loves a cheerful giver."

We are told in 2 Corinthians 9:10–11 that God multiplies and gives back to us according to our liberal giving. We can't give God more than He will give to us. God's ability to enrich our lives depends on our own generosity of giving into His kingdom, because God abides by His laws for kingdom living. He does not bless any kind of financial injustice.

Asking and Receiving

The other reciprocal agreement we have in the kingdom is the one of asking and receiving. In John 14:13–14, Jesus said, "Whatever you ask in My name, that I will do, that the Father may be glorified in the Son. If you ask anything in My name, I will do it."

There is a lot of controversy about this statement, because many people think they should get everything they ask for, and when it doesn't happen they become discouraged. Others believe we shouldn't ask for anything, even though Jesus told us to ask. The statement stands, but glorifying the Father is one of the prerequisites for receiving.

In James 4:3, we are told why we don't receive. "You ask and do not receive, because you ask amiss, that you may spend it on your pleasures." God will not answer lustful requests, for He knows they make us vulnerable to the enemy and we derive only momentary satisfaction from them. God will not let us have evil things that will bring us harm; that is why sometimes His answer is no.

Jesus told His disciples that God knows how to give good gifts to His children just like parents give good gifts to their children. God wants us to seek things that result in goodness on earth and eternal rewards in heaven. He desires that we have abundant life here on earth, and He knows what will bless us and what will bring evil on us. If we act like spoiled children, He is free to turn us over to Satan for punishment, just as we are free to punish our children when they pursue evil choices.

Knocking, Opening, Seeking, Finding

God has given us reciprocal agreements concerning knocking and opening, seeking and finding. Jesus talks about the persistent friend who knocked on the door of his friend's house at midnight because he wanted to borrow bread for a traveler who was visiting him at midnight. The man who had been asleep finally got up and gave his friend the bread because the knocking interfered with his rest. (See Luke 11:5–8.)

Jesus said, "Ask, and it will be given to you; seek, and you will find; knock, and it will be opened to you. For everyone who asks receives, and he who seeks finds, and to him who knocks it will be opened" (Matthew 7:7–8).

People who make good salespeople have to be good knockers. Many times their persistence pays off because they wear down the resistance of the buyer. I have bought many things from traveling salesmen because their door-to-door persistence paid off. When I was in college, I bought a set of pans for the kitchen and arranged to make payments on them. Another time, I bought a set of encyclopedias that I thought was the perfect solution to acquiring knowledge for children in school, even though I didn't have children for several years. My husband Norman once told me I was the perfect pigeon for a salesman, and I stopped letting them get a foot in the door after that. Then Norman said I was being rude turning people away. But I knew my weakness once they got inside my house, so rudeness seemed my only answer to their persistence.

I still have that weakness. I get so many calls for donations by phone, I've found myself getting rude with them too. I have a hard time saying no to people, and they recognize my weakness.

When it comes to selling your talents in music, singing, or the arts, knocking is important to get past the door in order to be heard. I believe success in these industries does not fall strictly to the talented, because we hear good talent in churches and many other places, and there are good artists all over the world who can't make a living with their artistic talents.

Except for people who know someone important who is able to help them, those who succeed in becoming wealthy or well known are persistent in their knocking. Success stories usually come from a person's own initiative.

All of God's reciprocal laws fall under the category of taking action before receiving results.

Chapter 37

Lending to God

The idea of giving originates from God. He is the greatest giver of all time. When we give back to Him, we are lending our money to further His kingdom. He gives back more than any bank or financial institution on earth can give—He owns the world! When we lend to God with our tithes and offerings, we are storing up rewards for eternity instead of using our money to pile up riches here on earth that can be burned by fire.

In Malachi 1:8 the Lord warned people that it was evil to offer a blind, lame, sick, or blemished animal as a sacrifice for Him. This would bring a curse on the giver instead of a blessing.

The Israelites were taught to give God the best of their flocks and the best of their fruit offerings. However, in time they became stingy and started giving God polluted fruit and blemished animals as their tithes and offerings. He accused them of robbing Him and said that He would curse the whole nation.

However, God always gives a second chance. In Malachi 3:10 He pleaded with them. "'Bring all the tithes into the storehouse, that there may be food in My house, and try Me now in this,' says the Lord of hosts, 'if I will not open for you the windows of heaven and pour out for you such blessing that there will not be room enough to receive it.'"

God went on to say that the vine would not fail to bear fruit because He would rebuke the devourer. Other nations would call the Israelites blessed because they would be a delightful land (Malachi 3:11–12). However, the people refused to listen to the message Malachi gave them from God, and they wouldn't change their backsliding ways.

Tithes and offerings have been given to God since Adam and Eve left the garden of Eden. However, God refuses to bless that which is given reluctantly or is defiled in any way. We give our tithes and offerings to honor God and to show Him that we are thankful for all He does for us. He honors our giving by continuing to bless us.

Assisting the Poor

Proverbs 19:17 talks about lending to God. "He who has pity on the poor lends to the Lord, and He will pay back what he has given." The churches would be greatly blessed if they concentrated on helping the poor instead of letting the government handle such problems. There was a time in our culture when only churches and charitable individuals looked after the poor.

Our country's government took over the task of helping the poor during the Great Depression. Since that time the cost of charitable giving has mushroomed, and state and federal governments are finding it difficult to meet the financial needs of the poor. There is a huge amount of waste when government takes on charity, because most of it goes to the salaries and expenses of government officials.

Proverbs 22:9 tells us that God will bless those who give to the poor. "He who has a generous eye will be blessed, for he gives of his bread to the poor." God's eyes are always on the poor and oppressed. Proverbs 22:16 warns against oppressing the poor by trying to make money off of them. "He who oppresses the poor to increase his riches, and he who gives to the rich, will surely come to poverty."

Unscrupulous people use various schemes to take money from the poor. Because many poor people lack good judgment, they become prey to rich people who have become shrewd in the ways of the world. God stands in the gap for the poor. We are told not to shut our ears to their cry (Proverbs 21:13). God will eventually cause the riches gained by an evil man to end up with a righteous man.

Jesus says, "If you do good to those who do good to you, what credit is that to you? For even sinners do the same. And if you lend to those from whom you hope to receive back, what credit is that to you? For even sinners lend to sinners to receive as much back. But love your enemies, do good, and lend, hoping for nothing in return; and your reward will be great, and you will be sons of the Most High. For He is kind to the unthankful and evil" (Luke 6:33–35).

Anytime we lend to those who cannot pay us, we are actually lending to God, and He promises that our rewards will be great. Proverbs 28:27 says, "He who gives to the poor will not lack, but he who hides his eyes will have many curses."

If we want to receive all of God's blessings for us, we have to be aware of what initiates curses and what institutes blessings. This information comes from abiding in the Word of God and gleaning it for His wisdom concerning prosperity.

Before we can take back the dominion of the earth and receive God's blessings, we must abide in God's Word. He wants us to inherit the blessings of the kingdom, not the curses.

Don't Rob the Poor or God

"Listen, my beloved brethren: Has God not chosen the poor of this world to be rich in faith and heirs of the kingdom which He promised to those who love Him? But you have dishonored the poor man. Do not the rich oppress you and drag you into the courts?" (James 2:5–6).

James admonished the rich man against hiring laborers for his field and not giving them the wages they earned. When the workers cried out because they had been defrauded, their cries reached the ears of the Lord and the rich man suffered punishment. (See James 5:1–4.)

We see the same injustice in our country today. Migrant workers from other countries are exploited; if they complain, they can be reported as illegal aliens and sent back to their original countries. However, God assures us that the cry of the poor will reach His ears, and men who exploit the poor will be cursed.

Make Use of God's Laws Concerning Prosperity

Many a business has gone belly-up not from financial problems but from management that refuses to follow God's laws of reciprocity of giving and receiving. Greedy management brought about union control in our country. Now the union is greedier than management in some cases. The depressions and recessions our country has experienced have been brought on by men who deal deceitfully with money.

Through His parables, Jesus taught us how to glean truths from God's wisdom so that we can overcome the sin and curses that affect our finances. Good character builds good relationships in business. It is the forerunner of godly success.

If we observe God's financial laws, we can develop mouse-free storehouses that will stay full of God's earthly blessings. He will meet our needs according to His riches in glory through Christ Jesus (Philippians 4:19).

Father, we thank You for the wisdom of Your Word concerning financial prosperity. We thank You, Father, that as we abide in Your Word, we will stop lustful spending and handling Your money deceitfully. We will lend to You by helping the poor. We will stop robbing You of tithes and offering so that You can open the windows of heaven and pour out Your blessings upon us. Amen.

A Forgotten Man

On this old earth a man is measured

By his money and by his fame.

He can buy love with earthly treasures

Or be wise as a mighty king.

But the love he buys fades and dies,

And he becomes a forgotten man.

If you want to be remembered forever,

Choose Jesus Christ for your Savior and Friend.

He'll introduce you to God the Father,

And you won't become a forgotten man.

Discipline #8: Health

God's wisdom and discipline help us maintain good health.

So you shall serve the Lord your God,
And He will bless your bread and your water.
And I will take sickness away from the midst of you.
(Exodus 23:25)

Chapter 38

The Body Is a Flesh-and-Blood Force

When my daughter-in-law Elaine was reading some material I had given her on health, her son's teenage friend asked what she was reading. She explained about the book I was writing on God's ten disciplines and said that she was interested in information concerning the body.

"What does God have to do with the body?" he asked.

Many people don't understand that God's disciplines are given to help us take care of our earthly home: the body. The soul and the spirit reside in the body, so the health of all three is important. If one is not well, the other two are affected.

Before God created man from the dust of the earth, He prepared a perfect environment for him to live in. He gave every green herb and the fruit from the trees for food for both man and beast. But Adam and Eve's sin caused God to curse everything that He had created. (See Genesis 1–3.)

God's curses affect the body, so we have to gain knowledge about the physical body as well as the physical and spiritual world in which it resides. Hosea 4:6 says, "My people are destroyed for lack of knowledge." We need God's wisdom to live on this earth and to help us keep our bodies healthy.

The Body Houses a Natural Force

God wants to help men and women live in good health and die peaceably at a ripe old age. Psalm 91:16 says, "With long life I will satisfy him, and show him My salvation." When I asked the

Lord why some Christians are satisfied with a long life but others die early deaths, He answered, *The body is a force.*

As I contemplated forces, I realized that they have energy and power. The body is regulated by its own system of natural energy and power. The curses God put on the earth cause stress that affects the body's energy and power, resulting in sickness and disease.

Centuries ago, the Chinese discovered the energy flow of the body and called it chi (pronounced "chee"). They believe that chi runs through the body in channels called meridians and that life energy energizes all cells and tissues of the body. When a channel of energy flow is blocked, the result is sickness, disease, or death.

The Chinese found pressure points on the body where energy can be stimulated. So they developed acupuncture, a method of placing tiny needles on the pressure points to unclog energy, which allows the body to heal naturally. Acupressure with the hands can also be effective, along with reflexology, in stimulating energy flow and blood circulation.

These natural healing methods are gaining momentum in the United States.[9] However, because of our fast-paced lifestyle, modern medicine still concentrates on man-made chemicals for healing the body.

The Electric Force in the Body

Dr. Robert O. Becker spent almost thirty years researching the electric force in our bodies and the ways its hidden energy regenerates and heals the body. His research also included the ways the electromagnetic fields of earth, moon, and sky, as well as the artificial fields from our machines, affect life. [10]

Electricity has been one of the forces in the universe since the beginning of time, but we were not able to harness electricity or

---

[9] Doug Dollemore, Mark Giuliucci, Jennifer Haigh, Sid Kirchheimer, and Jean Callahan, *New Choices in Natural Healing,* edited by Bill Gottlieb, editor-in-chief, Prevention Magazine Health Books (Emmaus, Pennsylvania: Rodale Press, Inc., 1995), 564–599.

[10] Robert O. Becker, MD, and Gary Selden, *The Body Electric: Electromagnetism and the Foundation of Life* (New York, NY: William Morrow and Company, Inc., 1985), 164–202.

understand it until modern times. Before that energy force was discovered, the world combated darkness through the use of man-made torches, candles, and gas. Now the darkness of the world has been illuminated by the simple invention of an electric light bulb. The discovery of electricity has helped us to explore the universe in astounding new ways.

Most of us do not understand electricity or how the light bulb works. But we are capable of plugging a lamp into an electric socket, thereby turning darkness into light.

Different kinds of light bulbs have different amounts of power and last for a different number of hours. Unless a greater force intervenes to shorten its life, the light bulb will give light for its programmed time. Like the light bulb, the body has a system of energy that lasts an anticipated life span. It's crucial that we understand how its systems work and learn how to keep its energy flowing to maintain good health until its natural life span abates. That way we can make the most of the power that lies within us.

The Body Is a Living Machine

The body's life span can be shortened through poor diet, environmental pollution, and the stress of life. We can learn how to help the body stay healthy through studying God's Word, using His discipline of common sense, and partaking of the nutritional foods that He put in this world.

People tend to abuse their bodies in the same way they misuse machinery. For instance, if a vacuum cleaner bag is not changed often enough, the circulation and suction of the machine is affected and it loses its ability to work efficiently. Consequently, the motor, the origin of its energy, dies more quickly from lack of proper attention.

Similarly, if a clothes dryer's lint trap is not cleaned out regularly, the dryer has to work harder, and drying clothes takes longer. Eventually its energy supply will stop because of the wear and tear on the machine.

Some people do not schedule regular maintenance service on their cars, such as oil changes, that help keep it running smoothly. They excuse their undisciplined ways by telling themselves they don't have the time, not realizing that unnecessary mechanical problems will surface to rob them of more hours when the car is in the shop for repairs.

If a car is neglected for long periods of time, the engine eventually burns up, and a new engine is required. Or the car is relegated to the scrap-metal yard long before it has used up its normal life span. Its good parts are put into other cars to keep them running efficiently.

The Body May Need Transplants

The body, like all machines, needs consistent maintenance and may sometimes need new organs to fulfill its life span on earth. Modern medical technology has advanced to the point where certain parts of the body—such as kidneys, hearts, and corneas— can accept transplants.

Some people donate one of their organs to a loved one. Others become organ donors at death. If a donated organ takes to its new body, it can save a life or cure blindness. Young people who donate organs and die in accidents have made their short lives valuable to others by the love they expressed for humankind through their donations.

Jesus told us there is no greater love than for a man to give his life that others might live (John 15:13). Those who donate organs to prolong the life of another, or to give individuals a higher quality of life, fall into that category.

The Power of Life Is in the Blood

The blood of man and beast is sacred to God. In Leviticus 17:11, God says, "For the life of the flesh is in the blood, and I have given it to you upon the altar to make atonement for your souls; for it is the blood that makes atonement for the soul."

God warned the Israelites not to eat the blood of any dead animal, but to pour it on the ground and cover it with dust, "for it is the life of all flesh. Its blood sustains its life. Therefore I said to the children of Israel, 'You shall not eat the blood of any flesh, for the life of all flesh is its blood. Whoever eats it shall be cut off'" (Leviticus 17:14).

When God told men not to eat the blood of animals, He gave them not only spiritual reasons, but also physical reasons. Disease can be transmitted through the blood of meat that is not cooked fully.

After God declared the blood of animals to be sacred to humans because it made atonement for their souls, He began preparing His people for the blood sacrifice of Jesus Christ. His blood would ultimately save mankind from Satan and his kingdom of darkness. God established that the blood is the power behind physical life as well as spiritual life.

Just like oil and gasoline provide energy to keep a car going, our blood gives us energy to keep our systems running smoothly. If the body is circulating polluted blood, or if the blood is stagnating in certain areas, the body develops diseases.

Develop Healthy Blood Naturally

Scientific research on the blood and its components leads to cures for disease. But hypertension or high blood pressure is becoming a problem for many people. Factors that lead to hypertension include obesity, smoking, alcohol, drugs, stress, and lack of exercise.

Elderberry extract and hawthorn berry are proven to lower blood pressure. Garlic and cayenne pepper are also healthy blood regulators. Minerals that help keep the blood healthy can be found in foods or taken in supplements.

The following are good food sources:[11]

---

[11] Frank W. Cawood and Associates, Inc., *Natural Cures and Gentle Medicines that Work Better than Dangerous Drugs or Risky Surgery* (Peachtree City, Georgia: FC&A, seventh printing, 2001), 217–218.

- Calcium—low-fat milk and yogurt, cooked turnip greens, canned salmon, and cottage cheese
- Magnesium—avocados, raw sunflower seeds and almonds, pinto beans, black-eyed peas, spinach, baked potatoes, and broccoli
- Potassium—dried apricots, avocados, dried figs, acorn squash, baked potatoes, kidney beans, cantaloupe, citrus fruits, and bananas.

Another simple way to reduce blood pressure is to increase water intake. Diuretics used in blood pressure medicine can cause a loss of important minerals, such as potassium and magnesium, and make the cells electrically unstable. Drinking more water helps the blood pressure stay normal.[12]

My sister Linda has been drinking the fresh juice of three large carrots, two celery sticks, and half an apple every day for years. Her doctor comments on how healthy her blood has stayed. She attributes it to that juice. Celery has magnesium, calcium, potassium, vitamin A, some B-complex vitamins, vitamin C, and a trace of iron. Carrots and apples have similar minerals and vitamins. The three juices have the necessary ingredients to keep the blood healthy, and they taste good together.

Healthy blood and healthy blood pressure are the keys to a healthy body, because the Word tells us that the life of the flesh is in the blood.

---

[12] Dr. Lynne Paige Walker and Ellen Hodgson Brown, JD, N*ature's Pharmacy* (Paramus, NJ: Prentice Hall Incorporated, 1998), 218–228.

Chapter 39

The Body Is a Flesh-and-Blood Building

The body is a homestead given to us by God. When homesteaders received land from the government, they had to build homes on it and continually improve and maintain their property. Homesteaders for God are obligated to take care of their bodies and use them for His glory, not to glorify or amuse themselves. The body is God's building, and after we accept Jesus as our Savior, it becomes a temporary home for the Holy Spirit. Paul says, "We are God's fellow workers; you are God's field, you are God's building" (1 Corinthians 3:9).

God has given us a homesteader's privilege to live in His flesh-and-blood building, the body. However, He warns us not to defile or misuse the building we share with the Holy Spirit. Paul says, "Do you not know that you are the temple of God and that the Spirit of God dwells in you? If anyone defiles the temple of God, God will destroy him. For the temple of God is holy, which temple you are" (1 Corinthians 3:16–17).

The length of our life and our happiness on earth will be determined by the wisdom we use in the upkeep of our temporary home. "The wisdom of this world is foolishness with God. For it is written, 'He catches the wise in their own craftiness'; and again, 'The Lord knows the thoughts of the wise, that they are futile'" (1 Corinthians 3:19–20). Unless we are willing to use God's wisdom in dealing with our flesh-and-blood bodies, we can't expect to experience God's best for our earthly life.

The Body Houses a Spiritual Force

Since the body lives in a natural and spiritual world, it needs the wisdom of God working with human wisdom to overcome the spiritual and physical problems that constantly plague it.

Paul talks about the difference between natural wisdom and spiritual wisdom when he says, "These things we also speak, not in words which man's wisdom teaches but which the Holy Spirit teaches, comparing spiritual things with spiritual. But the natural man does not receive the things of the Spirit of God, for they are foolishness to him; nor can he know them, because they are spiritually discerned" (1 Corinthians 2:13–14).

Christians are in a continual fight against the inward or natural man, who tries to sway him toward reason and rationalism instead of the Word of God. Because God planted a will in our soul, along with intellect and emotions, we are free to choose whom we will serve: God or Satan. Although the Holy Spirit and Satan can both influence us, they cannot override our will.

When Jesus was living in His earthly body, He was tempted by the devil just as all people are. Satan tried to tempt Him during his forty-day fast in the wilderness by offering Him all the kingdoms of the world if He would bow down and worship Him (Matthew 4:1–11). However, Jesus had already turned His will over to God, and by using the Word of God He was able to overcome Satan's tactics.

When Jesus was being harassed by the Jews, He said, "I can of Myself do nothing. As I hear, I judge; and My judgment is righteous, because I do not seek My own will but the will of the Father who sent Me" (John 5:30). To the multitude who had been following Him, He said, "For I have come down from heaven, not to do My own will, but the will of Him who sent Me" (John 6:38).

Since the will resides in the soul, it represents the final authority to the body and spirit. Colossians 3:1–2 tells us how to give our will over to God. "If then you were raised with Christ, seek those things which are above, where Christ is, sitting at the right hand of God. Set your mind on things above, not on things on the earth."

When we think, speak, and walk according to God's Word, we can keep our minds from concentrating on negative things and being overcome with worldliness. Scripture tells us to think on things that are of good report (Philippians 4:8). When we keep our minds on things above (things that pertain to God) and think on whatever is true, lovely, and of good report, we are walking in God's will for us.

The Body Is Temporary

The body is a temporary home; it returns to dust when we go to our eternal rest. The Word confirms that we won't have to live in a flesh-and-blood building forever. In Revelation 21:3–4, John heard the following words: "Behold, the tabernacle of God is with men, and He will dwell with them, and they shall be His people, and, God Himself will be with them and be their God. And God will wipe away every tear from their eyes; there shall be no more death, nor sorrow, nor crying. There shall be no more pain, for the former things have passed away."

The Body Can Be Born Again

Our eternal abode with God depends on us being "born again" with a new spirit that can enter into God's kingdom. When people refuse to be born again through the blood of Jesus, they keep their corrupted, sinful souls, which are eventually aborted into Satan's kingdom for eternity. Our free will gives us the choice of accepting or rejecting the Word of God.

Jesus said, "Most assuredly, I say to you, unless one is born of water and the Spirit, he cannot enter the kingdom of God. That which is born of the flesh is flesh, and that which is born of the Spirit is spirit. Do not marvel that I said to you, 'You must be born again'" (John 3:5–7).

Paul explains what it means when we are born of the Spirit. "Therefore, if anyone is in Christ, he is a new creation; old things have passed away; behold, all things have become new. Now all things are of God, who has reconciled us to Himself through Jesus Christ, and has given us the ministry of reconciliation" (2 Corinthians 5:17–18). Each Christian has the job of reconciling unbelievers to God through Jesus.

Because of sin, the flesh-and-blood force called the body is hard to control. The soul (mind, emotions, and will) is inclined to go along with the body's demands. The will can be hostile to the Holy Spirit, even after the born-again experience that occurs when the Holy Spirit is allowed to reside with a person in his or her renewed spirit.

People, like Satan, can fall from God's grace by using their free will against God's wisdom. Jesus left us the Holy Spirit, and it's His job to help us protect our body and soul from sensual and earthly desires that can harm us physically, mentally, and spiritually.

Romans 8:11 says, "If the Spirit of Him who raised Jesus from the dead dwells in you, He who raised Christ from the dead will also give life to your mortal bodies through His Spirit who dwells in you." Holiness resides in our physical bodies after we are born again.

The Body Gets Spiritual Energy from God's Word

Our physical energy comes from food, but the Word gives us our spiritual energy.

With the help of the Holy Spirit, we can use the Word of God to strengthen our spirit; otherwise, the flesh entices us into the playgrounds of the world. There the body and soul are easily manipulated and worn out in a manner similar to the tires of a car. Just as the tire was designed to withstand the bumps and dips of a road, humans were created for the road of life, even when we encounter constant friction that causes wear and tear on our bodies.

The Body Operates on Spiritual and Physical Truths

If we study the Word of God, use His spiritual wisdom, and concentrate on simple ways to support the flesh-and-blood body we have been given, we will be equipped to fulfill our appointed destiny here on earth. Psalm 91:14–15 says, "Because he has set his love upon Me, therefore I will deliver him; I will set him on high, because he has known My name. He shall call upon Me, and I will answer him; I will be with him in trouble; I will deliver him and honor him."

Certain physical and spiritual truths have to be obeyed before God's promises become a reality. Our success in dealing with the innumerable problems presented to us daily depends on our physical and spiritual disciplines.

The Soul and Spirit Help the Body Face Life and Death

When my mother-in-law Nellie was in her seventies, she began to talk about wanting to die, but she went to the doctor for every little ailment. She lived until she was eighty-seven. Her behavior prompted me to ask the Lord why some people say they want to die but keep on living. (This can happen when a person is ill or is getting old and feeling useless.) He explained that the body, soul, and spirit have to be in agreement before death occurs.

We can't know what a person is thinking when the mind and spirit are struggling to keep the body alive. However, many people who have overcome incurable diseases have told how their emotional and spiritual attitudes helped them heal their bodies.

The body clings tenaciously to life because it is programmed to survive. It will utilize its power against any force that would hasten its demise. If the body is in a coma, the will can agree with the body for life. Although the spirit might prefer to be released from its bondage, it yields to the body and soul until the body is ready to die.

The apostle Paul gives us insight into humankind's dilemma in choosing whether to live or die. Paul knew he was badly needed to establish a sound gospel for the people around him and for those who would come to live on the earth for centuries after his death. Even though death and torture were threatening him on every side, he focused on the needs of future Christians and said, "For to me, to live is Christ, and to die is gain. But if I live on in the flesh, this will mean fruit from my labor; yet what I shall choose I cannot tell. For I am hard-pressed between the two, having a desire to depart and be with Christ, which is far better. Nevertheless to remain in the flesh is more needful for you" (Philippians 1:21–24).

If we observe the elderly as they approach death, we will see the body, soul, and spirit working together to bring peace before death occurs.

When my mother discovered that she was dying with cancer, she moved into a trailer on my sister's property. She refused to talk about her impending death; instead, she spent the two months before her death musing over the kinds of flowers, shrubs, and roses she would plant around her new trailer home. She had devoted many hours of her life to the care of shrubs and flowers. Visualizing the beauty of a new flower garden in the spring was her way of dying peacefully.

Most people don't want to talk about their impending deaths, but there are exceptions. My family doctor told me of an elderly relative who was in reasonably good health but had started telling people she would be dying soon. Since there was nothing health-wise to indicate a quick demise, her daughter became perturbed when her mother insisted she could not attend a family wedding because that was scheduled on her day to die. Nobody believed her, although they conceded to her wishes and allowed her to stay at home. True to her prediction, she died quietly that very day.

If our spirit is in control of the body and soul, dying without a struggle is possible. That is the kind of death most people would choose. But it seldom happens, primarily because the body, soul, and spirit are separate entities that must be disciplined and dealt with individually until they are in agreement.

Our survival in this world depends on how well we train ourselves to listen to the call for help from the body. It can talk to us in many ways about its problems. We listen to its call when it's hungry, but we don't always choose the nutrition that will keep it functioning properly. It calls for help when it's ill, but we don't always choose the best methods for healing. We are inclined to keep it in a high level of stress and not exercise it enough or give it the proper amount of rest. As caretakers we can be our bodies' worst enemies.

If people who are terminally ill can heal their bodies with simple things such as adequate rest, good nutrition, exercise, reduction of stress, and spiritual help from God's Word, we too can use those methods to keep our bodies well.

Chapter 40

Fuel for the Body

In Leviticus 11, God gave the Israelites strong cautions concerning health and healing. He listed the specific foods they could eat that were clean and healthy for the body and foods that were considered unclean and unhealthy. His list of unclean foods included different insects and creeping things such as the mole, mouse, and lizard.

In Leviticus 11:45, God said, "I am the Lord who brings you up out of the land of Egypt, to be your God. You shall therefore be holy, for I am holy." The Israelites would defile themselves and became unclean if they didn't follow His instructions.

Some people today still adhere to these dietary prohibitions. But others eat things that crawl on their bellies (like rattlesnakes), insects (spiders, ants, and crickets are considered delicacies in Asian or African countries), and swine (pigs).

The blood of Jesus frees us from the old Jewish dietary laws; nevertheless, breaking those laws has consequences.

Prayer Helps Purify Food for the Body

God's Word says it is wrong to command people to abstain from food. "For every creature of God is good, and nothing is to be refused if it is received with thanksgiving; for it is sanctified by the Word of God and prayer" (1 Timothy 4:4–5).

Missionaries on foreign fields use prayer to cleanse the strange foods they may be obligated to eat. I have heard missionaries say they think they have eaten foods made with dog or horsemeat. Others have eaten insects the natives consider a delicacy. Missionaries try not to offend their hosts and hostesses, because they know they are being offered the family's best food. They represent Jesus, so they try to walk in love and not appear judgmental.

Food Is Used for Socialization

Food is fuel for the body, but it's also used for entertainment and to honor guests. For instance, a friend of mine who was teaching English to Greeks on the Island of Rhodes told me of an unusual eating experience she had. While she was on a picnic with her students and their families, they served cheese and bread. She gorged herself because she thought it was lunch.

Later, they spread out all kinds of other food, including lamb. Greeks reserve the eye of the lamb for honored guests. However, as my friend looked at the eye, she knew she couldn't swallow it. A small child was admiring the delicacy in much the same way an American child would drool over a lollipop. So when no one else was looking, my friend plopped the eye into the child's mouth.

People have always delighted in the food they eat. We use food as part of events such as parties, weddings, sports, and movies. The value of food for nourishment has been overshadowed by the desire to use it for entertainment purposes.

God prepared food for our enjoyment as well as for nourishment. He expects us to honor our bodies by striving to keep them healthy. We must develop discipline, integrity, and tenacity as we fuel our bodies with food.

The Body Can Act like a Spoiled Child

Instead of honoring our bodies as a creation of God, people often use them for exploitation, decoration, or amusement. Like a small child, the body craves an exorbitant amount of attention, and it will do anything to get that attention.

A child's desire for attention overpowers his common sense and good judgment, and he will pester his parents until he gets punished. This type of conduct can carry into adulthood, where poor diet, lack of exercise, sexual promiscuity, and other abuses of the body are considered normal behavior even though they create health hazards.

Due to the body's voracious appetite for attention, we sometimes use the body as a garbage disposal. We dump into it all kinds of comfort and junk foods that include a lot of sugar, fat, and calories, but lack good nutrition.

When the body is stressed because of the daily problems of life, the soul develops unhealthy, negative emotions such as anxiety, worry, anger, frustration, and self-pity that play a big part in a person becoming addicted to certain foods (such as chocolate or sugar), drinks (such as coffee, soda, or alcohol), drugs, or cigarettes.

Many people today struggle with overeating. The problem often starts when a baby is overfed and children are given fast foods instead of vegetables and fruits.

Instead of overeating or trying to placate the body with alcohol or drugs, we can use God's Word to calm the soul and revive the spirit. Jeremiah 15:16 says, "Your words were found, and I ate them, and Your word was to me the joy and rejoicing of my heart; for I am called by Your name, O Lord God of hosts." God's Word is our spiritual food and it helps heal the body, soul, and spirit.

Drunkenness and Gluttony Affect the Body and Society

A diseased liver usually shortens the life span of an alcoholic. Alcoholics may commit crimes while under the influence, including physical abuse against family members and drunk-driving accidents. The behavior problems of an alcoholic can result in an inability to retain employment, causing his family to end up in the welfare system.

A glutton sins against his own body and society too. Bad eating habits can cause excess weight that hinders the body's digestive and elimination systems, as well as blocking arteries and veins, thereby stopping the circulatory and other systems from working properly. These obstructions affect the flow of blood, which in turn deprives the body of energy and contaminates the blood that feeds the body's muscles, bones, organs, and cells.

An overweight person is more susceptible to various diseases, such as hypertension, diabetes, and heart disease. These diseases have affected society by causing an increase in the cost of pharmaceuticals and hospital bills.

We can help ourselves and our society if we keep our bodies healthy.

Chapter 41

Healing the Body Naturally

Very little money was spent on drugs or health care before World War II. The poor exchanged merchandise and services through bartering. They couldn't afford to go to medical professionals on a regular basis. Doctors were called for extreme illnesses, to deliver babies, or to take care of injuries or broken bones. Dentists were used mainly for pulling teeth or fitting patients for dentures.

The types of medicine found in my parents' home were typical of many poor families. We had iodine and other ointments for wounds, and salves to be put on chests for flu or a cold. If we stepped on a nail, the wound was soaked in kerosene. We didn't even have aspirin for pain. Yet we remained relatively healthy because our environment was clean and our food was not contaminated.

The discovery of antibiotics in the 1940s diverted the attention of the medical field to pharmaceuticals. In the United States, prescription drugs and over-the-counter medicines became a panacea for healing all diseases and illnesses. They are commonly used as the first option for maintaining the body's health.

But chemical drugs can produce serious allergic reactions. They can also harm the blood, bones, liver, kidneys, eyes, and more. In some cases, side effects show up quickly, and the drug has to be taken off the market. Other drugs may be used for years before problems appear.

When allergies, sinusitis, bronchitis, and arthritis began bothering me in my thirties, I went from not taking even an aspirin to taking multiple medications. Over the years, I developed allergies to many prescription and over-the-counter medicines.

In the 1960s I had a friend in her early forties who lost half of her stomach due to ulcers she received from the aspirins she took for arthritis.

My husband and I moved to Alaska in 1967, and the cold climate affected my arthritis. When the doctor recommended large doses of aspirin, I followed his advice even though I was aware of the side effects. I developed an unusually bad headache, then a rash erupted. I have never taken aspirin since that time.

The law requires that the dangers of drugs be exposed. In the last few years there has been an increase of advertisements for drugs on nightly television, including their benefits and side effects.

Many doctors are practicing alternative medicine, trying to cut down on drug use. But most doctors and their patients keep playing a dangerous game with drugs and hormone replacement to deal with pain and distress. They can be likened to Russian roulette players who keep pulling the trigger but escape the deadly bullet in the gun.

Antibiotics and other drugs have saved many lives, but they have also caused an alarming outbreak of viruses, diseases, and even death. Our bodies were made to absorb the natural substances found in foods and herbs, but they may reject or find it hard to assimilate the synthetic material found in drugs. Modern medicine improves health for some people but harms others.

Andy takes several prescriptions. They have extended his life. But I have to choose natural ways of healing as much as possible because I develop side effects from most medicine.

Food Can Be Harmful

The body is programmed by God to be healed with food. But food, like medicine, can have bad side effects for certain individuals.

Andy's grandson Jacob, at age ten, discovered he was allergic to many things, including certain foods. When he ate a pistachio nut it caused a swelling in his mouth and throat that threatened to cut off his breathing. He was rushed to an emergency room.

Allergies can develop at different ages. My daughter Mary Catherine ate eggs for years, but in her early twenties an omelet made her ill. She was able to vomit, but she still had to have emergency help with her breathing. From that day on she has been unable to eat any food that has egg in it. She and Jacob developed deadly allergies that no one else in the families had.

Eggs and nuts are healthy foods for most people to eat. They are both high in protein. Eggs help make healthy red blood cells that combat anemia and they can help prevent birth defects. Lutein found in carrots is also found in egg yolk. Eggs have been maligned because of cholesterol. But Jordan Rubin says in *Return to the Maker's Diet* that eggs that are high in omega-3 are an almost perfect food because they contain all known nutrients except vitamin C. They can reduce the risk of heart problems and cancer, as well as help prevent eye diseases such as macular degeneration.[13]

Bad Eating Habits Can Cause Disease

Bad eating habits, including overeating, can cause diabetes, heart disease, and high blood pressure. Bulimia (voracious eating then purging) and anorexia (not being able to eat enough to sustain weight) can cause disease or death. Medical and psychological assistance are usually required before these people can return to normal eating habits.

Fast foods and packaged foods have become the source of most meals for many people, but they contain all kinds of preservatives, which are harmful to the body. Packaged foods are usually loaded with sugar, salt, and fats. Many fast foods are fried, full of grease and oil that clog the circulatory system, low in nutrition but high

[13] Jordan S. Rubin, *The Maker's Diet* (Lake Mary, Florida: Siloam, A Strang Company, 2004), 153.

in calories. But people like the grease, salt, and sugar found in fast foods, and they like the convenience of packaged food, so it is not likely that many will change their eating habits.

Most children and adults consume great amounts of sugar, which can be more harmful to the diet than fat. Candy, soft drinks, cookies, cakes, and pies are a way of life for Americans. Our holidays find us stuffed with sugar.

I listened to a panel of doctors on TBN who were answering the question "How much sugar should we consume?" They agreed that no sugar is best. One doctor commented that our bodies need the natural sugar found in fruits and vegetables, but refined sugar is poison to the body because it causes a lot of diseases.

Many years ago artificial sugar was introduced for the purpose of helping diabetics enjoy sweets. But the chemicals used in the sweeteners are not natural. They add to other chemicals mixed with food and can cause more toxicity in the body.

Although as a nation we are hooked on cane sugar, there are two safe ways to cut some of it out of our diets. One is with xylitol, a natural type of sugar found in berries and birch bark that is as sweet as cane sugar, so it can be measured just like sugar. It is used in some toothpastes for the purpose of cutting down on cavities.

Stevia powder comes from a safe herb that has been used for centuries in other countries. It is much sweeter than cane sugar and has to be used sparingly in its powdered form. It can leave a bitter aftertaste. But I find it's an excellent substitute for sugar in any fruit pie as well as in pumpkin, sweet potatoes, or cranberries.

Both of these products can be found in health-food and grocery stores.

Body Needs to Relax While Eating

The short periods allowed for eating lunch in school or on the job cause children and adults to gobble their food. Eating fast puts the body under stress. Indigestion or heartburn can be the first signs the body calls to our attention, but ulcers of the stomach or intestinal problems can follow.

When my grandson James was in junior high school, he started getting a lot of headaches during the day. His mother discovered he was going without lunch, even though he took it with him. Because of his time schedule, he developed the habit of eating his lunch after school, but by that time the headache had started. This type of behavior could eventually produce migraine headaches.

Adults and children often prioritize education or work over health, not realizing that the energy they get from good dietary habits will aid in their quest to accomplish more.

Family meals should not be ignored, and fast foods or packaged foods should not be the basis for a family's diet just so extra activities can be added.

God's Food Is Healthy

Before the flood, God said, "I have given you every herb that yields seed which is on the face of all the earth, and every tree whose fruit yields seed; to you it shall be for food. Also, to every beast of the earth, to every bird of the air, and to everything that creeps on the earth, in which there is life, I have given every green herb for food" (Genesis 1:29–30).

After the flood God gave us meat to eat. Genesis 9:3 says, "Every moving thing that lives shall be food for you. I have given you all things, even as the green herbs."

All natural foods can be used to benefit the body. However, moderation is best. If we develop finicky eating habits, we lose certain nutrients that contribute to good health.

Beware of Carbohydrates and Chemicals in Drinks

Sodas have no nutritional value. They are carbonated water with either sugar or sugar substitutes that can cause cancer. Even though sodas are not nutritional, they remain the preferred nonalcoholic beverages for many Americans. They are introduced

328   *Discipline #8: Health*

to some children at a very early age, and the addiction becomes an ongoing lifestyle.

Sweetened teas have become the next unhealthy drink for children. Andy's great-grandson had several cavities at age three because his mother let him drink too much sweet tea in his bottle in place of milk, water, or diluted juice. The same thing happens to children's teeth when they drink too many sodas. The large intake of sugar from tea, sodas, or juice can also weaken the immune system and increase the chances of disease, among them sugar diabetes.

In her article on "Water Wisdom," Dr. Janet Maccaro says water is second only to oxygen for our survival. Water makes up 65 to 75 percent of the body. It flushes waste and toxins, transports nutrients for assimilation, regulates body temperature, and acts as a shock absorber for joints, bones, and muscles. It also curtails hunger. Yet people will substitute almost any type of liquid for water.

Dr. Maccaro says she strives to get her patients to drink six to eight glasses of water a day of bottled spring or mineral water. She teaches them the importance of drinking water that is free of certain chemicals like chlorine. Chlorinated, fluoridated, or otherwise chemically treated water, as well as the chemicals found in ground water, adds pollutants to our water supply. Toxicity in drinking water can be an irritant to the system instead of a blessing.[14]

Water filters that eliminate chlorine can be attached to the sink or to home water tanks. There are several types of water purifiers on the market. Some people are having them installed in their homes, adding to the value of the house. Hopefully, one day they will be found in all new homes, eliminating a lot of plastic bottle waste as well as cutting out chlorine in our showers and baths.

Milk is another natural liquid that has been polluted by people. Cow's milk (unless it is organic) contains growth hormones.

---

[14] Janet Maccaro, PhD, CNC, *Natural Health Remedies* (Lake Mary, Florida: Siloam, A Strang Company, 2003), 32–34.

Farmers give hormones to dairy cows to increase their production of milk. This throws the normal supply of hormones out of balance.

Soy milk, rice milk, and goat's milk are alternatives to cow's milk, especially for children who are allergic to cow's milk. But the pesticide sprays used on soy and rice can add to the toxicity. Organic milk will help cut down on some of the contaminants the body is exposed to.

Food and drink are fuel for our bodies, but we must be careful to eliminate as much toxicity as possible.

Chapter 42

Keeping the Body Healthy

Commitment and tenacity are required when dealing with the physical, mental, and spiritual needs of the body. You can't allow the winds of adversity to blow you about like the waves of the sea when it comes to physical or spiritual healing. James says, "Let not that man suppose that he will receive anything from the Lord; he is a double-minded man, unstable in all his ways" (James 1:7–8). If we are double-minded, we cannot hear from God, nor can we persevere in the art of helping the body heal itself.

Start off with Good Supplements

The digestion of vitamins and minerals is as important as the supplements themselves. Liquids and powders are easier to digest, so the body can absorb more of the nutrients than from capsules or pills. There are several powders and a few liquid supplements on the market. Their nutrients should be compared the same way we compare nutrients in food.

Powdered substances made from natural foods can be mixed with water or juice. They contain many of the proteins, enzymes, vitamins, and minerals that are needed for good health. I use Dr. Schulze's Super Food, distributed by American Botanical Pharmacy. I put two tablespoons of powder in a blender with a banana, orange juice, ice, and water. It makes a healthy and tasty breakfast.

I also get a formula called Nature's Fuel by NU-TEK from a health-food store. It's a powerful blend of minerals, vitamins, and antioxidants that support the immune system. It's easy to travel with because a small scoop of powder mixed with a little water is taken just once a day. Nature's Greens and Nature's Fruit are good too.

Know Your Super Foods

Researchers have identified plants they call super foods because they contain photo-nutrients (plant-based nutrients) that combat many illnesses such as cancer and heart and eye diseases. These super foods also build up the immune system so it can help ward off infection.

Any vegetable in the cabbage family—such as Brussels sprouts, cauliflower, and bok choy—help fight disease, but broccoli leads the list.

Spinach is rich in antioxidants such as lutein and beta-carotene, minerals like calcium, iron, magnesium, zinc, and omega-3 fatty acids. The cartoon character Popeye made spinach famous because he always ate a can of spinach when he needed extra energy to perform seemingly impossible tasks. Parents have used Popeye as an example to encourage their children to eat spinach. In reality, they were helping their children fight diseases.

Spinach is reported to help protect against lung, stomach, colon, ovarian, prostate, and breast cancers as well as cataracts and age-related macular degeneration. Tomatoes are also considered beneficial in fighting cancer and age-related macular degeneration. Kale, collards, Swiss chard, mustard greens, and romaine lettuce are helpful cousins of spinach.

Blueberries contain more antioxidants than any other fruit, and they are high in vitamins C and E. They have helpful cousins, such as red grapes, cranberries, blackberries, and cherries. Kiwis are antioxidant all-stars because they are rich in vitamin C, which helps neutralize the free radicals that damage cells, and they are low in calories.

Oats lead the pack as a nutritional powerhouse for grains. They are rich in minerals such as magnesium, potassium, zinc, copper, manganese, and selenium. Wheat germ and flaxseed are high in omega-3 fatty acids and, like oats, help reduce bad cholesterol. These high-fiber foods help heal diseases like diabetes, cancer, and heart problems.[15]

God has provided a diversity of fruits, nuts, vegetables, proteins, and grain products so that even finicky eaters can find foods that contain the nutrients necessary for their bodies.

People today are becoming ill from the things they eat and from the toxic environment in which we live. Kevin Trudeau, author of *Natural Cures "They" Don't Want You to Know About*, says we get sick because we have (1) too many toxins in the body, (2) nutritional deficiencies, (3) exposure to electromagnetic chaos, and (4) stress.[16] He believes the food industry and the pharmaceutical industry are more concerned about profits than good health. In his book he mentions many natural ways to stay well.

Poor Man's Diet Is God's Food

God made beans in many varieties such as navy, kidney, pinto, Northern, butter, and lentil. They used to be called the poor man's diet. Dried beans are considered a healthy meat because they are high in protein. They are especially good for people with diabetes because they can keep blood-sugar levels steady. They help lower cholesterol, so they are good for the heart. They have also been shown to inhibit cancer cell growth.[17] Beans are a good source of vitamins and minerals, including iron and potassium. They can be used in a variety of recipes.

The Old West was settled by American cowboys who could fight Indians and herd cows on their diet of beans. Dried beans

[15] Steven Pratt, MD, and Kathy Matthews, *Bottom Line's Super Foods RX* (Stanford, CT: Bottom Line's Books, Boardroom, Inc., 2004).
[16] Kevin Trudeau, *Natural Cures "They" Don't Want You To Know About* (Elk Grove Village, IL: Alliance Publishing Group, Inc., 2004), 67–119.
[17] Selene Yeager and the editors of Prevention: *Prevention's New Foods for Healing* (Emmaus, PA: Rodale Press, Inc., 1998), 65–70.

didn't require special care because they didn't rot like fruits or vegetables, and they were cheap.

My dad loved beans and ate them almost every day. He got his protein from eggs and beans because he ate very little meat. He lived to be almost ninety-eight years old.

Proverbs 23:1–3 says, "When you sit down to eat with a ruler, consider carefully what is before you; and put a knife to your throat if you are a man given to appetite. Do not desire his delicacies, for they are deceptive food."

Eating sweets during the holidays or at parties loads our bodies with fat and sugar. Foods like cakes, pies, candies, and cookies are high in calories and low in nutrition. Many meats are loaded with fats and gravies, and our pastas are covered with rich sauces.

Reese Dubin, in his book *Miracle Food Cures from the Bible,* says that God's simple foods of herbs, fruits, and vegetables are meant for the body. Health problems result from processed foods. He describes how to use God's foods for healing and keeping healthy. He presents an amazing history of diseases that a grape diet has healed, and he gives instructions on how to prepare for such a diet.[18]

Juice Is a Great Healer

One great way to find healing from many diseases is to juice organic fruits and vegetables. These foods help eliminate toxicity that has made the body ill. Juices also relieve the body from the stress of digesting raw whole foods.

Choose the combination of fruits and vegetables necessary for the disease you are afflicted with or for ways to keep specific parts of your body healthy. For instance, apricot juice helps with cancer, failing eyesight, and a sluggish liver. It's high in vitamin A. Asparagus juice is good for the kidneys and skin disorders. Dandelion juice helps restore the liver to good health. Watermelon juice (without the seeds) is good for skin problems, arthritis,

[18] Reese P. Dubin, *Miracle Food Cures from the Bible* (Paramus, NJ: Rewards Books, Prentice Hall, 1999), 217–225.

gout, and uremic poisoning. Peach and pear juice are good for the lungs.[19] Bananas can be added to other fruit juices to help the body heal itself from different diseases.

Foods Are the Body's First Line of Defense

We need to be aware of the simple, cheap foods that have good nutrients such as fruit and vegetable super foods, eggs, beans, and nuts.

Supplements should be chosen carefully because they are an added cost that many families can't afford. Eating properly and juicing can save money on doctor bills and drugs.

When we follow God's health plan, He can satisfy us with long life.

---

[19] John Heinerman, *Heinerman's Encyclopedia of Healing Juices* (Englewood Cliffs, NJ: Prentice Hall, Parker Publishing Company, Inc., 1994).

Chapter 43

Cleansing the Body Internally

My mom and dad used to say, when referring to a person who was always complaining, "He has more problems than Carter has pills." Carter's Little Liver Pills were quite popular at that time.

Their generation believed in cleansing the liver, as well as cleansing and purging the bowels. My aunts and grandparents talked about picking certain plants in the springtime to cleanse the body from the heavy wintertime diet of meat, potatoes, gravies, and pastries. They knew the nutritional values of many wild greens and mushrooms.

Jordan S. Rubin, author of *The Maker's Diet,* healed himself from Crohn's disease, an intestinal problem. He became ill when he was in college and went the medical route first, then he tried all kinds of alternative programs. He finally took the advice of a nutritionist who advised him to try the Bible diet. He ate a lot of raw fruits and vegetables and uncontaminated animal foods that were rich in nutrients, and avoided processed foods.

In chapter 3 of his book *Life and Death in the Long Hollow Tube,* he says that most Americans have neglected gastrointestinal health. He discusses the importance of the enteric or intestinal nervous system. He notes, "It has been said that death begins in the colon." But he adds, "And so does life."[20]

---

[20] Jordan S. Rubin, *The Maker's Diet* (Lake Mary, FL: Siloam, A Strang Company, 2004), 50–61.

Detoxify the Colon

Constipation causes old fecal matter to lodge in the intestines. This condition produces myriad diseases, including stomach and colon cancer. Parasites and worms hang out in the intestines, and some of these vile creatures may end up in the bloodstream. Parasites and worms can come into the body through unclean hands and from the water we drink or the food we eat. They add more problems to an already overtaxed toxic body. The only way to clean out the intestinal tract is to do a colon cleanse.

Cleansing the colon allows the nutrition of fresh fruits, vegetables, and juices to be assimilated properly in the body so healing can begin. The cleanse not only detoxifies to help the body heal, but you can lose weight as the body gets rid of a lot of waste.

I have been using a five-day colon cleanse three or four times a year for several years, and I lose a few pounds during each cleanse. I get this cleanse, and two others, from Dr. Schulze's American Botanical Pharmacy (800-437-2362), but health-food stores offer a variety of cleanses. They are also sold by private distributors.

New Health Colon Cleanser is distributed by the Health from Within Facility, located in Modesto, California (800-997-1655). This product is recommended by the *Harvard Medical Journal* and has been featured on CNN, *The Larry King Show* with Dr. Andrew Weil, and in the *Wall Street Journal*. The cleanser can be used a minimum of three months up to six months for maximum results for cleansing and weight loss.

Detoxify the Liver and Gallbladder

The main job of the liver is to detoxify and purify the blood. It also maintains healthy cholesterol levels. We live in a more toxic society than ever before. Our diet, environment, and the abuse of alcoholic beverages and drugs put tremendous stress on the liver.

Medication to lower cholesterol is constantly advertised on television. The side effects of the drugs are enormous. Some of them can even damage the liver they are supposed to be helping. Still, these drugs are perceived by the medical profession to help in preventing heart attacks. However, many doctors believe that the homocysteine (amino acid) level in the body causes strokes and heart attacks, not cholesterol.

Detoxifying the liver and gallbladder with natural supplements can lower the bad cholesterol and raise the good cholesterol. These cleanses can be found in health-food stores or from natural-health distributors. The cleanse I use from American Botanical Pharmacy helps me keep cholesterol levels down.

Detoxify the Kidneys and Bladder

Some herbal cleanses help dissolve gallstones and kidney stones. Periodic cleanses, along with a healthy diet, could make gallbladder and kidney surgeries a thing of the past.

Kidney problems are at an all-time high in the United States. A diseased kidney is extremely painful, and the medical treatment can be very expensive. If the kidney fails, a transplant may be necessary.

When you cleanse the kidney, bladder, liver, gallbladder, colon, and intestines, you rid them of toxicity and enable them to operate at their highest levels. Diseases such as diabetes, heart disease, and cancer, as well as dangerous surgery, can be avoided.

In a special report by Sam Biser, Dr. Schulze, medical herbalist, states his belief that until we cleanse our organs, God's food can't benefit the body the way it should.[21] He healed himself of heart disease as a young man by studying the natural methods of healing by older doctors, and by going to universities that promoted alternative ways to heal without medicine.

I. E. Gaumont's book on a nine-day inner cleansing of the body and blood says that blackstrap molasses, apple-cider vinegar, honey, and garlic are natural blood-washing foods with healing

---

[21] Dr. Richard Schulze, *Ancient Cleansing Formulas that Work—After Vitamins and Medicines Have Failed!* (Charlottesville, VA: The University of Natural Healing, Inc., 1995–1996).

power. He says that 10 percent of the total content of blackstrap molasses is minerals.[22]

Even if we eat a good diet, the body needs inner cleansing to reduce toxicity. Colon cleansing is the first step in detoxifying the body. Using a liver and gallbladder cleanse, and a kidney and bladder cleanse, will also help those vital organs stay healthy. Cleansing the body internally is a prerequisite for good health.

---

[22] I. E. Gaumont, *Nine-Day Inner Cleansing and Blood Wash for Renewed Youthfulness and Health* (West Nyack, NY: Parker Publishing Company, Inc., 1980), 23–47.

Chapter 44

Reducing Stress

Adam and Eve didn't know anything about stress until after they left the garden of Eden. They were forced to work for their own food, shelter, and clothing in an unfriendly environment. They had to deal with having one son murder the other. They came in contact with sickness and disease for the first time.

However, God did not abandon humankind. He spent a great deal of time teaching people how to live and deal with the stresses of life caused by sin.

Adequate Sleep and Rest

God programmed in us one of the simplest ways we have of dealing with stress, and that is sleep. Psalm 127:2 says, "It is vain for you to rise up early, to sit up late, to eat the bread of sorrows; for so He gives His beloved sleep."

Many people today are putting their health at risk by burning the candle at both ends. They are caught up in a hectic schedule of going to work, school, sports, church activities, and entertainment.

Healthy sleep is as important as healthy food. The body cannot survive without both. Sleep deprivation stresses the body so much that it is used against criminals when they are being interrogated. The amount of sleep a person requires can vary; however, the average adult can do well on seven or eight hours a night. Older people and children require more sleep than adults do. Health experts tell us that the body gets the most benefit from sleep between ten p.m. and two a.m.

It is important to wind down before sleep. This can be accomplished by reading tranquil stories or listening to soothing music or Bible tapes at bedtime. Taking a bath with placid essential oils like lavender, geranium, bergamot, chamomile and orange blossom is also beneficial.

Lack of sleep leads to health problems. However, stay away from prescription or over-the-counter sleep aids. For most people, natural sleep supplements, like melatonin and valerian tea, which are available in health-food stores, can assist in getting a good night's rest.

Start Good Sleep Habits with Children

Small children, even babies, should have a specific routine at bedtime and naptime. Going to bed at the same time each night prepares the body for rest. Children should not watch scary or disturbing movies on television, read frightening stories, or listen to loud music just before bedtime. If children develop unhealthy sleep patterns, they may become candidates for sleep clinics when they become adults.

Stress Can Cause Depression

The stress of life can result in a lack of sleep, which can lead to depression. On the other hand, depressed people often spend too much time sleeping. Both are debilitating problems with serious repercussions.

There is a tendency to give drugs to young people who develop depression, but suicide has been one of the side effects of prescription drugs. Suicide is the eighth leading cause of death in the United States, fourth in ages twenty-five to forty-four, and third in ages fifteen to twenty-four. S-adenosyl-methionine (SAMe) can be used to prevent depression and arthritis, and it is safe to take. Vitamin B12 is also an aid for those who are depressed.[23]

Dr. Libby's sublingual B12 helps battle fatigue as well as depression. I have seen it work on my own family members. My source for B12 is Tri Vita (800-991-7116).

A change in diet can heal depression, but so can simple exercise, such as walking. I have heard that people who feel depressed should walk three miles a day. They may concentrate on their problems for the first two miles, but after the third mile, the mind is at peace.

Be Sensitive to Your Child's Limitations

Our children are suffering terribly from poor diets and a polluted environment, sometimes to the point of causing them to commit suicide and crimes. It is crucial that we get them involved in their own health, teach them to enjoy nutritious foods, and give them natural supplements to enhance their diets. Then eliminate as many stressful activities as possible. Many children and adults have every hour in the day full of some kind of activity. There is no time for spontaneous relaxation

Some personalities can deal with a continuously on-the-go lifestyle, but others need more quiet time to relax and daydream. It is important to discover the temperament and personality traits of an individual and live accordingly.

Exercise Reduces Stress

Regardless of one's age, size, or physical stamina, the health of the body can be improved with exercise. Yet today, an increasing number of young people refuse to exercise on their own. To make matters worse, many schools do not have adequate exercise programs. Many children spend hours every day in front of computers or watching television.

---

[23] Frank W. Cawood and Associates, Inc., *Natural Cures and Gentle Medicines that Work Better than Dangerous Drugs or Risky Surgery* (Peachtree City, GA: FC&A, 2001), 111–116.

Lack of exercise and poor diets have caused a dangerous weight problem in our children and older people. It has resulted in illnesses that include heart disease, high blood pressure, and diabetes.

Numerous fitness clubs in the United States sponsor a variety of good exercise programs; however, membership in these clubs is costly. Exercises like walking, jogging, running, hiking, swimming, and sports can cost little or nothing.

The goal for exercise is to get the blood circulating better through the body. Keeping the body moving promotes good blood circulation.

When Andy was in a nursing home for six months, he had to have therapy to learn how to walk again. He and other patients did group exercises in their chairs twice daily. Since being released from the home, he has remained faithful in doing the chair exercises. He also walks two miles every day in a park by our house, using a walker, with Nicole at his side. Andy's regular exercise has greatly improved his mental and physical fitness.

Hydrotherapy Reduces Stress

Water therapy is a good stress reliever. It is used in expensive weight-loss and health clinics; however, simple, cheap alternatives are available.

Taking hot-and-cold showers can relieve stress as well as increase the circulation.

Start by alternating hot and cold temperatures for fifteen to thirty seconds each, eventually working up to a minute for each one. Make sure the hot water is not uncomfortably hot. End the shower with warm water.

A few minutes of a hot-and-cold shower in the morning energizes the way coffee does.

In cases of illness or unusual stress, these showers can be taken two or three times a day, up to a maximum of seven minutes for each temperature.

Laughter Reduces Stress

God programmed in all of us the easiest way to relieve stress and to heal the body. He gave us the ability to laugh. The closer you get in a relationship with Him, the more you notice His sense of humor. Learning to laugh at little distractions can be extremely helpful. It's healthy not to take yourself or your circumstances too seriously.

Proverbs 15:15 says, "All the days of the afflicted are evil, but he who is of a merry heart has a continual feast." Proverbs 15:13 says, "A merry heart makes a cheerful countenance, but by sorrow of the heart the spirit is broken." Laughter reduces stress and helps us overcome depressing situations and sorrow.

Instead of watching hours of televised sports or news programs every evening, encourage laughter with old comedies. Many good slapstick movies and humorous episodes of old television sitcoms are available on video. Old-time comedians used a combination of silly mistakes and funny incidents for laughter, and young people might find them as entertaining as the older generations did.

Today, many television sitcoms exploit sex topics, or rely heavily on sarcasm for humor. Though laughter can be used in a harmful way, good clean fun that produces giggles or boisterous laughs is healthy for the body and can restore an ill body to good health. To maintain good health, we all need at least one good belly laugh a day and lots of smiles and giggles.

Pets Can Relieve Stress

When you come home from a hard day's work, a pet can be an excellent source of delight and entertainment. For example, petting a dog, walking it through the neighborhood, or romping with it in the house or backyard are all great stress relievers. Health experts know that petting animals is beneficial to the ill, so trained dogs are taken into hospitals for children or adult patients.

When Andy was hospitalized once, a huge dog made Sunday afternoon rounds through the hospital. Andy beamed whenever the pet's big head rested on his bed.

Troubled children interact well with animals, so going to farms is good therapy for them. Animals accept people as they are, and this acceptance enables the elderly, the mentally ill, or abuse victims regain their self-esteem and reestablish a working relationship with humanity.

Children Can Relieve Stress

Though dealing with children may sometimes be stressful, they can also relieve stress because they see life simply. Watching them enjoy nature, playing games with them, reading to them, teaching them sports, and taking part in their daily activities are great for relieving adult stress.

Children love receiving attention in any kind of game or project. This gives parents opportunities for teaching certain aspects of life to them. It also produces plenty of giggles and hearty laughs that relieve pressures from a strenuous day.

Outdoor activities such as hunting, fishing, and boating are great stress relievers for children as well as adults. My husband Norman took all of our children on fishing and boating trips. He taught them how to water ski, fish, and shoot guns at an early age. They went to turkey shoots each year and became good suppliers for Thanksgiving and Christmas dinners.

My dad and brothers spent many hours hunting and fishing on our farm. Dad sometimes took us fishing at night. I can still remember seeing a snake swimming in the water toward the lantern in our boat. That extinguished my desire to be in a boat at night, even though it was fun to camp out on the river.

Dad continued to be an avid fisherman until he died. When he was unable to climb into a boat, he fished from the shore. Dad spent many hours walking outdoors. He also enjoyed his indoor hobby of playing dominoes. His hobbies relieved the stress of aging for him, and he never became a grumpy old man.

The simple things of life—such as adequate sleep, healthy food, laughter, games, exercise, enjoying family pets, and family activities—help eliminate everyday stress from our lives. Healthy lives help us enjoy God's creation.

Chapter 45

Spiritual Help in Healing

In helping our bodies stay healthy and well, we need to do what we can do, then let God do what He can do. Our spiritual resources come from God's Word, so the first step in spiritual healing is to sacrifice the body to God. We are reminded of this when Paul says, "I beseech you . . . that you present your bodies a living sacrifice, holy, acceptable to God, which is your reasonable service" (Romans 12:1).

God wants us to honor our bodies and acknowledge that they belong to Him. His spiritual wisdom must get into our spirits.

Negative thoughts bring sin into our hearts, and sin affects health. Proverbs 4:23 says, "Keep your heart with all diligence, for out of it spring the issues of life." An issue is something that comes forth from a specified source, and for people, the source of life is God's Word. His Word must spring forth from our hearts or spirits, not the mind or intellect.

If we choose to ignore the wisdom of God's Word, we will reap a whirlwind of illnesses and death. "Fools, because of their transgression, and because of their iniquities, were afflicted. Their soul abhorred all manner of food, and they drew near to the gates of death. Then they cried out to the Lord in their trouble, and He saved them out of their distresses. He sent His word and healed them, and delivered them from their destructions" (Psalm 107:17–20).

The Body Reacts to What It Hears

Since our wisdom can be influenced by sin, we need God's wisdom to help us stay healthy. Proverbs 3:7–8 says, "Do not be wise in your own eyes; fear the Lord and depart from evil. It will be health to your flesh, and strength to your bones."

Wisdom is as important to good health as it is to salvation or prosperity. Proverbs 19:8 says, "He who gets wisdom loves his own soul; he who keeps understanding will find good." The body listens to what we say, and its systems react accordingly. Using God's wisdom will keep us from sending negative messages to the body that cause it to react in ways that undermine its health.

Heal the Body with a Happy Heart

Maintaining good health is impossible without developing a happy heart. A positive attitude helps in healing the body. Proverbs 17:22 tells us, "A merry heart does good, like medicine, but a broken spirit dries the bones." We cannot keep a merry heart without walking in agreement with God's Word and walking in His will.

Isaiah prophesied about what Jesus' death on the cross would do for humanity. Isaiah 53:4-5 says: "Surely He has borne our griefs and carried our sorrows; yet we esteemed Him stricken, smitten by God, and afflicted. But He was wounded for our transgressions, He was bruised for our iniquities; the chastisement for our peace was upon Him, and by His stripes we are healed."

Peter, speaking about Jesus' death on the cross, said that He "bore our sins in His own body on the tree, that we, having died to sins, might live for righteousness—by whose stripes you were healed. For you were like sheep going astray, but have now returned to the Shepherd and Overseer of your souls" (1 Peter 2:24–25).

The beatings and the thirty-nine stripes Jesus took for us did more than save us from sin. He was wounded and bruised for our sins and iniquities so that we may live in His righteousness. His stripes represent healing for us.

An unforgiving and bitter spirit interferes with our peace of mind, causing us to think critical, judgmental, and fearful thoughts. The medical world agrees with God that these thoughts make us ill in many ways. The stress of living with an angry spirit can cause heart disease.

Peace is opposite of anger, and it is a great healer because it lets us have a happy heart. Jesus said, "Peace I leave with you, My peace I give to you; not as the world gives do I give to you. Let not your heart be troubled, neither let it be afraid" (John 14:27).

Pride and fear rob us of peace, joy, and a merry heart; consequently, we become ill emotionally and then become weak and sick physically. Nehemiah told the Israelites, "Go your way, eat the fat, drink the sweet . . . for this day is holy to our Lord. Do not sorrow, for the joy of the Lord is your strength" (Nehemiah 8:10). We can enjoy God's food, and have the Lord's joy in our lives, if we walk in God's disciplines and don't allow Satan to influence our thinking.

Resist the Devil with Faith

After we have done all we can do physically, we must have faith in God's healing power. Peter says, "Humble yourselves under the mighty hand of God, that He may exalt you in due time, casting all your care upon Him, for He cares for you. Be sober, be vigilant; because your adversary the devil walks about like a roaring lion, seeking whom he may devour. Resist him, steadfast in the faith, knowing that the same sufferings are experienced by your brotherhood in the world" (1 Peter 5:6–9).

Negativity is Satan's weapon. The devil wants to devour us in whatever way he can. His goals are to affect our health, our peace of mind, and our relationships with one another and with God. Between the devil and our natural environment, we will be in endless emotional, physical, and spiritual battles if we are not safely in the arms of God.

An Act of the Will Does Not Heal

Many years ago I was talking with a friend of mine about using faith for spiritual healing. She was concerned about a recent news report of a child who had died from appendicitis. Medical help could have saved the child. But the parents did not believe in doctors, so they refused to seek medical help but simply prayed.

I didn't have an answer for my friend as to why the parents' faith was not enough to save the child, so I presented the case to the Lord. His answer was: *It was not an act of faith, but an act of the will.*

When I told my friend what I had heard from the Lord, she replied, "There must be a fine line between the will and faith."

Faith puts God in charge of our will. Only then can the Holy Spirit come to our rescue with wisdom and spiritual healing.

Learn to Walk in the Way

When I asked the Lord how we can know if we are using our will or faith for healing, I heard in my spirit, *It's a way of life.*

Some people have been healed from an illness only to have it return. That's because they saw their healing as a quick solution to their illness, then went back to business as usual.

The Lord wants to teach us His way of life in His disciplines. We cannot walk in faith one moment and the next moment worry about situations.

Hebrews 11 gives examples of people who lived by faith in God's disciplines, even though it meant persecution and death.

Since Jesus was walking in God's will at all times, He was able to heal people spiritually. Jesus said, "These signs will follow those who believe: in My name they will cast out demons; they will speak with new tongues; they will take up serpents; and if they drink anything deadly, it will by no means hurt them; they will lay hands on the sick, and they will recover" (Mark 16:17–18).

God's Word does not return void but prospers in the thing for which it is sent (Isaiah 55:11). However, our lack of faith and discipline in His Word can make His promises void.

Know How to Resist Your Adversaries

When we cast out demons as Jesus did, we are overpowering the devil and his advocates. Countries like Africa, India, and China have many demon strongholds, but those countries also have some strong Christian missionaries who can deal with demonology.

Since demonology and spiritual healing have been largely ignored in our Christian heritage, modern countries have very few Christians with enough faith to cast out demons, to pick up serpents, or to lay hands on the sick so they can recover. Although faith is our shield, unless we use it persistently, Satan can rob us of God's blessings just as he was able to rob the Israelites when they refused to obey God's commandments.

Faith is our weapon from Jesus, and fear is the weapon Satan uses against us. Fear takes away our peace. Jesus said to the woman with the issue of blood, "Daughter, your faith has made you well. Go in peace, and be healed of your affliction" (Mark 5:34).

Even people of faith are faithless at times. We are just like the Israelites who died in the wilderness and were not allowed into the Promised Land.

In Psalm 103:1–5, David declares his faith in God's blessings. If we don't believe that God can heal our bodies, forgive our sins, redeem our lives from destruction, and renew our strength, then doubt, fear, and calamity will pursue us.

To encourage ourselves in our journey toward better health and a long life, we should repeat daily Psalm 118:17, which says, "I shall not die, but live, and declare the works of the Lord."

God needs soldiers trained in spiritual warfare in His end-time army to overthrow the forces of darkness and wickedness in high places. For the kingdom's sake, God's army must not be composed of sick, wimpy soldiers who will fall by the wayside.

The Body Belongs to God

God created all of the energy forces of the world, and He supervises all of them, with the exception of the body. The free will that God gave us allows us to dominate our own bodies, which are God's temporary homes for us.

The body is continually calling for help from its Owner and Creator to adapt to the stresses of its environment. Therefore, our relationship with God must be our number-one priority in life. Our second priority must be the home of the Holy Spirit—our bodies. The body needs to be loved, honored, and respected by its owner for the part it plays in the grand scheme of life.

Accept God's Grace

When I became apprehensive about various health problems in the family, I heard in my spirit, *When knowledge ends, prayer takes over.* That little phrase was God's way of comforting me and reminding me that after we have done all we know to do, then He, through our prayers, will do what knowledge can't do to help us overcome sickness and disease.

Later, I awakened from a deep sleep repeating the phrase "Healing is journey and grace." Another word for *journey* is *pilgrimage,* and grace is unmerited favor, something we haven't earned. As I meditated on the "and" in the phrase, I realized that our journey and God's grace are inseparable. We are on a pilgrimage of trying to keep the body in its healing cycle, and God's grace goes with us. We have to choose the path of discipline to keep the mouse from violating our temporary home, the body.

Father, in Jesus' name we pray for knowledge, wisdom, guidance, and grace as we strive to overcome the evil environment that we are subjected to on a daily basis. We are thankful that by the stripes of Jesus we are healed. We are thankful for the Holy Spirit, who helps us with all of our infirmities .We pray that we will be good caretakers of the temple of the Holy Spirit. Amen.

Jesus, Jesus, What's He All About?

Jesus, Jesus, what's He all about?

He's the name on which all miracles depend.

The blind can see, the lame can walk again.

He's the balm of Gilead; by His stripes we are healed.

Through His precious blood our sins are repealed.

Jesus, Jesus, what's He all about?

He's our Living Water; with Him we won't thirst.

He's our Bread of Life and our Manna on earth.

He's our joy, our strength; in Him we are strong

He's the joy that remains when all hope is gone.

Information for Better Health

Julian Whitaker, MD, editor of "Health and Healing," Whitaker Wellness Institute Medical Clinic. For brochure and information call 949-851-1550 (www.DrWhitaker.com).

Mathew Simmons, editor of Health Revelations, Baltimore, Maryland (www.HealthRevelations.com).

Dr. Robert J. Rowen (www.doctorrowen.com).

Dr. Robert J. Rowen's Second Opinion Newsletter (www. secondopinionnewsletter.com).

Nutri-Health Supplements, 260 Justin Drive, Cottonwood AZ 86326, 800-914- 6311 (www.nutri-health.com).

Dr. Nan Kathryn Fuchs, Women's Health Newsletter, PO Box 8051, Norcross GA 30091-8051, 800-791-3459 (www. womenshealthletter.com).

Michael Cutler, MD, *Heart Health News,* True Health, PO Box 3703, Hueytown AL 35023, 800-746-4513 (www.drcutler.com).

Dr. David G. Williams, Alternatives, PO Box 3277, Lancaster PA 17604, 800-888-1415 (www.drdavidwilliams.com).

Dr. Bruce West, Health Alert, 30 Ryan Court, #100, Monterey CA 93940, 888-525-5955 (www.healthalertstore.com).

Dr. William J. Yarwood, Electriclife, 2602 Northwood Drive, Suite 101, San Jose CA 95132 (www.electriclife.net).

Discipline #9: Prayer

Prayer helps us deal with the stresses of life.

The Lord will command His lovingkindness in the daytime,
and in the night His song shall be with me—
a prayer to the God of my life.
(Psalm 42:8)

Chapter 46

Develop Good Communication Skills

We have an open line to God's throne through our prayer life. We have the opportunity to fellowship with Him, to praise Him, and to seek His counsel. The amount of fruit we can produce for His kingdom depends on how successful our communication is with God.

Power in Communication

Communication is a two-way circuit. Something goes forward and something comes back.

There is power in communication—for evil or good. After the flood, when all human beings spoke the same language, they began to build a city in the land of Shinar with a tower that reached into the heavens, intended to glorify mankind. The city was called Babel, the Hebrew name for Babylon. "Gate of God" referred to Babel as well as to Babylonia, the country of which it was capital. [24]

When God came down to check on the Tower of Babel, He recognized their intentions were evil. "And the Lord said, 'Indeed the people are one and they all have one language, and this is what they begin to do; now nothing that they propose to do will be withheld from them'" (Genesis 11:6).

So God changed the language of the earth. After that, the name Babel became synonymous with babbling or confusion in communication. People were scattered across the earth, which kept them from promoting even greater amoral ideas.

[24] Madeleine S. Miller and J. Lane Miller, *Harper's Bible Dictionary,* seventh edition (New York: Harper and Row, Publishers, Incorporated, 1961), 55–56.

Even though the people were scattered, some of those who remained behind finished building the temple and used it to worship Murdock, their chief pagan god. Babylonia flourished and its culture influenced many countries.

Abraham lived in the city of Ur, which was part of Babylonia. When he left for the land of Canaan, he carried with him his language, his culture, and his faith. But through wars and captivity, idolatrous Babylonia continued to exert its influence on Jewish thought, business, and worship.

Jesus tells us that when two or more agree on earth concerning anything, it will be done by our Father in heaven. "For where two or three are gathered together in My name, I am there in the midst of them" (Matthew 18:20).

Terrorists, who are programmed to promote evil and glorify self, are in agreement on their agendas, just like the people of Babel were. They have a tremendous ability to communicate and thus achieve their destructive goals. The terrorists succeed because they are better communicators than most people on this earth. Agreement brings power and makes us bold in the things we are attempting, for good or for evil.[25]

Many people are poor communicators because they refuse to give up their points of view when others don't accept their conclusions. Terrorists, however, have one intention: to eliminate those who disagree with them so they can be masters in the world.

A self-centered person who wants to be right regardless of what is involved may become angry or abusive if he encounters obstacles to his way of thinking. Such people are not inclined to listen to God's point of view either.

Good Communication Is Not Boring

Good communication is not about having our way and focusing on what we want. Our purpose as Christians is to glorify God by

---

[25] Quin Sheerer and Ruthanne Garlock, "Agreement Brings Boldness," *The Spiritual Warrior's Prayer Guide* (Ann Arbor, Michigan: Servant Publications, 1992), 59–66.

following His examples in His Word and submitting our will to His.

As we communicate with God we receive the power we need to overcome everyday problems, to prosper financially, and to live healthy, fruitful, joyful lives in spite of disagreements, trials, and tribulations. Unfortunately, most of our time here on earth is spent seeking our own glory, spinning our wheels trying to please other people, or interfering in other people's affairs. None of these behaviors reflects the attributes of God or His will for us.

Good communication with God helps us build an exciting relationship with Him—one that never gets boring. If we are not bored with God, we will not be bored in our relationships with people.

After Jesus was resurrected, He left us power through the help of the Holy Spirit, who can make our relationship with God as close as the relationship Jesus had with His Father while He was on earth in human form.

Good Communication Requires Time and Effort

How do we develop good communication skills with people and with God? We begin by concentrating on *them,* not ourselves. What are they focused on? What are their goals? What are their likes and dislikes? What are their desires? What are their personality traits? What is their temperament or nature?

Good communication, with people or God, requires more time and effort than most people are willing to commit to. But such an investment is necessary to obtain the skills we need for our relationships to be healthy and fruitful. The fast pace of life in today's society doesn't leave much time for learning how to communicate with God; therefore, families fall apart and the world is in chaos.

Bad Communication Has a Domino Effect

God is not the instigator of individual and world chaos— Satan is. All negative emotions in people stem from pride, fear, and an unwillingness to forgive. These characteristics develop the self-seeking syndrome "It's all about me." Such an attitude blocks communication. Failing in interpersonal relationships has a domino effect because families, the business world, all forms of governments, and the world in general revolve around relationships.

Paul says, "Stand fast therefore in the liberty by which Christ has made us free, and do not be entangled again with a yoke of bondage" (Galatians 5:1). We have the freedom to submit to the yoke of Jesus, but we must not take the yoke of the world upon ourselves or try to hang our thoughts and opinions on others.

God has a hard time teaching us to think as He thinks. People tend to want others to think as they do. However, we are called to make converts for Jesus Christ, not for ourselves. We do this by living out the attributes of God, thinking and acting the way Jesus taught, and speaking and doing the Word of God.

Chapter 47

Seek to Know God's Attributes

Paul tells us that we are without excuse if we don't know God's attributes, because they can be found in His Word:

> Since the creation of the world His invisible attributes are clearly seen, being understood by the things that are made, even His eternal power and Godhead, so that they are without excuse, because, although they knew God, they did not glorify Him as God, nor were thankful, but became futile in their thoughts, and their foolish hearts were darkened. (Romans 1:20–21)

When we focus on God and walk in His Word, we will be less inclined to pick up Satan's attributes.

David was committing to a holy life when he said, "I will behave myself wisely in a perfect way. O when wilt thou come unto me? I will walk within my house with a perfect heart" (Psalm 101:2 KJV).

Terrorists have been fooled into thinking that they are working for God. They have developed the idea that God is wrathful; therefore, they walk in the Old Testament laws that required a life for life, "eye for eye, tooth for tooth, hand for hand, foot for foot, burning for burning, wound for wound, stripe for stripe" (Exodus 21:24–25).

Terrorists believe that God will reward them for the murders of men, women, and children, and the destruction of property, plus give them virgin women to be their wives in heaven. However, murdering innocent people is an attribute of Satan, not God.

Psalm 89:14 says, "Righteousness and justice are the foundation of Your throne; mercy and truth go before Your face." God is merciful and just, not vindictive as the terrorists are taught.

Light, Love, Peace, and Joy

It is inconceivable to Christians that terrorists could be so confused and deceived about the attributes of God, or about His will and His ways. However, these people have never been taught that God is love. Even some Christians today fail to grasp the enormity of God's love for mankind. They tend to think His love is based on their performance. But our righteousness comes from Jesus, not from our works. The apostle John said, "In this is love, not that we loved God, but that He loved us and sent His Son to be the propitiation for our sins" (1 John 4:10).

When we place our hope in God, we can say to Him in times of trouble, "O send out thy light and thy truth: let them lead me; let them bring me unto thy holy hill, and to thy tabernacles" (Psalm 43:3 KJV).

God revealed His attributes of love, peace, and joy to mankind when He sent Jesus Christ to redeem us from sin. Those who haven't accepted Jesus as the Son of God can't understand the fullness of God's love.

Righteousness and Power

God tried to reveal His true nature to the Israelites in the Old Testament. But it took the teachings of Jesus, and His death on the cross, for God to get the attention of humankind and show them how much He loves each individual. The Scripture teaches us to focus on God's Word, His love, mercy, and grace.

The Ten Commandments are the laws that God gave to Moses for the Israelites to obey. Jesus said, "Do not think that I came to destroy the Law or the Prophets. I did not come to destroy but to fulfill" (Matthew 5:17). Four of the Ten Commandments are about our relationship with God: we are to worship one God, not make or worship idols, not profane the name of God, and rest on the Sabbath.

The other six commandments have to do with our relationship with one another. We are told to honor our fathers and mothers, and not to murder, commit adultery, steal, bear false witness, or covet anything that belongs to another person.

The Ten Commandments were useful in helping people to understand the attributes of God. However, because we are born in sin, we are unable to keep the Ten Commandments. So God gave us Jesus, who intercedes on our behalf for the sins we commit daily. Jesus, "being the brightness of His (God's) glory and the express image of His person, and upholding all things by the word of His power, when He had by Himself purged our sins, sat down at the right hand of the Majesty on high" (Hebrews 1:3).

Hebrews 1:13 says, "To which of the angels has He ever said: 'Sit at My right hand, till I make Your enemies Your footstool'?" We have been made ambassadors of Christ, and we are the righteousness of God if we have accepted Jesus as our Savior.

Wisdom and Knowledge

God and Satan have opposite personality traits, characteristics, and natures. For instance, God is a positive thinker and manifests such things as love, peace, joy, long-suffering, honesty, honor, humility, kindness, patience, gentleness, faith, grace, mercy, favor, and even good humor. Satan, on the other hand, is a negative thinker and manifests pride, fear, unforgiveness, criticism, hate, bitterness, condemnation, selfishness, dishonesty, envy, jealousy, impatience, prejudice, anxiety, and all manner of sin.

In the Old Testament, God revealed to the Israelites His loving nature, as well as His wrath, by giving them good advice and pleading with them to walk in His counsel. History records that His warnings and advice were refused—in the same manner as we do today.

Proverbs 24:5 tells us that a wise man is strong and that knowledge increases strength. Knowledge of the attributes of God and His Word gives us strength to fight off all enemies, including the terrorists who are plaguing the world today.

Grace and Forgiveness

Jesus was sent in the form of man to experience what living as a human being is like. His death on the cross was preordained from the foundation of the earth. In spite of Satan's input, God has revealed to mankind, through His attributes, how to enjoy this life here on earth. We can, if we choose to, have power through the Holy Spirit to bear fruit for God's Kingdom and enjoy a happy life.

Many times Christians display some of Satan's attributes in their daily lives. The result for Christians can be the same as for those in the world: disobedient children, family squabbles, divorce, sickness, disease, sexual promiscuity, drugs, poverty, etc.

We are saved by God's grace, not by our works. Yet God expects good works from His children. He wants us to imitate His way of life just as good earthly parents try to teach their children the excellence of a life devoted to obedience through godly behavior that manifests love, honor, respect, wisdom, mercy, and forgiveness.

Fulfill the Love Commandment

God's attributes are like a many-faceted diamond. Each facet helps the diamond shine more brilliantly. For instance, peace radiates joy, which produces contentment. Grace illuminates mercy, gentleness helps kindness glow, and honesty causes honor to gleam. All of God's attributes garner into one luminous light of love, the very essence of God.

Paul sums up God's attributes for us in 1 John 4:7–8: "Beloved, let us love one another, for love is of God; and everyone who loves is born of God and knows God. He who does not love does not know God, for God is love."

PART THREE: BATTLEFIELDS OF LIFE

God's glory is reflected by the many sparkles that His love generates. It lights up the darkness of the world just like firecrackers light up the night on the Fourth of July in the United States. Psalm 27:1 tells us that God is our Light. Matthew 5:14–16 remind us that Christians are the spiritual light of the world; we are not to hide our light, but let it shine so that we might glorify our Father in heaven.

Through our communication with God, we can manifest God's attributes in our lives. Then God can take us with Him from glory to glory as we help Him penetrate His light into one person at a time, starting with us, until the light of His love illuminates His glory around the world. The amount of spiritual light a Christian reflects is based on how much of God's love he allows to shine through him.

Chapter 48

Resist Carnality

Paul spent much of his time trying to help the believers of his day overcome carnality. When we are careless in everyday activities, we develop bad habits that are hard to break. Romans 6:16 says, "Do you not know . . . you are that one's slaves whom you obey, whether of sin to death, or of obedience to righteousness?" We become slaves to ourselves when we walk in the flesh instead of the spirit.

Carnality Leads to Carelessness

In the July 31 devotion of his book *My Utmost for His Highest,* Oswald Chambers writes, "Beware of becoming careless over the small details of life. . . . Whatever it may be, God will point it out with persistence until we become entirely His."[26]

Chambers says that our carnality leads us to be careless in our walk with God. He maintains that our carelessness insults the Holy Spirit. He also states that we should be careful in the way we worship God, even in the way we eat or drink.

Chambers was born in 1874 in Scotland. He died in 1915 in Zeitoun, Egypt, following surgery on a ruptured appendix. Even though his life was short, he left the world a legacy of God's wisdom, and that wisdom applies from generation to generation because it is ageless. His insights came from constant communication with God and walking in His Word.

---

[26] Oswald Chambers, *My Utmost for His Highest* (Discovery House Publishers, 1992).

We cannot communicate with God, achieve His purposes, or connect to His power unless our spirits are willing to abide by the disciplined power given to us through the Holy Spirit and God's Word.

Carnal Law Cannot Deliver Us from Sin

The apostle Paul often despaired over the carnality of the Israelites. They wanted to establish their righteousness through the old law and religion, not through the righteousness given to humankind by Jesus' death on the cross. They felt the covenant of circumcision set them apart as God's people, not the grace of God.

Paul admitted that he fought against carnality himself, even while he struggled to bring his brethren out of their carnal ways. The Ten Commandments and the various laws given to Moses were to help the people live godly lives before Jesus came, but they could never save people from their sins. The hundreds of laws the Israelites tried to practice concerning the washing of hands, eating certain foods, practicing prescribed rituals, keeping various holy days, and making elaborate prayers in public places were done to glorify man, not God.

Paul speaks of his and the Israelites' dilemma concerning carnality under the Mosaic laws.

> We know that the law is spiritual: but I am carnal, sold under sin. For that which I do I allow not: for what I would, that do I not; but what I hate, that do I. If then I do that which I would not, I consent unto the law that it is good. Now then it is no more I that do it, but sin that dwelleth in me. . . . For the good that I would I do not: but the evil which I would not, that I do. (Romans 7:14–19 KJV)

We have to renew our minds through God's Word to represent the mind of Jesus Christ.

Paul was one of the greatest Christians on earth, but even he struggled with carnality. Knowing that everyone struggles with the sinful ways of the world, he did his best to teach against being a carnal Christian. In Romans 8:6–8 Paul says, "To be carnally minded is death, but to be spiritually minded is life and peace. Because the carnal mind is enmity against God; for it is not subject to the law of God, nor indeed can be. So then, those who are in the flesh cannot please God."

The Holy Spirit Helps Us in Our Weaknesses

How do you know if you are a carnal Christian? The carnal Christian lacks peace, contentment, joy, and love for others. Carnality is caused by pride, strife, arguments, anxiety, fear, pride, unwillingness to forgive, and worldliness.

How do we get out of this enmity toward God? By seeking the attributes of God through His Word, and letting the Holy Spirit reveal the things of God to us. Paul says, "The Spirit also helps in our weaknesses. For we do not know what we should pray for as we ought, but the Spirit Himself makes intercession for us with groanings which cannot be uttered. Now He who searches the hearts knows what the mind of the Spirit is, because He makes intercession for the saints according to the will of God" (Romans 8:26–27).

Seeking God's glory while living in a carnal world is impossible without prayer. Before we can overcome our carnal ways, we must immerse ourselves in God's Word and listen to the Holy Spirit as He intercedes on our behalf and helps us in our prayer life.

Busyness Leads to Carnality

Christians can reflect the weakness of carnality in their endeavors to do something for God. They can become so preoccupied in doing things that look good to the world that their communication with God suffers from busyness. Communication in Christian families and worldly families alike deteriorates when we are involved in too many activities.

Lack of good communication with God has caused the fall of many churches and ministries, plus failure among pastors to properly look after their families and their flocks. When communication with God is not our first priority, communication with family suffers, and our children become easy prey for the influences of Satan.

Carnality is the first thing the world spots in most Christians, and the result is that much of the world is unimpressed with Christianity. The only way we can minimize our carnal ways and develop positive attitudes toward one another is to improve our communication with God.

Chapter 49

Make Use of God's Gifts

There is a diversity of gifts for Christians, and each one is important. There are words of wisdom and knowledge, gifts of healing, working of miracles, prophecy, discerning of spirits, different kinds of tongues, and interpretation of tongues. They all work together through the power of the Holy Spirit, who distributes His gifts to each person as He wills (1 Corinthians 12:4–11).

We are one body in Christ even though we are separate individuals—one body working together for the glory of God. Some of us may be toes or fingers in the body of Christ. However, just as a toe or finger is important to a physical body, the body of Christ is hampered when its toes or fingers are not working to their fullest capacity.

As Paul talked about spiritual gifts, he mentioned praying in an unknown tongue. This type of prayer is unfruitful to others and should not be used in church unless the tongues can be interpreted so that all can understand the prayer. However, praying in an unknown tongue—or praying in the Spirit, as it is called by some Christians—can help a Christian develop a stronger relationship with God.

Speaking in Tongues Is a Gift for Believers

In 1 Corinthians 14:2, Paul says, "He who speaks in a tongue does not speak to men but to God, for no one understands him; however, in the spirit he speaks mysteries."

Communicating with God in an unknown tongue is meant to edify the believer. "When the Day of Pentecost was fully come, they were all with one accord in one place. . . . And they were all filled with the Holy Ghost, and began to speak with other tongues, as the Spirit gave them utterance" (Acts 2:1–4 KJV). After that incident Peter spoke to the multitude and explained what had happened. About three thousand people were baptized in the name of Jesus and received the gift of the Holy Spirit.

I was introduced to the speaking-in-tongues phenomenon when I was fourteen years old. I attended an outdoor Pentecostal meeting led by a young man who felt he had the calling to preach. When he prayed in an unknown tongue, he became so emotional that he jumped over the benches among the congregation.

He later held a revival in a country church next to the home of an elderly couple with whom I was staying. Since my bedroom window faced the church, I could hear him preaching and praying in tongues. He sometimes preached to an empty church.

The opinion of the adults around me was that speaking in tongues was not necessary for the church today. I agreed with their philosophy. Since the young man was not educated in a seminary, we felt his emotions were not genuine.

I clung to this opinion for many years, even though I married into a Pentecostal family. I felt a strong conviction against that when I stated to a family member that I felt I was as good a Christian as anyone who spoke in tongues—as if our goodness depends on anything we do to serve God. The blood of Jesus is the only thing that makes us good enough or pure enough to fellowship with God.

Speaking in Tongues Edifies the Believer

A couple of years later a problem occurred in my life, and I cried out to God for special help. At that time, a cousin in the family said I needed to be baptized in the Holy Spirit. I agreed to lay aside my prejudice and pray with her and a small group of ladies from different denominations. I received the gift of speaking in tongues, but I didn't feel anything different. There was no lessening of my burden, and nothing changed in my life.

A few days later I felt an insatiable desire to read the Word. The Old and New Testament came alive for me in ways I had never encountered, even though I had been a born-again Christian for almost thirty years and had been a Sunday school teacher for several years.

This experience led me to study the Pentecostal movement. I read that individual members of different denominations, including Catholics, had received the gift of speaking in tongues. Many Christians left their denominations because of disagreements about speaking in tongues. They joined Pentecostal churches, which caused the movement to expand. Different Pentecostal denominations were established, and nondenominational charismatic churches were added to the reformation. In the beginning, many poor people were attracted to the movement because of the emphasis on God's blessings and a closer walk with Him.

One day, after picking up some books in a Christian bookstore, I was driving home and thinking about the things I had been learning about the Pentecostal movement. "Lord," I prayed, "why did You let something as wonderful as the baptism of the Holy Spirit get misused by poor, ignorant people?"

I didn't really expect an answer, but in my spirit I heard, *I've always worked with the poor and ignorant.* Realizing that I was one of those poor, ignorant people, I quickly readjusted my thinking. I didn't want pride to keep Him from working with me or interfering with my growth as a Christian.

Confusion about Tongues Began in the Early Church

Paul speaks a great deal about the confusion in the church from people speaking in tongues and getting out of order. He said that even though he spoke in tongues more than anybody, he would rather speak five words with understanding so that he could teach others (1 Corinthians 14:18–19). Teaching others edifies the church.

Paul tells us that singing and praying in the Spirit edifies us and glorifies God just as much as praying and singing in our language does. The gift of praying and singing in tongues is a powerful aid to the individual Christian. It brings unspeakable joy to the believer and helps him to grow spiritually if he doesn't use it in a foolish way.

Larry Christenson, in his book *Speaking in Tongues,* says, "The cure for *abu*se is not *disuse*, but *proper use.*"[27] The foreword for his book, written by Corrie ten Boom, says, "The Lord did not in any way give His gifts as a means to quarrel about, but He gave His gifts that we should enjoy them."

Exercise God's Gifts

Just as a baby learns to speak a language slowly, the vocabulary of a spiritual language increases gradually. As more time is spent with God, talking with Him through our spirits to His Spirit, the gift of speaking in tongues becomes a great comfort to the believer. A sensitive believer can be used in his prayer time by the Holy Spirit for someone who is going to be attacked by the enemy. Many missionaries have reported such incidents from people who have prayed for their safety.

Those who pray in the Spirit a lot will occasionally sense a sudden urge to pray. They pray until they feel at peace. They may not know who or what they are praying for, but reports might come to them later, letting them know their prayers were effective in a certain situation.

Such an incident happened in our family recently. One night I was experiencing a restless leg syndrome along with sciatic pain in my leg, so I took a pill that was supposed to help that condition. However, I became ill from the pill and felt I was going to vomit. As I stood in front of the kitchen garbage disposal, I fainted. When

[27] Larry Christenson, *Speaking in Tongues and Its Significance for the Church* (Minneapolis, MN: Bethany Fellowship, Inc., Dimension Books, 1975), 19.

I came to my senses, I crawled back into bed, not realizing I had experienced a concussion.

That night Andy's daughter Dwnell experienced an uneasy feeling during her evening prayers, so she prayed in the Spirit until she felt peace. Her prayers did not stop the accident that I had put in motion, but I do believe they saved my life because I barely missed hitting the stove. If I had been cut and started bleeding, no one would have known it. The fall caused such dizziness that I had to be hospitalized for five days. It took months for the dizziness to subside.

Two other times Andy's daughter was used like that for family members. In each case the accidents could have been fatal but were not.

If praying in the Spirit is used wisely, Christians can derive many benefits from it, just as Paul did. However, Paul assures us that prophesying is more fruitful for the body of Christ while we are in church. Even though it is not widely used today, prophecy remains a good tool for the church.

Prayer Is a Powerful Mystery

Although praying in the Spirit is done on a small scale among believers, even praying in our understanding is not done on a large scale. Most people would rather spend their time doing works for the Lord that can be seen and admired by others. Playing music, singing, drama, speaking, and teaching Sunday school or Bible classes fall into this category. All of these wonderful talents are openly appreciated and enjoyed by the body of Christ.

But prayer remains a mystery. Like the wind, prayer is powerful. But like the wind, you can't tell where it comes from or see its presence—you can only feel and see its effects. Still, prayer remains the backbone of the church, and the success of the church rises or falls in its service to the Lord depending on the prayer going forth from the congregation as well as the pastors, deacons, elders, administrators, and those in charge of youth groups. Prayer is a mighty tool to be used for protection, healing, relationships, finances, wisdom, and guidance in the affairs of life.

Chapter 50

Seek Wisdom and Counsel in the Word

Proverbs 1:7 tells us, "The fear of the Lord is the beginning of knowledge, but fools despise wisdom and instruction." The first thing we must seek from God's Word is wisdom, and that wisdom will aid us in our prayer and meditation. Without prayer, we would be adrift in a sea of sorrow, grief, and every evil thing that Satan could manage to throw at us. We need to develop a strong defense against our adversary, the devil.

Wisdom obtained from the Word of God and used in prayer is our greatest weapon of spiritual warfare.

God Created the World with Wisdom

Proverbs 8 says wisdom was before the water, mountains, or hills, before the fields, even before the primeval dust of the world. Wisdom was the master craftsman when God prepared the heavens, established the clouds, strengthened the fountains of the deep, assigned the sea to its limit, and marked out the foundations of the earth.

Wisdom says, "When He marked out the foundations of the earth, then I was beside Him as a master craftsman; and I was daily His delight . . . rejoicing in His inhabited world, and my delight was with the sons of men" (Proverbs 8:29–31).

People who presume that they do not need God or His wisdom to survive are foolish indeed. Yet few, including Christians, seek God's wisdom or His council for everyday problems. That is why Satan can inflict his ills in the daily affairs of life.

Proverbs 4 is an excellent passage to memorize because it teaches us the importance of wisdom. In this great proverb, a father speaks to his son. Proverbs 4:7–9 says, "Wisdom is the principal thing; therefore get wisdom. And in all your getting, get understanding. Exalt her, and she will promote you; she will bring you honor, when you embrace her. She will place on your head an ornament of grace; a crown of glory she will deliver to you."

We need wisdom to grow in the attributes of God so we can reflect God's values; otherwise, we will absorb Satan's characteristics and become negative in ways that affect our fruit as Christians.

As we seek to communicate with God through prayer and the Word, we will be able to climb up on higher ground instead of wallowing in the muck and mire of the world.

God's Word Has Power to Prosper or Destroy

Jeremiah 23:29 says, "'Is not My word like a fire?' says the Lord, 'and like a hammer that breaks the rock in pieces?'" God's Word has the power to prosper and to destroy.

God desires that we do everything according to His Word. When He gave the laws to the Israelites, He commanded them to continually teach them to their children (Deuteronomy 6:6–9). However, they refused to follow His instructions and walked in their own counsel. Many Christians are like the Israelites. They fail to see the importance of God's Word in their everyday activities, including prayer. This lack causes them to suffer the consequences of their actions.

In Philippians 2:13, Paul reminds us of the importance of God's will. "It is God who works in you both to will and to do for His good pleasure." God's counsel teaches us that His power in our prayers comes from His Word, which is His will for us.

Chapter 51

Plug into God's Power through Prayers of Petition

If we want the power of electricity, we must plug into an outlet that is connected to the electrical currents in the atmosphere. If we want power from God, we need to plug into Jesus, because He is connected to the spiritual currents of God. Prayer is the plug that brings God's power into the lives of people.

Seek God's Favor by Knocking and Asking

A petition prayer is one that asks a favor or makes a request known to God. For instance, we may ask for protection, justice, deliverance from addictive behavior, help in relationships, wisdom in handling specific problems, or spiritual renewal. Whatever situation we are in, it is important to pray. Jesus actually commands us to pray for our needs (Matthew 7:7–11).

Hannah, a woman of God, was sorely afflicted because she was barren. Her husband loved her dearly, but his affection was not enough for her. Women of her day felt dishonored if they could not bear children. She had knocked on God's door many a time, yet she had not received an answer to her request.

One day, when she visited the temple in Shiloh and presented her petition, she did something unusual. As she wept bitterly and prayed silently before the Lord, she made a vow that if God would give her a male child, she would give her son to Him and that no razor would be used on his head all the days of his life (1 Samuel 1:11).

Eli the priest heard Hannah's complaint and saw her grief. He said her request would be granted and told her to go home in peace.

After Hannah's baby was born, she was true to her vow. She kept Samuel until he was weaned, then gave him to Eli at Shiloh. Samuel became a great priest and God gave his mother other children.

Pray the Answer to Your Petitions

As we put our petitions before the Lord, we can pray the Word that pertains to that need. I discovered this in the 1980s when I was fretting over a specific problem. I heard in my spirit, *Present your problem and pray the answer.*

I shared this revelation with one of my prayer partners, and she wondered what it meant, but I knew the Lord was telling me to pray the Word over my problems. So I memorized a few relevant Bible verses.

One Scripture I used to build my faith was Mark 11:24, where Jesus said, "Therefore I say to you, whatever things you ask when you pray, believe that you receive them, and you will have them." Many people misuse that prayer. They act like little children, asking for things they want that are not good for them or that are not of God.

For example, one person may want something that belongs to another person—a man might like to have another man's wife or something even more foolish or detrimental to him. Some people are always praying for a million dollars, but most people are not equipped to handle money well, and God knows this.

There is an old saying that a fool and his money are quickly parted. Many people who become fast millionaires become penniless as time goes by. If God gave money to a foolish man, He would be increasing the man's problems.

The Word assures us that our petitions are always heard (1 John 5:14–15). But praying in the will of God is crucial to having our prayers answered. The answer may be yes, no, or wait. In Hannah's case she had to wait a long time, but the answer was eventually yes.

For every problem a person has, God has a Scripture that can be used to bring His power into the situation. Psalm 118 has many good verses to use in prayer. For fear or worry, you can pray verse 6: "The Lord is on my side; I will not fear. What can man do to me?" Verse 17 can be used when we are worried about health: "I shall not die, but live, and declare the works of the Lord." Job 34:28 tells us, "He hears the cry of the afflicted."

When in Doubt, Pray God's Will and Way

Some problems arise that no Bible verse seems to address, so you may be unsure of how to pray. As I was praying about a family conflict once, I didn't know what the best solution would be. Each time I thought of the problem, I found myself praying, "Lord, let Your will and Your way be done." Within a few days there was a complete turnaround in the situation, and the positive changes were completely unforeseen.

When we don't know how to pray, we can always pray for God's will and His way. That kind of petition can never be wrong. Even though months or years may pass before a situation is resolved, it is in God's hands. His will and His way eventually bring results if we don't despair and give up praying.

Look for God's Word in Prayer Books

In 1986, I came across a delightful book by Germaine Copeland called *Prayers that Avail Much*. In 1976 Ms. Copeland was praying with a group of ladies, and they were finding it hard to find answers to certain problems. So they worked through the Scriptures and came up with a number of prayers, which they compiled into this book.

This book had excellent Scriptures for various problems, and I gave many copies to my family. Today there are several good prayer books on the market with specific prayers for women, families, fathers, mothers, children, etc. They contain Scriptures that help us know how to pray when we are faced with certain problems. If we want healing, we look for healing Scriptures; if we want help in finances or relationships, we look for the Scriptures that pertain to those problems. Then we present the problem and pray the Word answer.

Isaiah 55:11 says, "So shall My word be that goes forth from My mouth; it shall not return to Me void, but it shall accomplish what I please, and it shall prosper in the thing for which I sent it." God's Word does not return void, because it is accompanied by His power. It is His power in His Word that brings answers to our prayers.

Chapter 52

Throw Out the Lifeline with Intercessory Prayer

For centuries hedges and walls were the means for protecting farms, cities, and homes. A gap in the hedge or wall meant a breach in security. Something had to be put in the gap until the hedge or wall could be replaced.

A prayer intercessor is someone who spends a great deal of his time standing in the gap before God on behalf of those who are walking in unrighteousness or who are in stressful situations.

In Old Testament times God used prophets and priests to intercede between Him and the people who were committing sin. However, at times even the priests were involved in unrighteous behavior and profaned the laws of God. In Ezekiel 22:30–31 God said, "I sought for a man among them who would make a wall, and stand in the gap before Me on behalf of the land, that I should not destroy it; but I found no one. Therefore I have poured out My indignation on them."

The intercessory prayer warrior will stand in the gap for salvation of family members or friends, as well as for addictive behavior with drugs, alcohol, or cigarettes, for bondage of various sins, for healing of diseases, or for financial purposes.

We need Christians who will intercede for the healing of nations, for godly governments throughout the world, and for protection and wisdom for our president.

There is a need to pray for the military men and women who give their all for our country. Christians around the world can stand in the gap against terrorist attacks by calling on the Word of God for protection.

We must also pray for those in public service such as police officers, fire fighters, teachers, lawmakers, governors, and mayors.

Most of all we should intercede for the ministers of our churches and for the missionaries who are carrying a heavy load trying to reach the lost.

Intercede for Missionaries

Many wonderful Christians have left their own countries to preach the gospel to people in foreign lands. We can't all go, but through prayer we can support those who are called for this special work.

I became interested in praying for missionaries when a church I attended gave the congregation a list of 365 missionaries to pray for on their birthdays. I set aside a special time of prayer each day. I prayed for their needs, their relationships with their families, and protection.

One night in prayer, God thanked me for my prayers. I felt truly blessed to have the honor of praying for those missionaries and their families.

Intercede for Better Laws

In 1895 Amy Carmichael, a twenty-eight-year-old single woman, went to India. After living there a few years, she discovered that many children and babies were being forced into prostitution and trained to dance and entertain the temple gods and men.[28]

Diseased old men could buy children for brides as young as five years old. After the husband died, the young widow, who could be ten or twelve years old, was left alone without financial or moral support. Their families rejected them or were unable to help.

---

[28] Lois Hoadley Dick, *Amy Carmichael: Let the Little Children Come* (Chicago, IL: Moody Press, 1984).

If the young widows had children, the babies were improperly cared for; many died because the mothers could not support themselves or their children. Some of those girls were given to the temple gods.

Amy made it her goal to rescue as many of these mothers and babies as she could provide for financially. She had to leave her burdens in the hands of God when it came to food, clothing, and medicine. However, the children always had enough motherly love, and intellectual and spiritual training, to help them become useful citizens.

With God's help Amy brought worldwide awareness to the plight of these children. She eventually acquired property and a hospital to care for thousands of unwanted children and young widows.

Amy had many years of heartbreaking experiences along the way, but her faith never wavered. If she didn't receive a special word from God about something, she prayed for His will to be done. Sometimes attempts to rescue a child failed; at other times court cases were brought against her. On one rescue mission a special aide traveled a thousand miles to rescue a child who later died. These situations were hard for Amy to accept, but she never questioned God's mercy or will. She knew she had God's favor.

Due largely to Amy and her intercessory prayer warriors, a law was passed in 1947 that made it illegal to dedicate a child to the temple. Children were no longer legally allowed to be married before maturity.

Intercede for the Children of the World

India is not the only nation to have desecrated its children. There are many black pages of history for children in countries such as England, South America, Africa, Turkey, China, and Japan, not to mention the United States.

In the 1980s, when I was praying with an intercessory group in St. Louis, Missouri, we heard reports that children were being kidnapped for child prostitution in our own nation. I felt a heaviness in my spirit to intercede in prayer on behalf of these children.

Regardless of laws to protect children against sexual predators, children are still being abducted for use in pornography or for sexual activities. It seems there are more sexual vultures circling the globe than ever before in our history. Modern technology has made it easier for them to locate their prey.

Andy and I have several children in our families, and we continually cover them with protective prayer. I think those prayers were at work when a four-year-old great-grandchild got lost in a Chicago hotel. He had opened the hotel room door after his dad had gone on an errand and his mom was still asleep. Though the child was found unharmed, it would have been a different story if a child molester had been around. The hotel staff spotted him wandering around and protected him until the parents arrived.

Intercede for Repulsive Sins

Regardless of how revolting a sin is to us, the death of Jesus on the cross washes it white as snow. We are told in 1 John 5:16, "If anyone sees his brother sinning a sin which does not lead to death, he will ask, and He will give him life for those who commit sin not leading to death."

The sin unto death concerns the enlightened Christian who has been given all of the Holy Spirit's special gifts, then decides he prefers Satan's kingdom instead of God's kingdom. If he does this he can never repent.

> It is impossible for those who were once enlightened, and have tasted of the heavenly gift, and were made partakers of the Holy Ghost, and have tasted the good word of God, and the powers of the world to come, if they fall away, to renew them again unto repentance; seeing they crucify to themselves the Son of God afresh, and put him to an open shame. (Hebrews 6:4–6 KJV)

An intercessor cannot be hypocritical by criticizing others. He is called to worship God and let God give life to those who have not committed the unpardonable sin of putting the Holy Spirit to shame.

This means we must intercede for even the most repulsive sinner, including the sexual deviate, the terrorist, the murderer, or those who commit any sin society finds repugnant, as well as the ordinary Christian who finds himself involved in sexual sins and other bad habits.

Abraham Threw Out the Lifeline

Abraham is a good example of an intercessor in the Old Testament. Born with the name Abram, he was the son of Terah and he had two brothers: Nahor and Haran. After Haran died, Terah took his son Abram and his grandson Lot and moved to the land of Canaan. When the Lord spoke to Abram and asked him to leave his father's land, Abram took his nephew Lot, and all of Lot's family and possessions, and moved to the south.

Lot's servants and Abram's servants were unable to work together, so Abram told Lot to pick the place he wanted for his family, herds, and servants. Lot chose to live in the city of Sodom, and Abram went to Hebron. God made a covenant with Abram and told him he would be the father of many nations; at that time He gave him the name Abraham.

After some time had elapsed, the sins of the cities of Sodom and Gomorrah came to God's attention, and He told Abraham he was going to destroy them. Since Lot and all of his family lived in Sodom, Abraham interceded for the cities. He asked God to spare them if fifty righteous men could be found. The Lord agreed, but there were not fifty good men in the area. So Abraham started bargaining with God for their salvation.

He went from fifty to forty-five, forty, thirty, twenty, then ten. Finally, Abraham had to stop interceding. The only people who were spared were Lot and his two daughters, who fled to the mountains for safety. They were told not to look back at the carnage, but Lot's wife looked back at the city that held her possessions and she was turned into a pillar of salt (See Genesis 12–19.)

God's Prophets Threw Lifelines to the Israelites

Moses was probably the greatest intercessor for the Israelites. He spent his life praying on behalf of the people to keep God's wrath turned away from them. God gave Moses the laws that the people were to obey, and Moses was continually begging God not to do great harm to the people for their disobedience.

Because of His covenants with Moses and Abraham, God did not destroy the Israelites. However, many tragedies befell the people due to the sins they committed and the laws they ignored. Their wayward ways caused Moses to stumble, too, and he was not allowed into the Promised Land. Moses died in the mountains, after which Joshua took care of the people and helped them settle in the land God designated to them.

All of God's prophets lived hard lives as they interceded on behalf of the people and tried to teach them to walk in the ways of God. The prophet Jeremiah said, "Oh, that my head were waters, and my eyes a fountain of tears, that I might weep day and night for the slain of the daughter of my people!" (Jeremiah 9:1).

Jeremiah pleaded with the people to change their ways. "But," he said, "if you will not hear it, my soul will weep in secret for your pride; my eyes will weep bitterly and run down with tears, because the Lord's flock has been taken captive" (Jeremiah 13:17).

Jeremiah pronounced God's judgment on the people who did not believe that his prophecies were from God. Regardless of the many hours spent on his face, weeping and praying for the people, he had to watch the people suffer for their sins as the prophesied calamities descended on the nation of Israel.

Throw Out the Lifeline with Fasting and Prayer

The book of Esther is a fascinating story about intercession. Esther was a Jewish girl who was chosen to be the wife of

Ahasuerus, King of Persia. When her uncle Mordecai discovered a plot to destroy the Jewish people, he asked Esther to plead for her people before the king. She was fearful for her life—first, because the king did not know she was a Jew, and also because a law was in place that said anyone who went before the king without being summoned could be put to death.

However, Mordecai prevailed upon Esther and said, "Who knows whether you have come to the kingdom for such a time as this?" (Esther 4:14). Esther answered Mordecai's requests by telling him to have all the Jews in Shushan fast for three days and nights, and said that she and her maids would be fasting too.

After Esther made her preparations for fasting, she went before the king and found favor with him and was able to save her people from destruction. The book of Esther is a wonderful story of people fasting and praying together during a time of enormous crisis and overcoming seemingly insurmountable odds with great victory. We have access to this same kind of power when we intercede for the United States against the threats of terrorism and attacks on Christians in our own country as well as other parts of the world.

Fasting can be personal or done in groups. The first time I tried to fast by myself, I started a three-day fast on water. I lasted two days. Later, I realized that a liquid fast can include juices, coffee, and soft drinks. You can also fast from meat or sweets. I know one church where the intercessors fasted during the day and ate a salad in the evening. The length of time can be one to three days. Longer fasts should not be attempted until the person becomes adept at fasting and understands his or her body's strengths. People with health conditions should consult their doctors before fasting.

Jesus fasted and taught His disciples to fast. When the disciples were unable to cast out a demon, He told them that it was necessary to pray and fast for results in certain situations (Matthew 17:21). When we fast we are humbling ourselves before God and letting Him know we are serious about hearing from Him. We are willing to give up something important to us to receive His favor.

David humbled himself in sackcloth and fasted for people when they were ill (Psalm 35:13).

As Jesus pointed out, fasting brings in special anointing and is crucial in certain situations.

Fasting strengthens our faith in the same way prayer does. Faith gets our prayers answered.

The Prayers of Elijah

James 5:17–18 tells us that Elijah was a man like us, but he prayed to withhold rain for three years and six months; then he prayed again and the rains came.

Elijah lived during the reign of Ahab and Jezebel. His life was always threatened by those two, but he kept interceding on behalf of the people and trying to get them to remember their God instead of following the false god Baal.

When God relieved Elijah of his burden, he passed his mantle and a double portion of his spirit on to Elisha, who was present when God took Elijah to heaven in a chariot of fire in the midst of a whirlwind (2 Kings 2:9–11).

Numbers Help Strengthen Intercessory Prayer

Even though one person can make a big difference with intercessory prayer, there is more power in numbers. Deuteronomy 32:30 says, "How could one chase a thousand, and two put ten thousand to flight, unless their Rock had sold them, and the Lord had surrendered them?" With Jesus as our Rock, one can put a thousand to flight, but two can put ten thousand to flight.

A spouse or a friend can be a daily prayer partner. When one becomes weak, the other can bring in reinforcements through the power of the Word and prayer.

The prayers of two believers have the power to put ten thousand to flight. Just think of multiplying two by ten thousand several times over, and you can see how powerful a small group is in the spirit world.

Intercessory Prayer Fulfills the Law of Love

Christ wants us to help and uphold failing or falling Christians. Galatians 6:1–2 says, "Brethren, if a man is overtaken in any trespass, you who are spiritual restore such a one in a spirit of gentleness, considering yourself lest you also be tempted. Bear one another's burdens, and so fulfill the law of Christ."

The Word also tells us to "consider one another in order to stir up love and good works, not forsaking the assembling of ourselves together, as is the manner of some, but exhorting one another, and so much the more as you see the Day approaching" (Hebrews 10:24–25).

Jesus Christ is the greatest intercessor in the history of man. When God saw that there was no intercessor for man, "His own arm brought salvation for Him; and His own righteousness, it sustained Him" (Isaiah 59:16).

Jesus is our High Priest, seated at the right hand of the throne of God, continually making intercession for the body of Christ (Hebrews 8:1). Jesus intercedes for us, so it is imperative that we do our part as intercessory prayer warriors here on earth.

In Revelation 3:21 Jesus says, "To him who overcomes I will grant to sit with Me on My throne, as I also overcame and sat down with My Father on His throne." Intercessory prayer helps us to overcome the enemy and fulfill Christ's commandment to walk in love.

Chapter 53

Stir Up the Sleepy Church with Revival Praying

Merriam-Webster's dictionary says *revive* means "to bring new life into something" or to "become active or flourishing again."[29] For Christians, it means to stir up the church, which has become despondent, complacent, and self-centered.

Revival Requires Repentance

Revival takes a great deal of effort, and its success comes through the power of prayer and repentance.

In the Old Testament, God asked the prophet Jonah to visit the city of Nineveh, a part of Assyria. It was a wicked city full of every abomination imaginable, with no respect for human life. However, God wanted to give the people a chance to repent. So He asked Jonah to go to Nineveh and warn them of their coming judgment if they did not change their evil ways. Jonah knew how horrible the people of Nineveh were, and he didn't want them saved, so he tried to run from God (Jonah 1:1–4).

When Jonah hid on a ship going to Tarshish, God prepared a big fish to swallow him. While in the belly of the fish, Jonah repented of his actions, so God had the fish vomit Jonah up on dry land, and Jonah went on to Nineveh.

When the king of Nineveh heard Jonah's message, he commanded all the people to fast, pray, and give up their evil ways. A great revival hit the city (Jonah 3:5–9).

---

[29] *Merriam-Webster's Collegiate Dictionary,* 11th ed., (Springfield, Massachusetts: Merriam-Webster, Inc., 2007).

Jonah became angry with God. He thought God should have annihilated the city on the spot after he prophesied against them. But God said to Jonah, "Should I not pity Nineveh, that great city, in which are more than one hundred and twenty thousand persons who cannot discern between their right hand and their left—and much livestock?" (Jonah 4:11).

God desires cities and nations to repent so that He does not have to judge them. But this can only happen when revivals break out and the hearts of people are changed. Even though Nineveh was spared for more than a hundred years, God prophesied against them again when they fell back into their evil ways.

Backsliding Brings Judgment

Nahum prophesied against Nineveh, saying, "Woe to the bloody city! It is all full of lies and robbery. Its victim never departs" (Nahum 3:1).

Even though Nineveh had become the mightiest city on earth, with one-hundred-foot-high walls, Nahum predicted that Nineveh would end with a flood (Nahum 1:8). The Tigris River eventually overflowed its banks and the flood destroyed part of Nineveh's wall. This left them vulnerable to the Babylonians, who plundered the city and burned it to the ground in 612 BC.

Nahum also prophesied that Nineveh would be hidden (3:11). The site did remain hidden until it was discovered in AD 1842.

From the example we get from Nineveh, we can see the need for revival to break out periodically among cities and nations. Throughout the centuries God has anointed great men to call His people to revival.

The Holy Spirit Leads Revival

Jesus made sure there would be a revival after His death. The disciples were sorrowful, yet they didn't question Jesus when He told them He was going away. Jesus said, "Nevertheless I tell you the truth. It is to your advantage that I go away; for if I do not go away, the Helper will not come to you; but if I depart, I will send Him to you" (John 16:7).

Martin Luther saw the need for men to know what the written Word said so they could have the promises that the Word has for them. At that time lay people did not read the Bible, so it was difficult for them to have a personal relationship with God. Christians were encouraged to do penance and pay for their sins, and the priests told them what they needed to do. However, Luther encouraged men and women of faith to know God and His Word personally.

As a result of his efforts and prayers, people learned to read the Bible, and this caused the biggest revival of all time. The Protestant movement came out of that revival, and many denominations of churches have sprung up since then.

Revival Brings Denominations Together

Every century God puts special men and women in place to bring revival to His church. Hope springs from those revivals that mankind can fight off the enemies Satan brings forth. God works mightily with people who pray and repent of their sinful ways.

When those of us who were born before World War II think of revival, we visualize tent meetings. These old-time revival meetings often lasted up to four weeks, depending on the speaker and the area. People from many small churches of the same denomination or similar faiths came together for prayer and worship, usually concluding with a dinner on the grounds, plus baptisms in local creeks or lakes. Rural and small-town Americans stayed close to God because of the emphasis on revival and prayer.

Today television and radio evangelists hold large meetings across the country, usually in big stadiums or in air-conditioned auditoriums. Different denominations attend their meetings. Some Christians use their vacation time to attend a week-long meeting in an area away from their homes. These revivals have a significant impact on churches in the United States as well as other countries. However, some little churches still cling to the idea that revival meetings should be held at specified intervals with special speakers.

Regardless of how Christians get together, it is imperative that we continue meeting in large numbers to call upon God, because this world is coming closer to the end-time calamities predicted in the Bible. The book of Revelation gives us the final chapter for mankind. We have a lot of revival praying to do before we will be ready for the return of Jesus.

Revival Praying Helps Restore Joy after Disaster

In 2001, three planes commandeered by terrorists hit the Twin Towers of the World Trade Center in New York and the Pentagon in Washington DC. These triggered an outbreak of prayer and togetherness in our nation not seen since World War II. People all across the United States met in churches and homes to pray for our country and the families affected by the tragedies.

In 2004, tsunami floods affected the lives of millions of people, and many countries banded together to help relieve the enormous human sufferings. Doctors, nurses, food, medicines, money, and building supplies were sent from all over the world. The greatest benefit was the power that went forth from churches as Christians prayed for the suffering people.

In 2005, Hurricane Katrina almost wiped out New Orleans and parts of the Gulf Coast. More hurricanes devastated Florida and the East Coast. We are in a time of siege for disasters, it seems. Other countries are experiencing outbreaks of earthquakes, hurricanes, fires, floods, and mud slides. Christians have responded to these tragedies with sympathy, prayer, and money to help the afflicted. However, these events are taking a toll on finances and energy throughout the world.

Recently, as I was pondering these adversities, I felt in my spirit the darkness surrounding our nation as well as the rest of the world. Through the Holy Spirit I heard these words: *There is coming a time when there will be no joy in the world except in the hearts of Christians.*

I was reminded of the Scripture that says, "Do not sorrow, for the joy of the Lord is your strength" (Nehemiah 8:10). One day we may have to greet one another with that phrase to keep joy abounding, because the world is fast becoming a place of darkness that denies the power of Christ and the love of God.

Revival praying must break out across our nation, as well as the rest of the world, in churches everywhere, regardless of denominational differences. Without a united front, Christians will become weak and worthless as soldiers for Christ. The devil will try to divide and conquer, just as he did when Jesus was on earth and even more so after He was resurrected.

Satan has had some great moments in history, but Christians have had some great moments too. Evangelists throughout the centuries have been like the prophets of old, reminding us of our power in Jesus and the Word of God. But God will use His foot soldiers to win the war in spiritual battles, just as foot soldiers are used to win the war in physical battles.

Revival Praying Makes Better Warriors

Years ago, when big ministries were getting into trouble, I asked the Lord what was going on. In my spirit I heard these words: *Some will increase and others will decrease.* (See John 3:30.) He continued, *I am not looking for big ministries to solve the problems of the world. I want Christians to take their territory (wherever their feet trod) for Jesus—so that under every rock, in every hole, and behind every tree the name of Jesus will be heard.* This is the great commission Jesus left for us, to cover the earth with His word (Mathew 28:19–20). Every single Christian is needed for this job.

This will not happen with a weak, sleepy church, The only way Christians will be stirred up to take territory for Jesus is if they strengthen themselves with revival praying. Individual Christians must unite with other believers so they can be as devoted to doing the work of Christ as the terrorists are to working for their evil causes.

Terrorists continue to attack country after country, burning and bombing in all kinds of places where people congregate in large or small numbers. They pick unlikely places that have nothing to do with war. Innocent people in stadiums, malls, parks, hotels, trains, airplanes, and buses can be their targets at any moment around the world.

In the face of this kind of terrorism, people never feel safe in any situation. Yet we must not fear, because that will bring defeat for the world and victory to the terrorists. We are not defenseless in battle. Revival praying will help keep the terrorists at bay.

Revival Praying Is Our Weapon of Warfare

Every Christian church, community, state, and country must come together in these days of great peril, because the power to defeat this ungodly foe lies in revival praying. We must pray for our leaders and all the people who are putting their lives on the line every day so that we might live comfortable, happy lives.

Just as we need generals in a physical army, we need spiritual generals in God's army. But God expects each individual Christian soldier to pick up the cross of Jesus and engage in spiritual battle for Him. We do this by walking in love with one another, speaking the Word of God, and praying for all nations in these crucial days before Christ returns.

Diplomacy, love, and reason are not part of the vocabulary of the terrorists. They are under the power of Satan as he strives for global dominion. Our world will remain like this until Jesus comes. But He said, "When these things begin to happen, look up and lift up your heads, because your redemption draws near" (Luke 21:28).

Revival praying can bring the changes we need to prepare the world for Jesus. It is a tremendous weapon in the body of Christ, and every Christian should become an intercessory prayer warrior. We don't have to be powerful in the body of Christ, just willing to be used by God to intercede for Him here on earth the way Jesus intercedes for us in heaven. We are to "pray without ceasing" (1 Thessalonians 5:17).

Prayer warriors will receive great rewards in heaven. Jesus told us, "The last will be first, and the first last" (Matthew 20:16). It's possible for a faithful prayer warrior to bear more fruit than a successful evangelist. Jesus told His disciples to pray in a secret place, "and your Father who sees in secret will reward you openly" (Matthew 6:6).

Chapter 54

Growing Spiritually through Praise and Thanksgiving

The Word tells us that God inhabits our praises (Psalm 22:3). What does that mean? I believe that something supernatural is let loose in our spirits when we praise God, and that is the Spirit of God who dwells in us. As we relinquish ourselves to the spirit of praise, the joy of the Lord we receive is a minute portion of His glory that Christians can experience here and now.

Praises Glorify God

Many years ago, while worshiping in church, the congregation was singing about the glory of God. As we sang, I wondered, *Lord, what is Your glory?*

He told me to look at the people around me. He asked me what I saw on some of the faces.

I see joy.

He replied, *That's my glory.*

Our joy is an intrinsic part of God's glory.

Revelation 7:11–12 paints a portrait of praise given to God continually in heaven. We are shown another picture of praise in Revelation 19:4–5, where twenty-four elders and four living creatures fell down and worshipped God, saying, "'Amen! Alleluia!' Then a voice came from the throne, saying, 'Praise our God, all you His servants and those who fear Him, both small and great.'"

Though praises go forth continually before God in heaven, He is just as interested in hearing our praises from earth. The glory of God comes upon us through His joy when we praise Him.

A Thankful Heart Glorifies God

Psalm 100:4 tells us to enter His gates with thanksgiving and His courts with praise, to be thankful to God and to bless His holy name. God loves it when His children are grateful to Him, just as parents are pleased when their children develop thankful hearts.

Psalm 105:1–5 tells us to give thanks to the Lord, call upon His name, sing to Him, sing psalms to Him, talk of His wondrous works, glory in His holy name, seek His strength, seek His face, and remember His marvelous works.

Even though King David committed some bad sins, he was quick to repent and ask for mercy. In Psalm 25:11 he said, "For Your name's sake, O Lord, pardon my iniquity, for it is great." David praised, worshipped, and thanked God so much, from his youth through his old age, that God said, "I have found David the son of Jesse, a man after My own heart, who will do all My will" (Acts 13:22). That is why God chose to send Jesus through the seed of David and establish his kingdom forever.

Psalm 104:33 gives us an example of how David worshipped God. "I will sing to the Lord as long as I live; I will sing praise to my God while I have my being."

While David was in the wilderness of Judah, he sought God. In that dry and thirsty land, his soul thirsted for God and his flesh longed for God. Even in his misery he still raised his hands and praised God with a joyful spirit (Psalm 63:1–5). God tells us, "Whoever offers praise glorifies Me; and to him who orders his conduct aright I will show the salvation of God" (Psalm 50:23).

Hannah did not forget God after He granted her prayer and gave her a male child. When her son was weaned, she took him back to Shiloh and left him with the priest. As she worshipped the

Lord, she gave a long prophetic prayer that included rejoicing and thanksgiving (1 Samuel 2:1–10).

Praising God Strengthens Our Faith

One of the greatest weapons we have in times of trouble is our praise and thanksgiving to God. That is how David was able to survive in the wilderness when King Saul was trying to kill him. He praised God by saying, "I will sing of Your power; yes, I will sing aloud of Your mercy in the morning; for You have been my defense and refuge in the day of my trouble. To You, O my Strength, I will sing praises; for God is my defense, My God of mercy" (Psalm 59:16–17).

Psalm 148 admonishes all creation to praise the Lord: all His angels and hosts, all the stars of light, the heavens, the heights, the heaven of heavens, and waters above the heavens. Psalm 149:5–6 says, "Let the saints be joyful in glory; let them sing aloud on their beds. Let the high praises of God be in their mouth, and a two-edged sword in their hand."

Psalm 150 tells God's people to praise Him for His mighty acts and greatness with the trumpet, lute, and harp, with the timbrel and dance, with stringed instruments and flutes, with loud, clashing cymbals, and to let everything that has breath praise the Lord.

We are told to speak to one another in psalms, hymns, and spiritual songs, singing and making melody in our hearts continually to the Lord, and to give thanks to our Father in all things (Ephesians 5:19–20). When we give thanks to God, and worship Him with our songs and praise, we can walk in God's will and ways much more easily. If our spirits are full of joy, God seems closer to us, and the problems of the world don't look so foreboding.

Psalm 67 tells us to let all the people praise God and let the nations sing for joy with gladness. Then the earth shall yield her increase and God shall bless us.

God Considers Praise a Sacrifice

If we try to live without the power or joy of the Lord as our strength, we become weary and weak, struggling in a world that delights in sucking us into its muck and mire. When we get bogged down in worldliness, we lose some of God's blessings and we produce less fruit for His kingdom.

Since Satan is the god of this world, the only way we can experience joy unspeakable, which is full of God's glory, is through the power of the Holy Spirit that lives in each of us. However, before we can experience His joy, we must give God the sacrifice of praise.

Praise is not something we do only when we feel good; otherwise, it would not be called a sacrifice. Even though we may feel like crying, the minute we begin to praise God, the burden is lifted and the tears stop. We can enjoy giving God our praises whether we are on top of the world or in the pits of hell. The sacrifice of praise through our lips lets God know how much we appreciate what He has done for us, and it helps us to produce more fruit for His kingdom.

Communication with God Requires Prayer and the Word

Before we can communicate well with God, we have to be aware of His attributes. We understand God through His Word.

Jesus told a parable about a woman who wanted a judge who did not fear God or man to avenge her from her adversary. He procrastinated. When she kept pestering him, the judge finally consented to help her. Jesus used this parable to teach people to pray and not lose heart (Luke 18:1–8).

Without God's help through prayer, our world would be even more chaotic and full of carnality than it is today. We would fall into idolatry, imitating the Israelites, with each person seeking to do his or her own will and doing what was right in his or her own eyes.

Failure to Communicate with God Produces Carnality and Judgment

After God destroyed the earth with a flood, mankind still walked in wickedness and refused to communicate with Him. God destroyed the Tower of Babel and the cities of Sodom and Gomorrah as examples of what could happen to those who do not seek His attributes and walk in His will and His way.

He chose the nation of Israel to show them how to live according to His disciplines. But they failed to walk in His judgments, so they lost their status as a chosen nation.

After Jesus rose from the dead, He left us the Holy Spirit to guide and direct us so Christian men and women can be stable and strong physically, mentally, spiritually, and even financially. He teaches us how to have good communication with Him, know His attributes, and walk in His disciplines. However, only men and women who are willing to pour themselves out through prayer and the study of God's Word can be helpful in getting the world ready for the return of Jesus.

Abandon Yourself to God with Praise and Thanksgiving

Praising God glorifies Him and helps us become strong Christians. Praise gives us joy, not happiness as the world knows it. The world's happiness is a momentary fleeting experience that does not create strength. God's joy remains in us. Jesus said, "These things I have spoken to you, that My joy may remain in you, and that your joy may be full" (John 15:11).

Thanksgiving is another way of receiving an overflowing of joy from God. One day after praying awhile, I started thanking God for the sun, the stars, the moon, flowers, trees, grass, birds, and many of His other creations when suddenly I found myself thanking Him for worms. Now, I detest worms. So for me, giving thanks for worms was a true act of love and adoration. I felt good about being able to thank God for something as lowly as an earthworm; after all, He made fish love them!

If I had not been abandoned to God at that moment, it would have been inconceivable for me to thank Him for something I loathed looking at or touching. That may seem like an insignificant example. But forsaking ourselves to God in praise and thanksgiving can have an unfathomable and far-reaching effect on us as children of God.

Philippians 4:6–7 tells us, "Be anxious for nothing, but in everything by prayer and supplication, with thanksgiving, let your requests be made known to God; and the peace of God, which surpasses all understanding, will guard your hearts and minds through Christ Jesus."

Praise, thanksgiving, and prayer can bring God's peace and power into any problem or situation, no matter how insurmountable it may seem. However, this type of communication with God requires discipline and obedience to God and His Word.

Prayer Is a Mighty Weapon in the Hands of God's People

In this section we looked at main ways we can pray for change: petition prayer, intercessory prayer, and revival prayer.

In petition prayer, we present a problem to God. His answer may be yes, no, or wait. If we are praying in God's will, the Word can be used as our surety for an answer. Probably the hardest thing in a petition prayer is accepting God's will in a matter. We know God delights in giving good gifts to His children, and we are delighted when the answer to our requests is yes. But the only way we can accept a no answer is by trusting in God's will. "Wait" can be an equally frustrating answer because God's timing is often chafing. Like little children, we want answers immediately or sooner.

With intercessory prayer, we approach God on behalf of the needs of others. This requires a great deal from the intercessor. We may feel as if we are doing physical labor when we pray. We have to be close to the heart of God, because in intercessory prayer we are asking God to bring about changes in situations that without

Him would be impossible tasks. Intercessors are "gap standers" until God moves through their prayers.

Revival prayer is a wake-up call on behalf of the body of Christ. It is a mighty weapon in the hand of God—one the church could move mountains with if they stood together under the banner of God and marched forward as Christian soldiers dedicated to their Savior, Jesus Christ.

Prayer is a mousetrap we can use for ourselves and others to keep the mouse out of our spiritual houses.

Father, Your Word tells us that those who come to You through Jesus Christ You will not cast out of Your kingdom, as long as they have not sinned the sin unto death. Help us not to despise the sinner, only the sin, and bring all the lost to You. May we concentrate on Your will and way as we continue to serve and glorify You. Amen.

Joy in Jesus

We will pray, pray to our Father,

Praise, praise God forever.

We will sing, sing a song for Jesus,

For there's joy, joy in serving the Lord.

O there's joy, joy in Jesus,

Joy, joy way down in our souls.

Let's make the hallelujahs roll.

For there is joy, joy in serving the Lord.

PART FOUR

GOD'S TOOL FOR OVERCOMING

As we journey through life to our eternal home,
God has equipped us to stay the course.

Why are you cast down, O my soul?
And why are you disquieted within me?
Hope in God, for I shall yet praise Him
for the help of His countenance.
(Psalm 42:5)

Discipline #10: Perseverance

Perseverance is the key to living in God's disciplines.

Blessed is the man whose strength is in You,
whose heart is set on pilgrimage.
(Psalm 84:5)

Chapter 55

Start from Scratch

The only way we can become disciplined is to persevere. All of God's disciplines require that we polish up the tool of perseverance that He has equipped us with. Perseverance is necessary whether we are attempting a small feat or a large one.

Expect to Persevere in Exercise

Each day that I enter the pool for my water-aerobics class, I am confronted with a big poster of a swimmer getting ready to plunge into the water. Under the picture are these words: "Before you can accomplish something, you must expect it of yourself."

The message reminds me of my first water-aerobics class in St. Louis. I was enrolled in a new YMCA, and we didn't have the usual supply of noodles to work with for balance and strength as we performed certain exercises. We improvised by taking two empty plastic gallon-sized milk bottles and filling them with the amount of water we thought we could balance our body weight with. For several sessions, I was either spitting water out of my mouth from sinking or popping up out of the water like a corkscrew. After a few weeks, I managed to get the right amount of water in the bottles for my strength.

I've never been the kind of person who persevered in exercise. I do it in spurts. I worked out to a few television programs for a while, then graduated to tapes. Then I tried walking a half hour a day three days per week. I bought a jump-rope in my fifties because I enjoyed jumping rope when I was a kid. But after working on any program for a short period, I always came up with an excuse to give it up.

After my husband Norman died when I was sixty-two, a relative told me I needed to do something that would help me mentally and physically. She recommended the water-aerobics class because she enjoyed it. I'd heard water programs were good for people with certain health problems. I had been suffering with arthritis for over twenty years. So I decided to give it a shot.

I signed up for a class that met three times a week. I found the program surprisingly appealing, which made it easy to be faithful to the regimen.

When I moved to California I took a YMCA class in water aerobics that was specifically geared for arthritis and similar problems. After a year of that, I wanted to join a more advanced class, and the teacher encouraged me to try it. That class did about forty minutes of their program jogging in place while they performed certain exercises in the water. My first attempt at jogging lasted about three minutes, after which I barely had enough energy to crawl out of the water. But each day I managed a few minutes longer. Eventually I was able to stay in the advanced class for the full hour.

A few years ago, when a health club opened close to me, I changed pools again because I had been driving thirty minutes each way to class. My new water-aerobics class had exercises geared to the young, but we were told to do things according to our abilities. At the ripe old age of eighty-three years, I smile when I see young people half my age floundering around in the water when they first enter our class.

That "expect it of yourself" sign has kept me going in this class for the last ten years. As long as I can get in and out of a pool, I expect to stay in a water-aerobics class.

Exercise plays an essential part in helping the body stay healthy. It strengthens the bones, and it helps the lungs, heart, and circulatory system work better.

Expect God's Help When Persevering through Trials

God led me to study perseverance for six months before He asked me to research the other nine areas of discipline. During that period of time, my mother-in-law was diagnosed with Alzheimer's disease, my mother was operated on for stomach cancer, and my youngest son signed up for six months in the naval reserves to see if he wanted to join the NROTC when he entered college.

My mother's situation became critical, so I concentrated on her recovery from surgery. As I stood by her bedside, watching the uneven lines on her heart monitor, the Lord told me that perseverance is a steady heartbeat of faith, not like the erratic heartbeat my mother was experiencing at that moment.

Later, when her monitor registered the smooth, steady beat of a normal heart, I realized how different the body works when it's under pressure. I understood what God meant when He said that perseverance is a steady heartbeat of faith; not faith that can be tossed about like the waves of the sea when we are being swamped by the stresses of life. I certainly was not persevering when I bounced in and out of exercise.

After my mother received her man-made stomach, she was able, with the Lord's help, to keep her faith steady as she persevered through the terrible aftermath of cancer chemotherapy.

In spite of the setback of a small stroke, she won the battle against that cancer. She persevered and enjoyed the next seven years before a different type of cancer struck in the esophagus area and took her home quickly.

During the tumultuous experiences with my mother, my husband Norman and I were helping my mother-in-law, Nellie, in her battle with Alzheimer's disease and the glaucoma that eventually led her into blindness.

After months of dealing with her problems ourselves, we found a lady to care for her. Virginia was experienced with elderly people and had been approved by the state to look after three or four adults in her home.

Before I heard of Virginia I spent many nights in prayer, expecting the Lord to find some way for Nellie to be looked after properly without being sent to a nursing home. At that time I had never heard of anyone who would care for an Alzheimer's patient in her home. Later, I found there were two or three in the St. Louis area, but they would not look after a patient over the weekend.

We had tried to keep Nellie in our home, but with my husband's illness, it was impossible. So when I discovered Virginia through my hairdresser, whose grandmother was being cared for by Virginia, I saw it as an act of mercy from God.

Regardless of what trials we are facing or what feats we are trying to accomplish, God will do His part if we expect it of Him. But we must expect to do our part, too, and that means persevering until God arranges to intervene on our behalf.

Military Training Develops Perseverance

In the meantime, our son was having his own trials in boot camp at the naval reserve in Orlando, Florida. The first morning, he woke up to a horrible noise made by a garbage can rolling against the bunk beds. For a teenager who had lived only in the comfort of his home, it was a nerve-shattering way to start a new day.

Then he discovered that some men in his class used drugs. Most of the boys did their best, but the entire class suffered humiliation and consequences as a result of the actions committed by these undisciplined classmates.

When I heard about these issues in his phone calls home, I was upset. But my husband had been a military officer, and he had told me many stories of his boot-camp experiences in the naval reserve. His class exasperated their chief because their undesirable attitudes caused them to flunk tests and not pass inspections. So when I tearfully expressed my worries about Norman Jr., my husband smiled and assured me he would be okay and nobody would harm him.

He was right. Our son got through the bad experiences and graduated.

Despite his rough introduction into military life, Norman Jr. finished NROTC in college. After some extra stateside training he joined his ship in the Persian Gulf. He missed the battles there, but his ship was in the Persian Gulf several months during Desert Storm.

A few years later he was called back for a year of active duty because of the Iraq War. Many times he wanted to quit the naval reserves, but like many young men today, he felt an obligation to serve in spite of the hardships. He became a commander in the naval reserves, and recently retired after completing twenty-three years of service.

None of this would have happened without his learning to accept incidents such as being awakened by a garbage can hitting bunk beds. Receiving harsh treatment and learning how to handle ridicule helped him develop the disciplines that were important for his welfare. He refused to be unduly influenced by his harrowing boot-camp experiences as a teenager because he wanted to follow in his father's footsteps.

When Norman Jr. gave his retirement speech from the Navy, he honored those who had served with him, and he honored his step-dad, Andy, for his service in World War II. He honored his father by developing the persevering spirit that helped him succeed as a military man.

After his dad died while he was still in college, he had only me to lean on. Years later, as we laughed about my tears through all of his hardships, he said, "Mom, you always were my bleeding heart." Even though it might be comforting to have a bleeding-heart mama, it is imperative that children be taught how to persevere with honor and dignity while they learn how to stand on their own two feet.

David Expected Great Things of Himself

When I think of someone trying to accomplish something that he is expecting of himself and God, I am reminded of David when he fought the Philistine giant as a youth. David was a shepherd boy, but his father occasionally sent him to take supplies to his brothers, who were fighting the Philistines with King Saul. One of these times, as David reached the camp, he heard about Goliath and his challenge to fight any soldier of the Israelite army. Without hesitation, David volunteered to kill the giant. Since God had helped David kill a lion and a bear, he expected to kill the giant with the Lord's help too. However, the soldiers and his brothers laughed at him.

With confidence and great expectations, David informed the giant that the Lord would deliver him into his hand. He told Goliath that he would strike him and take his head from him. He added that he would give the uncircumcised carcasses of the Philistine camp to the birds and wild beasts, for they dared to defy the armies of the living God. He told Goliath that the battle belonged to the Lord, and all the earth would know that there was a God in Israel.

David killed the giant with a sling and a stone, and the other Philistines fled, with the Israelites in hot pursuit. (See 1 Samuel 17.)

Eventually, God promoted David to become the second king of Israel, and Jesus came through David's lineage.

Expecting to accomplish something through God and ourselves will bring us great rewards on earth and in heaven.

Chapter 56

Persevering in Small Things

The first step in learning to persevere is to expect to accomplish the task at hand. We must not become overwhelmed by seemingly impossible projects.

In 1983, when the Lord gave me the ten disciplines in this book, I couldn't see myself writing a book on these subjects, even though I'd studied them for my own growth for three years. As time has gone by, I have come to see that a continual commitment is required for each discipline. We never arrive, but must consider each responsibility one day at a time, sometimes one hour or one minute at a time.

Think Small When Things Look Gloomy

When my husband Norman was ill with an incurable lung disease, he wanted to take a trip to Brownsville, Texas, where we had been stationed when we were young. During that time of reliving the past, I became distraught as I thought of the troubled years that lay ahead of us. One night, as I tossed and turned on my bed in Brownsville, the Lord spoke to my spirit and said, *Think small.* At the time I was confused by His remark. Nevertheless, like the mother of Jesus, I pondered the message in my heart (Luke 2:19). After some contemplation, I realized that the Lord wanted me to think about daily activities and not become overwhelmed by tomorrow's problems.

Don't Despise Small Beginnings

Months later, I came across the following Scripture that the Lord spoke to Zechariah:

> The hands of Zerubbabel have laid the foundation of this house; his hands shall also finish it; and thou shalt know that the Lord of hosts hath sent me unto you. For who hath despised the day of small things? for they shall rejoice, and shall see the plummet in the hand of Zerubbabel with those seven; they are the eyes of the Lord, which run to and fro through the whole earth. (Zachariah 4:9—10 KJV)

When the temple and the city of Jerusalem were destroyed, the Israelites were carried into captivity to the Babylonian Empire, where they remained servants for seventy years according to the prophecy given to Jeremiah by the Lord. Most of the temple treasures were carried to the palace of the king in Babylon (2 Chronicles 36:13—23).

Persia overthrew the king of Babylon in 539 BC. In the first year of the reign of King Cyrus of Persia, the Lord stirred up the king's spirit to command that the temple in Jerusalem be rebuilt. The king also commanded that the articles of silver and gold that the Babylonians had taken from the destroyed temple should be returned to Jerusalem and used in the new temple.

God chose Zerubbabel to oversee the rebuilding of the temple. Before he began work on the temple, Zerubbabel restored the altar and reinstated the religious feasts.

After construction on the temple was started, opposition by certain people around Jerusalem caused the work on the temple to stop for fourteen years. When King Darius discovered the decree written by King Cyrus that commanded financial help in rebuilding and restoring all things in the temple, Zerubbabel was allowed to finish the temple (Ezra 1:6–11).

The building of the temple may have been a small thing to the pagan Jews, but the eyes of the Lord were upon the project.

Rebuilding the temple was the first step in getting His people back to worshipping Him. The Jewish people had been in a pagan environment long enough to worship pagan gods, marry pagan women, and beget pagan children. Only after the temple was restored and the new wall built around Jerusalem did the Jews truly desire to return to the one true God.

The jobs undertaken by prophets like Ezra, Nehemiah, Haggai, and Zechariah were for a specific reason: to get the people to return to God. However, it took years of hard work, prayer, and many tears before the people responded and the temple and the wall of protection around the city of Jerusalem were finished.

Even though the people were finally cured of idolatry, their spiritual progress was greatly hampered because of sin, corruption among the priests, cheating on tithes, developing legalistic rituals, and an insensitivity to the ways of God. After the prophecies of Malachi, the people experienced four hundred years of prophetic silence, and they continued to live under their own legalistic bondage until Jesus came on the scene.

Mothers and fathers know that the parental tasks they perform are for the benefit of the whole family as well as for the next generation. When we see our children grown up and have children of their own, we know we have produced fruit for the kingdom of God. Our main goal in raising a family is to see our children serve the Lord. We must not become dismayed at the many tasks we have to finish before we can enjoy the fruits of our labor. God wants us to "think small," because the duties that lie ahead can seem overwhelming if we look too far down the road.

Psalm 34:15 says, "The eyes of the Lord are on the righteous, and His ears are open to their cry." Verse17 says, "The righteous cry out, and the Lord hears, and delivers them out of all their troubles."

God does not despise the day of small things. His eyes are on our everyday activities. He is not impressed with religious rituals or church attendance. His desire is that we walk in His will and His way. In order to persevere in His disciplines, we must continue to pray and live according to His Word, regardless of circumstances.

Chapter 57

Laughter

Once we have learned the discipline of perseverance, we can discover how to enjoy ourselves as we continue down the road of life.

Let Your Tickle Spot Prevail

Have you ever noticed how easy it is to make a child laugh? One way you can get a child's attention when he is crying or acting out bad behavior is to find his tickle spot. It might be a rib or a foot or the back of his neck. Usually you can get him started laughing while searching for his tickle spot. This little endeavor lets good humor prevail and diminishes his and your problems for a while.

I remember playing the tickle game with my siblings and girlfriends. The goal was to pretend we didn't have a tickle spot so we wouldn't have to laugh. With young children, especially girls, trying to hide the tickle spot is an act of perseverance because young girls love to giggle. Yet we persevered until the tickle spot was found and the game ended with peals of laughter.

Laughter is the most healing and rewarding activity that God has given to mankind. God Himself has a great sense of humor. He is not a God of stern commands, as some people have portrayed Him to be. He knows that a merry heart will help us persevere in all kinds of problems, so He enjoys making His people laugh.

Let the Holy Spirit Tickle You

After my husband Norman died, I was planning my first trip home to see my mother and father for my mother's birthday. I woke up in the middle of the night, and as I lay there in a sleepless state, I spoke to God about my fears. I reminded Him of the storm of heavy ice and snow that had blanketed the Missouri highways. I lamented that it would be dark by the time I made the two-hundred-plus-mile trip, and that I had no "backup."

Since we had lived a military life, I had taken many trips alone or with the children. However, I always knew my husband would be on the other end of a telephone to give me instructions for any dilemma I might face.

Suddenly, in spite of my tears and conjured up "maybes," the Holy Spirit got my attention by asking me questions.

Who gave Norman to you?

"You did."

Who's your source?

"You are."

In His gentle voice, He said, *If I am your Source, I can be your backup as well. Even though Norman is with Us now, We will find someone else to help you. So just let Us know what you need. You can call Us "Twinkle Toes."*

When He used the expression "Twinkle Toes," I imagined God, Jesus, and the Holy Spirit, with my husband in tow, scurrying around in heaven and saying to one another, "Now what does she want?" With that image in my mind, I burst out with tears of laughter instead of tears of self-pity and was able to go back to sleep.

Persevering Over Fear with Godly Laughter

As I expected, the drive to my parents' house was hazardous. I spent the last hour of my trip driving in snow-flurried darkness on a two-lane highway, but I had another car in front of me most of the way to help illuminate the road. I felt as if God had placed that car on the highway to help me see and to keep me from feeling isolated.

When I reached my parents' home, I saw the hill their house was on covered with snow and ice. I parked the car at the top of the hill, got out, and made it to their front door by slipping, sliding, and crawling. When I told my dad where I had left the car, he told me that nobody had been up or down that hill all day.

I didn't want to leave the car in the road at the top of the hill all night. Even though I was afraid I couldn't make a left turn into their driveway and might end up in the deep ditch that bordered each side of the drive, I told my dad I wanted to make the effort.

In spite of my feelings of agitation and trepidation about the ice-covered street and ditch, I began my slippery ascent back up the hill, crawling on my hands and knees most of the time. I stayed in the ditch as much as possible, because the leaves kept the ice from being as slippery. When I reached the car I prayed for a while, then smiled when I thought that help would surely come from "Twinkle Toes" when they saw my predicament.

Remembering what I had learned about ice- and snow-covered hills when I was living in New York and Alaska many years before, I turned the key, put the gear in neutral, and allowed the car to creep down the hill on its own momentum, without touching the gas pedal. Occasionally I tapped the brakes to control the speed. (I knew from experience that braking a car too hard on ice would cause the car to slide sideways.) I slowly turned into the driveway. I had to shift into low gear, accelerate enough to pull the car up the gradual incline, and park without hitting the house or sliding off the driveway into a tree.

My eighty-seven-year-old dad stood on the porch like a sentinel, watching my efforts, knowing he couldn't do anything to help. After we entered the house, and both breathed a sigh of relief, I gave my mom a big hug. I laughed at the distraught look on my dad's face.

Later, as I relived the drama, I realized that expecting myself to make it and thinking only of each immediate problem made the scenario a success.

When I snuggled up safely in a warm bed that night, I smiled as I gave "Twinkle Toes" my thanks and blew them a kiss that I am sure traveled all the way to heaven. After all, it was God's good humor that got me through that day!

Godly Laughter Helps the Psyche

Not all laughter is of God. Malicious humor is detrimental to a person's psyche or well-being. Such teasing can affect the overall health of an individual, whether a child, teenager, or adult. This kind of humor has caused a lot of tragedies, especially in schools. Hurt feelings from improper humor can run so deep in a teenager or child that he remembers the pain for the rest of his life. Adolescents tend to be especially vulnerable to ridicule because those are the years when they are trying to establish themselves as adults. Any negative laughter or criticism can decelerate the normal growth process.

Proper amusement has to be humor that all the participating parties enjoy, not choosing one person or group for malevolent buffoonery. Those who enjoy making others squirm with their jokes, or criticisms in the form of jokes, may be involved in pride. Some people feel better about themselves if they can find a scapegoat to ridicule; therefore, they vent their frustrations on helpless victims who are more fragile than they are. This form of humor is not to be exercised by followers of Christ. Laughter should help cure, not kill.

Chapter 58

Faith and Endurance

God wants us to be faithful in the simple things of life, but He also wants us to walk in His disciplines so that He can bless us. As we strive to walk in godliness, we need to remember how much He loves us. Our righteousness with God comes through the blood of Jesus, not how well we persevere in anything.

Heroes of Faith Persevere

Lest we forget what it was like for those who have traveled before us, we have the "Hall of Faith" in Hebrews 11 to remind us of true godliness and faithfulness.

Our first example of Old Testament righteousness is Abel, Adam and Eve's son. He offered up a more excellent sacrifice to God than his brother Cain did. However, Cain's jealousy caused him to murder his brother.

Next we find Enoch, a man who was perfect in his walk with God, so God transported him to heaven without him enduring a physical death.

Abraham, the father of our faith, offered up his son as a sacrifice, knowing that God was able to raise him from the dead. Because of Abraham's faith we can receive all of God's promises through the seed of Abraham's son Isaac.

When the men of Israel went to Jericho to spy out the land, a harlot named Rahab hid them from the king. By faith, Rahab believed that the God of Israel, who had delivered the Israelites from the Red Sea and the Egyptian soldiers, would give them

Jericho too. Consequently, she and her family did not perish when the city fell. God rewarded Rahab with her family's deliverance from slavery or death, and she became the mother of Boaz, who married Ruth and begot Obed, who begot Jesse, and Jesse begot David, through whose lineage Jesus was born. Rahab's faith and her small deed put her in line to be one of the ancestors of Jesus Christ.

Numerous other faith-filled men—like Gideon, Baruck, Samson, Jephthah, Samuel, David and the many prophets who subdued kingdoms, worked righteousness, obtained promises, stopped the mouth of lions, quenched the violence of fire, and escaped the edge of the sword—were made strong out of weakness and became valiant in battle. Many were tortured, scourged, imprisoned, stoned, and slain (Hebrews 11:31–37). The people mentioned in Hebrews 11 persevered in godly righteousness through their faith.

Simon Peter, the apostle of Christ, tells us that we have obtained faith like those mentioned in Hebrews 11 through the righteousness of God and Jesus Christ. We have been given Christ's divine nature so we can escape the corruption that is in this world. Peter says, "But also for this very reason, giving all diligence, add to your faith virtue, to virtue knowledge, to knowledge self-control, to self-control perseverance, to perseverance godliness, to godliness brotherly kindness, and to brotherly kindness love" (2 Peter 1:5–7).

Peter tells us that if we do these things we will be neither barren nor unfruitful in the knowledge of our Lord Jesus Christ, for we will be abundantly supplied with everything we need to keep us from stumbling.

Persevering in Unrighteous Behavior Brings Judgment

If we don't walk in God's disciplines, we will be shortsighted even unto blindness (2 Peter 1:9). Peter warns us not to turn away from God's righteousness once we have accepted it. That would be like a dog returning to its vomit or a sow returning to wallowing in the mire (2 Peter 2:20–22).

Jerusalem and Judah exhibited that kind of behavior; therefore, God brought His judgment on them. He said that when a land sins against Him by being unfaithful, as Judah had done, He would stretch out His Hand against it. He will remove its supply of bread, send famine on it, and cut off man and beast from it. Even though Noah, Daniel, and Job were in lands corrupted by sin, they delivered themselves by their righteousness.

God went on to say that if wild beasts passed through the land and emptied it and made it desolate, or if a sword went through the land and cut off both man and beast, even if Noah, Daniel, or Job were in it, they alone would be delivered. He would not save their sons or daughters, and the land would be desolate. If He sent a pestilence on the land and poured out His fury in blood, they could not save their sons and daughters; their righteousness would deliver them alone. (See Ezekiel 14:12–23.)

What made these three men so special in God's eyes? They habitually walked in righteousness and godliness despite all obstacles, persecution, and the ungodliness that surrounded them.

Noah was the only godly man left in his day. When the Lord saw the wickedness of the people on earth, and that their thoughts were evil continually, He was sorry He had made them. (See Genesis 6:1–8.)

Noah found grace in God's eyes because he was a just man and perfect in his generation, and he walked with God. So God told him to build an ark. Noah tried to talk to the people about getting on the ark for salvation, but only eight family members were on the survival list. Noah, his wife, his three sons, and their wives did as God commanded; they entered the ark and were saved from the flood that covered the earth (Genesis 6–7).

Even though God let Noah and his family replenish the earth after the flood, He became so angry with the Israelites that if Noah had been on the earth during that time, God would not have saved his family.

As ungodly as the world is today, we cannot imagine how Noah was able to walk in God's righteousness by himself. Apparently, his family was not that righteous. Yet God had a purpose for their lives: they were to replenish the earth.

That is why we can be sure that our children can be saved today. Even if our right standing with God is not causing them to take a stand for righteousness, and they appear to be more interested in worldliness, we can claim the promise that was made to the Israelites: "I will contend with him who contends with you, and I will save your children. . . . All flesh shall know that I, the Lord, am your Savior, and your Redeemer, the Mighty One of Jacob" (Isaiah 49:25–26).

Persevering in Righteousness Brings Rewards

After God had enough of Judah's wicked ways and Jerusalem fell, most of the people were sent into captivity to Babylon. The king of Babylon wanted some healthy, good-looking young men full of wisdom to serve him in his palace, and Daniel and three of his friends were among those chosen. The youths were expected to eat the sumptuous fare from the king's table. This might seem like a small thing, but God does not despise the small things.

Daniel convinced the chief eunuch that he and his friends could stay healthy with vegetables and water. Even though Daniel and his friends maintained their Jewish traditions, they were promoted to excellent positions in the Babylonian Empire.

However, their desire to remain true to God caused them some difficulties. When Daniel's three friends refused to bow to Nebuchadnezzar, they were thrown into a fiery furnace. But God delivered them.

Daniel was cast into the lions' den for praying to God on his knees three times every day in front of an open window. King Darius had been tricked into making a decree that no one could bow to any god or man except him for thirty days. Darius was greatly relieved when God did not allow the lions to harm Daniel. After Daniel's miraculous protection, King Darius decreed that in every dominion of his kingdom men must tremble before the God of Daniel. He stated that Daniel's God is a living God who delivers, rescues, works signs and wonders on earth and in heaven, and was able to deliver Daniel from the power of the lions (Daniel 6:25–27).

Daniel prospered under Darius and under the reign of Cyrus, the Persian. More important, Daniel became a mighty prophet for God. The book of Daniel is the story of a young man thrown into slavery and ungodliness, but who maintained an outstanding relationship with God through it all.

Job Represents the Ultimate in Perseverance

When we think of a man with many problems, most Christians consider Job. Satan was so jealous of Job's righteousness that God allowed him to persecute Job to prove that there was no one like Job on the earth, a blameless and upright man who feared God and shunned evil (Job 1:8).

Job's children, servants, and all of his livestock were killed. After these calamities Job gave his famous speech: "Naked I came from my mother's womb, and naked shall I return there. The Lord gave, and the Lord has taken away; blessed be the name of the Lord" (Job 1:21). During this time Job did not sin or curse God.

Next Satan was allowed to smite Job's body with horrible boils. Still Job refused to curse God. Instead he said, "He knows the way that I take; when He has tested me, I shall come forth as gold" (Job 23:10).

To make matters worse, Job had to listen to his friends' accusations about why he was being tested.

After Job had gone through all the trials and tribulations caused by Satan and his friends, God blessed the latter days of Job's life more than the beginning. He was given more livestock and servants than he had before. He had three beautiful daughters and seven sons. Job never ventured away from godly behavior, and he was able to enjoy his children and grandchildren for four generations, dying at a ripe old age (Job 42:12–17).

Righteous Perseverance Brings God's Mercy and Grace

Even though God hates unrighteousness and wickedness, He is a God of mercy and justice for people who are willing to change their ways. Proverbs 14:34 says, "Righteousness exalts a nation, but sin is a reproach to any people."

God promised restoration to the nation of Israel after they were exiled into captivity. He said, "I will betroth you to Me forever; yes, I will betroth you to Me in righteousness and justice, in lovingkindness and mercy" (Hosea 2:19).

Hosea 14:9 says, "Who is wise? Let him understand these things. Who is prudent? Let him know them. For the ways of the Lord are right; the righteous walk in them, but transgressors stumble in them."

When we realize what Noah, Daniel, and Job went through to walk in the righteousness of God, we realize why He chose them as examples of righteous people. These three men stood alone in their faith and trust in God regardless of severe misfortunes and hazards. They ran the race of life with godly endurance.

Jesus Persevered in Enduring the Race

Regardless of what we have to endure on this earth, we should remember Jesus. "Consider Him who endured such hostility from sinners against Himself, lest you become weary and discouraged in your souls. You have not resisted to bloodshed, striving against sin" (Hebrews 12:3–4).

Jesus started out life in a small way. When he was twelve years old, His parents took Him to Jerusalem for the feast of the Passover, as they had done every year. When they left to go home, Mary and Joseph traveled a day's journey, thinking He was with some relatives, but Jesus had lingered behind in Jerusalem.

During the three days it took for them to find Him, He sat in the midst of teachers in the temple, both listening and asking questions of them, and they were astonished at His understanding and answers (Luke 2:41–48).

When His anxious parents found Him, Jesus said, "Why did you seek Me? Did you not know that I must be about My Father's business?" (Luke 2:49).

Although His parents did not understand Jesus, His mother kept all His sayings in her heart, and Jesus continued to grow in favor with men and God daily (Luke 2:51–52).

When John the Baptist was baptizing people in the Jordan River for the remission of sin, Jesus went there to fulfill the Scriptures and be baptized by John. After that He went into the wilderness and spent forty days fasting. Satan was allowed to torment Him, but Jesus used the Word of God every time Satan tried to tempt Him to accept his earthly kingdom and reject God's kingdom.

In spite of the weakened condition Jesus was in, He prefaced His answers to Satan with "It is written," then He gave Satan the Word of God. (See Matthew 4:1–11.) By so doing, He endured all attempts by Satan to lure Him away from God the Father. When the testing ordeal was over, the angels brought food to Jesus and ministered to Him. It was only the beginning of His many trials and tests of endurance.

Jesus Persevered in Teaching

After His forty days in the mountains fasting and praying to strengthen Himself spiritually for the ordeals of His ministry, Jesus began His mission of teaching and performing miracles. He taught about the kingdom of God in parables to the multitude and to His disciples. He warned them of the cost of discipleship and what it meant to be a faithful steward. He said:

> I came to send fire on the earth, and how I wish it were already kindled! But I have a baptism to be baptized with, and how distressed I am till it is accomplished! Do you suppose

that I came to give peace on earth? I tell you, not at all, but rather division. (Luke 12:49–51)

One day, as He and His disciples were traveling down the road near Caesarea Philippi, Jesus told His disciples that He would have to suffer a lot of things, be rejected by the elders and scribes, and be killed, but that He would rise again in three days. Peter took Him aside and rebuked Him. But Jesus rebuked Peter, saying, "Get behind Me, Satan! For you are not mindful of the things of God, but the things of men" (Mark 8:33).

After this bout with Peter, Jesus called the people and His disciples together and talked about the cost of discipleship. He informed them that whoever wanted to follow Him must take up his cross and deny himself, and that whoever desired to save his life would lose it, but those who lost their lives for the gospel's sake would save their lives.

He asked them to think about what it meant to gain the whole world but lose their soul. He told the people that whoever was ashamed of Him and His words here on earth would cause Him to be ashamed of them when He came back in the glory of His Father with the angels (Mark 8:34–38). Jesus said that "a disciple is not above his teacher, but everyone who is perfectly trained will be like his teacher" (Luke 6:40).

The Holy Spirit Helps the Least Persevere Over the Greatest

Regardless of our trials on earth, Jesus went before us to make the way easier and to help us enter into His Father's kingdom, just as John the Baptist went before Jesus. John said, "This is He of whom I said, 'After me comes a Man who is preferred before me, for He was before me'" (John 1:30). John the Baptist told his disciples that he came to bear witness of Christ and said, "He must increase, but I must decrease" (John 3:30).

Jesus said John was a bright and shining lamp. "But I have a greater witness than John's; for the works which the Father has given Me to finish—the very works that I do—bear witness of Me, that the Father has sent Me" (John 5:36).

John was beheaded because of his teachings, and Jesus was crucified because He brought the word to us from His Father. Jesus said He spoke only on the authority and command of God. "And I know that His command is everlasting life. Therefore, whatever I speak, just as the Father has told Me, so I speak" (John 12:50).

John the Baptist endured the race set before him by preparing the way for Jesus. However, Jesus said, "Among those born of women there is not a greater prophet than John the Baptist; but he who is least in the kingdom of God is greater than he" (Luke 7:28).

Why would Jesus say that the least Christian was greater than John the Baptist in the kingdom of God? Because the Holy Spirit could not come into the spirits of men until after Jesus was resurrected.

Jesus appeared in a natural body to His disciples after His death. They were able to touch Him, and He ate fish and honeycomb in their presence to let them know that He was alive. He talked to them about the Law of Moses, the Prophets, and the Psalms concerning Him. He told them that He had to suffer and die for them so that men could have repentance and remission of sins.

Then He said, "Behold, I send the Promise of My Father upon you; but tarry in the city of Jerusalem until you are endued with power from on high" (Luke 24:49). Later, Jesus said, "John truly baptized with water, but you shall be baptized with the Holy Spirit not many days from now" (Acts 1:5). He went on to say that they would receive power through the Holy Spirit so they could be His witnesses to the end of the earth (Acts 1:8).

The Holy Spirit lives in us, comforts us, reminds us of Jesus, and gives us the unspeakable joy that Jesus left for us. Peter said to the people, "Repent, and let every one of you be baptized in the name of Jesus Christ for the remission of sins; and you shall receive the gift of the Holy Spirit" (Acts 2:38). When the storms of life beset us, we have power through the Holy Spirit to persevere and endure each trial as we walk in the way, keeping our eyes on Jesus, the Author and Finisher of our faith.

Testing of Faith Requires Perseverance

After Jesus' death on the cross, the disciples learned what it meant to run the race with perseverance as they struggled to teach people the disciplines of righteousness that Jesus had taught them. The Pharisees and Sadducees wanted people to live by the old laws, rules, and regulations, and many Jews wanted to continue in the old religious ways, even when trying to accept the blood of Jesus for their sins.

Christ's disciples were persecuted, but they endured with perseverance, even unto death. Later they had help from the apostle Paul, who had been a Pharisee named Saul. For months he had persecuted those who followed Jesus, even putting some into prison. Then one day, on the road to Damascus, he was blinded by a light and heard a voice saying, "Saul, Saul, why are you persecuting Me?'

And he said, "Who are You, Lord?"

And the Lord said, "I am Jesus, whom you are persecuting." (See Acts 9:4–5.)

Regardless of Paul's persistence in denying Christ, God chose him to bring the Word of God to the world. After Paul received Jesus as his Savior, power from the Holy Spirit made him one of the greatest of all men, and God used his intellect and persevering nature mightily. Paul did most of his work among the Gentiles.

No man suffered more or was persecuted more for the kingdom of God than Paul, yet he exhorts us by saying:

"I am persuaded that neither death nor life, nor angels nor principalities nor powers, nor things present nor things to come, nor height nor depth, nor any other created thing, shall be able to separate us from the love of God which is in Christ Jesus our Lord" (Romans 8:38–39).

Wherever we are on the road of life, Paul can be a powerful witness for us in finishing the race that is set before us, regardless of the cost. And there will be cost, as Paul reminds us:

As it is written: "Behold, I lay in Zion a stumbling stone and rock of offense, and whoever believes on Him will not be put to shame" (Romans 9:33).

If we continue to endure the race set before us, we will not be put to shame, regardless of how many times we stumble or fail. That is a wonderful promise.

However, Peter warns us not to suffer shame as evildoers: "If anyone suffers as a Christian, let him not be ashamed, but let him glorify God in this matter" (1 Peter 4:16).

As we continue in the footsteps of the great cloud of witnesses who ran the race with endurance before us, including the greatest witness of all, our Savior, Jesus Christ, we should be proud of our legacy, never ashamed of our inheritance.

Chapter 59

Plodding Through the Valleys

Life is like a rose garden, full of beauty but plagued with thorns. However, the thorn plays a special part in the development of a rose, just as tribulation can play a special part in developing perseverance and a beautiful character.

When roses are afflicted by various diseases and insects, they lose their luster. They will become blighted flowers unless they receive attention from someone who knows how to help them maintain their God-given beauty. Roses require special nutrition and sprays that will kill insects. Without that attention, a rose garden will not produce beautiful blossoms.

The Valley of Tribulation

People sometimes develop angry, resentful personalities that make them blighted or unattractive. Instead of being beautiful roses in God's garden, they allow sorrow and suffering to wither their souls. Yet Paul reminds us that there is Someone who knows what we need.

> We also glory in tribulations, knowing that tribulation produces perseverance; and perseverance, character; and character, hope. Now hope does not disappoint, because the love of God has been poured out in our hearts by the Holy Spirit who was given to us. (Romans 5:3–5)

Paul tells us that regardless of any charge against us, Christians are God's elect people, and we are justified by Christ, who died for us. In Romans 8:35 he says, "Who shall separate us from the love of Christ? Shall tribulation, or distress, or persecution, or famine, or nakedness, or peril, or sword?"

As we persevere in God's disciplines, they will build godly character that will produce hope. Paul says, "If we hope for what we do not see, we eagerly wait for it with perseverance" (Romans 8:25).

If we don't persevere in God's disciplines, we cannot build character that will produce hope. An undisciplined spirit is weak because hope is deferred. As long as we have hope before us, we can accomplish our goals.

The Valley of Change

I believe the greatest discipline problem that most Christians face today is not a specific sin, but our inability to make lifestyle changes that would benefit our health.

Personally, I find it much easier to part with my money and give tithes and love offerings than to change my lifestyle for healthier living. God gave me these ten disciplines in 1983, but I still find myself floundering when it comes to changing my eating habits. Yet I still have hope that I will eventually do the things that I know I should do.

Many Christians struggle with the issue of good health and end up dealing with cancer, heart disease, diabetes, and other problems, even though lifestyle changes can bring healing to the bodies of those suffering with such afflictions.

When God started talking to me about good health, His first remark was "Drink plenty of water." The next thing He said was that He did not want me to drink another Diet Coke as long as I lived. That was a real shocker because I disliked the taste of tap water and I had begun to use Diet Coke as my main intake of fluid. So I bought a water purifier to use in St. Louis and drank bottled water after I moved to California.

Diet Coke now tastes worse to me than tap water. I persist in trying to drink more water, though I vacillate in that endeavor, and

I still occasionally drink a regular Coke. Yet I am persevering in working on other areas of health now that I have learned so much about alternative medicine, exercise, and good eating habits.

Shortly after my husband Norman died, I came down with the flu and a sinus infection. In my misery, I cried out to the Lord, saying that I was sorry I couldn't stay healthy the way I felt I should be able to. His response was *You're doing better.*

"But I still flunk."

But you're flunking better.

No one but the Lord would ever encourage someone by saying she is "flunking better." However, God was reminding me of an episode in my husband's life that had happened years before, when he was in engineering school. The entire class was having trouble with a subject, as well as with the teacher, who spoke with a thick accent. The professor would tell them they were doing better, but they still flunked. I always enjoyed the way my husband told the story, imitating the professor's accent.

The Lord got me to laugh instead of feeling sorry for myself.

Even in failures, God is concerned with perseverance.

The Valley of Failure

One day, as I was sitting in a class at church listening to various conversations, I heard this message in my spirit: *To fail is to succeed.* When I ran that by my husband and a few other people, they pointed out that failure could not be taken as success.

Nevertheless, that is exactly how we succeed—when we keep trying regardless of how many times we fail. Then one day we will achieve the goals we want. We persevere and run the race regardless of the odds against us. We might keep flunking better indefinitely in some cases; in others, success comes more easily, without so much failing.

Both Christians and non-Christians fail to look after their bodies properly. They eat unhealthy food, maintain high stress levels, and still expect to lose weight. Diets to lose weight don't work. A lifestyle change is required before weight control can be accomplished or certain diseases prevented.

A changed character recognizes the importance of hope and does not give in to despair. The Word promises us that a person who preserves in godly discipline will succeed in changing his or her character.

Regardless of the success or failure in making changes in our lives here on earth, our goal as Christians is to spend eternity with our heavenly Father. Jesus, through His blood, has already paid the final price for our mistakes.

The Valley of Poor Health

I can't think of anything more debilitating to the human spirit than mental or physical ill health. We can be financially poor, but if our health is good, we can still be happy. We can enjoy the simple pleasures of life, such as a beautiful sunset, snow on the mountains, the wild waves of the ocean—all of God's creation— plus the innumerable pleasures of happy relationships with our loved ones. If we are wealthy but plagued with illness, we cannot enjoy the things that wealth can buy.

So why do we pursue things that produce bad health, like eating and drinking things that are not appropriate for good health, or stressing ourselves out with worldliness in the search for material possessions and pleasures? I believe the answer is that we are not properly connected to our loving Father. We haven't really understood the power that lies within us to change into the image of Jesus Christ.

If the ten disciplines in this book are followed, God will bless us with good health, loving relationships, and the abundant finances that will bring us happiness here on earth.

Sickness, disease, and death are a reality of life here on earth. They originate from Satan, the god of this world. Nevertheless, if we turn to God, He will help us develop the perseverance we need for our health issues, then sustain us as we persevere in helping a loved one through an illness or death.

Many years ago, when I was praying for a miracle in a certain situation, the Lord said, *Perseverance is the greatest miracle you can have.*

We must learn to persevere in the new covenant with God that helps us deal with illness. We have to abide by God's Word to help us deal with stress, and we must persevere in good health habits to keep from inflicting ourselves with disease.

The Valley of Caregiving

My second husband, Andy, has been ill with heart trouble for years. He also has a severe hearing loss and is considered legally blind. Even though he can see to get around, he hasn't been able to drive a car for ten years. He has to use a walker because he has developed Parkinson's disease. To make matters worse, he has an early case of Alzheimer's. Yet he is one of the most persevering people I have ever known.

Driving was Andy's first love; next was walking. For twenty years, he walked as a form of exercise. When driving was taken from him, he walked even more. During the last two years, he has shuffled around the sidewalks in our neighborhood shopping center with his walker, moving like a turtle. He can't manage a wheelchair because of his mental and physical disabilities. Still, he persists in his goal to walk a little each day if his health permits. The people who notice his daily efforts are encouraged by his tenacity.

Andy's health problems have increased in severity since I started writing this book, and my own health has suffered too. He spent six months in a nursing home for Parkinson's and Alzheimer's, but by God's grace, his mental and physical condition improved enough for us to bring him home. There have been months when I haven't touched my writing. Through all this, the Holy Spirit has patiently stood by in His role as Comforter.

I want to be able to persevere as a caregiver. The wisdom that God imparts to me gives me confidence that He will perfect that which He has called me to do. I want to be like Job and come forth like gold when all of life's testing is over.

After Satan had taken Job's children and wealth, he felt sure ill health would make Job blame God. He said to the Lord, "Stretch our Your hand now, and touch his bone and his flesh, and he will surely curse You to Your face!" (Job 2:5). Job's greatest miracle was his ability to persevere. "In all this Job did not sin with his lips" (Job 2:10).

Sinning with our words is one of the major problems facing God's children. When Satan puts negative thoughts in our heads, they materialize into negative words that come out of our mouths when we least expect them to.

The Valley of Procrastination

God is our supreme example of perseverance as we read about how He dealt with people throughout the Old Testament. Now, however, God allows the Holy Spirit to do the work. The Spirit perseveres with Christians the way God did before He sent His Son to die for the sins of humankind.

The Holy Spirit has waited twenty-six years for me to come to grips with His ten disciplines and put them in a book. I have used everything at my disposal to procrastinate in the jobs set before me, including ill health, death, remarriage, children, worldliness, rebellion, busyness, and just plain old laziness. Yet God's timing is always perfect. I know that each trial Andy and I go through, or watch as our children endure, produces a steady heartbeat of faith in both of us. We have a great number of family members to stand in the gap for, and we cannot afford to be procrastinators in that area.

When we use God's Word, we can crush the head of the serpent, who is our enemy. He comes as a thief in the night, sneaking in like a mouse to defile our spiritual houses. But all things are possible with God.

The Valley of Menial Tasks

After having some bad days with Andy, I cried out in frustration to the Lord that I hadn't done anything but wait on people all my life. He gently informed me that when I was waiting on people, I was waiting on Him.

No mother ever thinks that all the long hours she spends doing things for her family are being noticed by anyone. However, her rewards are greater than she could ever imagine, because she is continually waiting on the Lord.

The Lord notices everything, even changing diapers, picking up dog poop, helping children with homework, and the endless chores it takes to keep a family clean, healthy, and happy. He also watches the struggles a father has in supporting his family. The Word tells us to do all things from the heart, "with goodwill doing service, as to the Lord, and not to men, knowing that whatever good anyone does, he will receive the same from the Lord, whether he is a slave or free" (Ephesians 6:7–8).

Paul says, "Whether you eat or drink, or whatever you do, do all to the glory of God" (1 Corinthians 10:31).

The accolades we receive from people will not necessarily bring us accolades in heaven. A slave can receive more rewards from God than his master does because God rewards menial tasks, though the world rewards fame and accomplishments.

When my mother used to complain that she had not done anything special in her life, I told her what a wonderful person she was, that she had done a good job of taking care of her eight children. After her children were grown, she finally had the time to work on the arts and crafts that she loved. She also taught Sunday school to a youth group for many years.

I wish I had been able to comfort her with the wisdom the Lord gave me about the many rewards she had earned while waiting on Him. But now she has more stars in her crown than she ever dreamed of. Praise the Lord! His ways and His thoughts are far above anything that we could dream up in trying to obtain rewards for our work.

Mothers and fathers have to perform endless menial tasks in raising their children. They also endure many heartaches. But the valleys we find ourselves in as we deal with our children's problems bring us closer to Jesus. He will help us contend with Satan and save our children (Isaiah 49:25).

The Valley of Loneliness

During a Christian Women's Fellowship meeting, I heard a testimony from a lady who had been married three times, and all three of her husbands had died from different causes. She shared in her talk how she had dealt with the heartbreaking experiences of death. After the meeting, an angry lady came up to her, saying she didn't think the speaker had much to complain about since she had been given three husbands in her lifetime.

The lady from the audience shared that she had spent her life alone, with no one to share her joys or sorrows with. She had allowed her loneliness to affect her in a way that made her miserable and angry at the world. She didn't understand how death affects those who are close to it. When a loved one dies it feels like a piece of us died with them. No other human being can fill that void; we must allow Jesus to fill that empty spot in our souls.

Nevertheless, a lonely person does have a unique problem, because all people need love and attention from others. A person who lives alone may look at the future as a barren desert, filled with bleakness and desolation and lifelessness.

However, if you walk through a desert, you will see plenty of life there. God created special creatures that love the desert and beautiful flowers that thrive in the arid climate. Like everything else God created, there is both beauty and ugliness in the desert. It's up to us to seek the beauty among the ugliness.

If lonely people look for the beauty around them, they will find that a good life exists for them, even if they remain single. They must draw close to God in complete abandonment on His mercy and love. No human relationship can compare to being totally surrendered to God, waiting on Him to take you to a higher level in your growth as a Christian.

The apostle Paul spent much of his time in the valley of loneliness, yet his experiences with the Lord revealed his abandonment to Jesus. Paul said, "We are troubled on every side, yet not distressed; we are perplexed, but not in despair; persecuted, but not forsaken; cast down, but not destroyed; always bearing about in the body the dying of the Lord Jesus, that the life also of Jesus might be made manifest in our body" (2 Corinthians 4:8–10 KJV).

Chapter 60

Developing Self-control

Second Peter 1:6 tells us that knowledge helps us in the area of self-control, and self-control aids in perseverance. We may not be able to choose our tribulations and trials in life, because many times there are forces involved that are beyond our control. Yet we do have control over self, because God has given us a free will. Even though we gain knowledge from the Word of God and the world, the choice of how we use it is ours.

Self-control Is a Matter of Choice

In the Old and New Testaments God continually tried to give His people knowledge. He knows that His people perish from lack of knowledge, whether it is for spiritual or physical use (Hosea 4:6). When God chose the nation of Israel and gave them the Ten Commandments, He asked them to use their knowledge for self-control. However, they refused to persevere in God's knowledge and lost their godly self-control.

After spending forty days on Mount Sinai listening to God's voice and getting the Ten Commandments written in stone, Moses witnessed God's people worshipping a golden calf they had made while he was gone. Left to themselves, the people lost their self-control, even though they had seen the smoke on Mount Sinai and knew that God was on the mountain.

Before Moses went up on the mountain to receive the Ten Commandments, God made a covenant in blood with the people.

He took the Book of the Covenant and read in the hearing of the people. And they said, "All that the Lord has said we will do, and be obedient." And Moses took the blood, sprinkled it on the people, and said, "This is the blood of the covenant which the Lord has made with you according to all these words." (Exodus 24:7–8)

God prepared the people to worship Him, allowed them to witness Him in their midst, and gave them Aaron to be their leader in Moses' absence, yet they disregarded Aaron's admonitions about making a golden calf. They couldn't maintain self-control on their own for forty days while Moses and Joshua were on the mountain where Moses was hearing from God concerning His disciplines for them. Instead, they chose to run amok with immorality and sin.

They were like small children left alone who decide it would be fun to destroy property and make messes even though they have been taught to honor their parents' teachings and were warned that such antics will bring harsh discipline on them.

Anger and Impatience Affect Self-control

When Moses saw the people dancing and worshipping the golden calf that they had made, he probably felt like God was asking too much of him, trying to keep that bunch of renegades godly. He was so angry, he threw the tablet of stone at the mountain and broke it, even though it was in God's own handwriting!

God's harsh judgment fell upon the Israelites that day, and three thousand people died because of their bad choices. However, Moses did what many of us tend to do: he took the blame for what others had done. He probably felt he had failed the people in some way, just like we often feel guilty when our spouses, children, or other family members make bad choices. "And the Lord said to Moses, 'Whoever has sinned against Me, I will blot him out of My book'" (Exodus 32:33).

After the golden calf fiasco, Moses pitched his tent outside the camp and called it a tabernacle of meeting. There, through the pillar of a cloud, the Lord spoke to Moses "face to face, as a man speaks to his friend" (Exodus 33:11).

Lack of self-control and bad choices caused the Israelites to set a pattern that stayed with them until God finally had to send them into exile. They were scattered among different countries and lost their status as a nation.

One thing we can learn from the trials and tribulations of the nation of Israel is that lack of patience is the first evidence that we are not walking closely enough with God. Even though the Israelites had the prophets of God and direct intervention from Him in their lives, they refused to listen to His advice and allowed impatience to keep them from living godly lives and making right choices.

Today Christians have help through the Holy Spirit who lives in us. But not listening to the Word of God and allowing our negative emotions to overcome God's disciplines make us impatient with one another and with God.

When several small problems beset us in close proximity, our first impulse is to lose our patience and complain. I recently faced this dilemma when the cable for my TV was being repaired and my computer crashed while I was viewing my e-mail. That night the dishwasher overflowed. After I called the plumber and started cleaning up the mess, I actually laughed when I wondered what other problems could happen.

The next day a kind motorist warned me that a tire on my car was going flat. I immediately drove to the tire shop. The flat couldn't be fixed, so I bought two new tires. A few days later my printer stopped working, and I had to get a new one. The constant troubles were taxing my patience. I felt anger trying to surface, but I chose to allow God's wisdom to prevail with His peace.

A few days later fires started burning in areas close to our home. Many people lost their homes, but our town escaped any type of structural damage. The small problems I had been dealing with were nothing compared to the threat of losing a home. Being thankful to God for His blessings caused my impatience to disappear quickly.

Troublesome situations can make us unpleasant to be with. But when we deliberately walk away from God's wisdom and Word, as the Israelites did, our impatience can lead us into sin that can affect our finances, health, and relationships.

Impatience is an act of the will—then self is in control, not God or His wisdom.

Self-pity Affects Self-control

Every time we allow our thinking to bring us into the realm of self-pity, self-control flies out the window. A mother working with small children, after tending to a dozen small jobs all day, can become so harried that she loses her self-control and yells at the kids. At other times, she reprimands them in a more constructive way. Her reaction depends on whether she is developing self-pity or if she is able to keep the peace in herself and maintain peace around her.

The Bible says, "Great peace have those who love Your law, and nothing causes them to stumble" (Psalm 119:165).

Before we can maintain peace in our hearts and around us, we have to develop patience. We can cry out to God for help when we feel self-pity or anger overtaking us and say, "My tongue shall speak of thy word: for all thy commandments are righteousness. Let thine hand help me; for I have chosen thy precepts" (Psalm 119:172–173 KJV).

Self-pity is a hard master because it promotes anger. It rears its ugly head in many situations. At work, people who are more conscientious than others end up being assigned extra work. There is an old saying, "If you want something done, ask a busy person." After a while you begin to resent the extra work, and self-pity kicks in.

Some people lose their self-control when they are driving and someone cuts them off. They develop what is commonly called "road rage." This type of behavior is becoming more common because of the stress people are going through on the job and at home. The road is becoming unsafe. Frustrated drivers get on a roller-coaster-ride of uncontrolled thinking that leads to negative words and negative actions that may end up in physical violence, accidents, and jail time for the one who loses his or her temper.

Self-pity Causes Us to Question God

God wants us to do all things for Him, not people. That is the only way we can overcome self-pity. So if you think you are not being treated properly or overworked, take your problems to Him in prayer. He will sustain you and help you overcome and deal with stressful problems.

Once, when I was complaining that I could not do a particular thing, the Lord said, *I will never ask you to do anything you cannot do. However, I may ask you to do some things you don't want to do.*

Many times when we don't want to do the will of God, we are reacting out of fear, unforgiveness, self-pity, or anger. Or we may think that God is wrong and we are not capable.

When we are confronted with such situations, we can relate to Jonah when he didn't want to go to Ninevah to call the people to repentance. He felt that God could handle the problem without him, so he tried to run from God and ended up in the belly of a whale. Later, he repented and did God's will, but he sat under a tree and pouted after God spared the people. He thought God shouldn't withhold His judgment because they had been so wicked. (See Jonah 1– 4.) Jonah felt God's will was wrong in that situation.

Christians today are inclined to question God's judgment when they think His will is not the best for their lives. I have certainly found myself pouting like Jonah. I thought God was asking too much of me when He wanted me to write a book on

His disciplines. I even suggested a person to Him whom I thought could do the job better. His answer to my idea was that He wanted His disciplines tempered with mercy, and He had given me that gift. He also commented that He had given me the material for the ten disciplines.

As the psalmist said, God never makes a mistake. "As for God, His way is perfect; the word of the Lord is proven; He is a shield to all who trust in Him" (Psalm 18:30).

Even when we are being reviled, we need to exhibit good conduct so we can have a clear conscience. "It is better, if it is the will of God, to suffer for doing good than for doing evil" (1 Peter 3:17).

Jesus said that He always did the will of His Father, and He proved it by going to the cross and being crucified for our sins. It was the will of His Father.

Many people promise to do things but never follow through, usually because they want to avoid any confrontation concerning their conflict of interest with people or God. They are set on doing their will even if it harms them.

Love of Money Causes Loss of Self-control

A love for things that money can buy can cause people to lose control over their spending. "The love of money is a root of all kinds of evil, for which some have strayed from the faith in their greediness, and pierced themselves through with many sorrows" (1 Timothy 6:10).

Many people are so involved in worldly things that they incur phenomenal debts. They live far above their means, and easy credit prevents them from changing their spending habits. People spend money on travel, send their children to expensive schools, purchase expensive furniture and big homes, own one or more expensive cars, buy name-brand clothing, eat out in fancy restaurants, etc. There is nothing wrong with those things if you can afford them, but it is wrong to let spending get out of control.

At the present time, our economy is facing serious hardship because many people bought houses they couldn't afford and lenders wanted to make money, regardless of the risks. The evils of overspending have not only affected the United States but the world's economy as well.

The apostle Paul learned how to abase and how to abound, to be content whether he had a little or a lot of material possessions. Christian families are just as guilty as non-Christians when it comes to living "high on the hog," as farmers in the Depression used to say.

The love of money makes some people steal, others cheat on their income taxes, some even swindle the public. Entire families are involved in making and selling drugs to get the things they see others enjoying. However, Timothy tells us to flee these things and pursue righteousness, godliness, faith, love, gentleness, and patience (1 Timothy 6:11). The man who cannot develop self-control in the ordinary things of life will find himself straying from his faith in God and plunging deeper into sin.

Patience Develops Self-control

James says, "My brethren, count it all joy when you fall into various trials, knowing that the testing of your faith produces patience" (James 1:2–3). Patience is the key to learning how to develop self-control. But virtuous traits like patience are not born in us; we acquire them through daily struggles. Some people have to struggle harder than others to develop self-control. Individuals react differently to similar situations of stress. Some act in a negative way, while others approach the same problems in a more relaxed manner.

James says, "If any of you lacks wisdom, let him ask of God, who gives to all liberally and without reproach, and it will be given to him" (James 1:5). When we are being tested by trials and tribulations, we can develop self-control with God's help in any area of need: finances, health, or relationships.

Luke 8:15 tells us that seed sown on the good ground of a noble and good heart can keep the word and bear fruit with patience.

In speaking to the Romans, Paul said, "Whatever things were written before were written for our learning, that we through the patience and comfort of the Scriptures might have hope" (Romans 15:4). Hope strengthens our faith, and faith helps us persevere, and perseverance produces self-control.

Chapter 61

Mountaintop Experiences

Habakkuk was a prophet and minister who lived in a time when God was preparing to bring His final judgment on Judah. He questioned why the Lord was ignoring the evil things that people were doing all around him. When the Lord told him that Jerusalem would fall to the Babylonians and most of the people would be exiled into Babylon, Habakkuk couldn't understand why a nation more evil than Judah would be allowed to win over God's people. God told him that Babylon would pay for its misdeeds someday.

Dare to Develop Hinds' Feet

Even though Habakkuk was fearful of the coming events, he decided to rejoice in the salvation of God. He realized that he could trust God through perilous times. Even if the fig trees didn't produce fruit, if the olive fields yielded no food or the flocks were cut off from the fold and there would be no meat from them, God would be in control. When he knew God would save him from the pending disasters of famine and war, he said, "Yet I will rejoice in the Lord, I will joy in the God of my salvation. The Lord God is my strength, and he will make my feet like hinds' (deer) feet, and he will make me to walk upon mine high places" (Habakkuk 3:18–19 KJV).

Saul was the first king of Israel when the twelve tribes were in the same kingdom. However, his disobedience to God resulted in God anointing David to be king after Saul died; therefore, Saul was constantly trying to have David killed.

David was thankful to God for helping him escape all the snares Saul set for him. Like Habakkuk, he decided to rejoice in the Lord even during times of great peril. David said, "I will call upon the Lord, who is worthy to be praised; so shall I be saved from my enemies" (Psalm 18:3).

David also talked about developing hinds' feet. "It is God that girdeth me with strength, and maketh my way perfect. He maketh my feet like hinds' feet, and setteth me upon my high places" (Psalm 18:32–33 KJV).

Even thou David and Habakkuk lived centuries apart—one when the nation of Israel first started, and the other when the last of the Israelites were sent into captivity—they both had the same desire. They wanted God to bring them out of the valley of tribulation, to help them develop hinds' feet so they could travel with God on higher ground. The trials these men experienced increased their perseverance and gave them the hinds' feet they wanted. They learned to maintain their joy during times of sorrow and look to the Lord for their salvation and strength before experiencing the ecstasy of walking with God on the mountaintops.

Glory in Tribulation

Persevering in the ten areas of God's disciplines will aid in our endeavors to climb up on our high places and go from glory to glory with Christ like David and Habakkuk did. The disciplines that help us to develop hinds' feet are given to us by Jesus, His first-century disciples, and Paul, who wrote many of the books in the New Testament.

Paul tells us that he had a mountaintop experience when he was caught up to the third heaven, but it was not proper that he should boast or glory in the experience. To keep him from exalting himself, God sent a messenger of Satan to harass him. Paul asked the Lord three times for it to depart.

> And he said unto me, My grace is sufficient for thee: for my strength is made perfect in weakness. Most gladly therefore

will I rather glory in my infirmities, that the power of Christ may rest upon me. Therefore I take pleasure in infirmities, in reproaches, in necessities, in persecutions, in distresses for Christ's sake: for when I am weak, then am I strong. (2 Corinthians 12:9–10 KJV)

Paul was able to have joy in his tribulations because his imprisonment was helping instead of hindering the preaching of the gospel. Paul said, "It has become evident to the whole palace guard, and to all the rest, that my chains are in Christ; and most of the brethren in the Lord, having become confident by my chains, are much more bold to speak the word without fear" (Philippians 1:13–14).

Jesus taught His twelve apostles and the seventy He chose to send from city to city and gave them all power and authority over demons and diseases before He sent them to preach the kingdom of God. After He appointed the seventy men He told them, "The harvest truly is great, but the laborers are few; therefore pray the Lord of the harvest to send out laborers into His harvest. Go your way; behold, I send you out as lambs among wolves" (Luke 10:2–3). He also informed them that whoever heard them heard Him, and whoever rejected them rejected Him (verse 16).

The seventy met with excellent success in healing and teaching people about the kingdom of God. When they returned, they told Jesus that even the demons were subject to them in His name. However, He told them not to rejoice because they had power over spirits, but because their names are written in heaven (Luke 10:19–20).

If we try to serve the Lord without the proper preparation that Jesus gave His twelve disciples and the seventy, we may become prey to the wolves of the world. When we develop hinds' feet, we too can have power over the enemy in the name of Jesus.

God created deer to be sure-footed, nimble creatures, at home in the valleys or on the rocky slopes of mountains and hillsides.

He equipped them with the power they need for their survival. Men have always marveled at their agility to run and leap over obstacles.

As Christians, we need hinds' feet to escape from the enemy that constantly pursues us.

Perseverance Prepares Us to Minister in the Valleys

If we want to be at home in the valleys and on high places in this life, we must allow the Holy Spirit to help us develop spiritual hinds' feet. We do this by drawing closer to God and planting our feet on firm ground with the disciplines He gives us.

Before we can change, we must prostrate ourselves, humbly cry out to God for strength, glorify Him in prayer, sing songs of love to Him, praise Him, and thank Him for His mercy, goodness, love, kindness, and salvation. If we do this, we are assured of developing the hinds' feet that will enable us to walk with God on the high places where He will take us so He can pour out His Spirit of love upon us, renew us, and restore us.

Mountaintop experiences not only enable us to be refreshed and reinvigorated, they also equip us to succor those who are not spiritually strong. Jesus often went into the wilderness or mountains to pray and be alone with God, away from His disciples and the people. He needed God to restore His physical and spiritual strength because He was constantly being persecuted and in the midst of trials and tribulations.

Before we can joy in tribulation the way Paul did, and do the works that Jesus left for us to do, we have to let God breathe new life into us through our mountaintop experiences with Him.

Chapter 62

God's Righteous Cause

Many people commit a portion of their time and money to some kind of cause. God's cause can bring change into our lives and produce results for His kingdom. Worldly causes may or may not help God in His kingdom.

Persevering in Earthly Causes

Some causes are associated with cures for cancer and other diseases. Some causes relate to helping the poor, feeding starving children, or providing shelter for the homeless. Then there are causes that help people in disastrous situations such as hurricanes, tornadoes, floods, and fire.

The World Trade Center bombings resulted in the deaths of many firefighters and police officers, and several charitable organizations sought donations to help their family members.

Due to the war in the Middle East and other recent wars, we have a large increase in military causes to help disabled, wounded, or paralyzed veterans.

Environmental causes strive to keep pollution from the earth's atmosphere, to protect the forests, land, water, fish, animal, and insect life God created in this world. We even have causes to protect cats and dogs and other pets.

We also have causes that try to change the government's view on certain situations. The abortion issue is a long-standing problem in our society, and great numbers of people have put time and money into trying to save children who are being aborted because of unwanted pregnancies.

The Danger in Earthly Causes

Unfortunately, even good causes can have bad results. Different groups fight for their own opinions, often leading to anger and violence. Causes appeal to a wide variety of people. Many are seeking to make a difference in life or government. Many religious affiliations draw people to a man or organization that helps the poor and needy. But a cause can turn into a cult.

Cults develop their own religious philosophy with rules and regulations that don't have the Bible as the final authority. Their proponents are not interested in God's will but in developing a "group will." There is no freedom of choice. The leader of a cult is a charismatic, domineering, strong-willed individual who keeps a tight control over his followers with subtle intimidation and fear.

Many young people enjoy belonging to groups, and they can be pulled in over their heads because they don't understand the deceptive manipulations of the leader they have chosen to serve.

A cult is led by an individual with an authoritarian disposition, and he is aided by others with similar traits. He seeks to break off family ties and to control his followers' finances and social activities. He may know a few biblical truths and do a few good deeds, but he completely abandons God's wisdom and operates with his own set of rules and regulations.[30]

When we know God's Word, we can walk in His will for us by "casting down arguments and every high thing that exalts itself against the knowledge of God, bringing every thought into captivity to the obedience of Christ" (2 Corinthians 10:5).

Jim Jones was a charismatic person who fooled many important people with his ideas of social reform. Even though he was a communist, he become an ordained minister, and in 1956 he started a church of his own called the People's Temple. They

---

[30] http://www.leaderu.com/common/cults.html.

established themselves in several locations throughout California. They were widely accepted in the 1970s when their bus caravans traveled across different parts of the United States. They collected thousands of dollars on each trip.

Jim Jones saw the church as a way to escape taxes and raise money for his social goals. He earned a reputation for aiding the cities' poorest citizens, especially racial minorities and drug addicts. But his underground activities for the Communist Party finally got attention from the federal government. When he was threatened with exposure, he fled to Guyana, South America, and established Jonestown there. Several hundred people followed him.

Congressman Leo Ryan from the San Francisco area went to Jonestown to investigate abuse within the temple. He and several members who tried to leave with him were killed at the airport on November 18, 1978. A few hours later Jones had his followers drink cyanide-laced Flavor Aid. His and his followers' deaths shocked the world.[31]

Paul warns Christians by saying, "Beware lest anyone cheat you through philosophy and empty deceit, according to the tradition of men, according to the basic principles of the world, and not according to Christ" (Colossians 2:8).

Today, many young men and women are devoted to terrorist causes because they are told they are doing God's work. Because they believe they have found a cause greater than self, they are willing to lead a martyr's life and die a martyr's death. They are taught that God approves of their evil, destructive ways.

Peter tells us that there are false prophets and false teachers who will bring in destructive heresies, and many will follow their destructive ways. By covetousness they will exploit men with deceptive words. Peter tells us that God will bring judgment on them, just as He did on the unrighteous world in Noah's day, and just as He did with the fallen angels. (See 2 Peter 2:1–5.)

---

[31] http://en.wikipedia.org/wiki/Peoples_Temple.

The Mystery of God's Cause

When we are looking for a cause greater than self, we must look to the One who died on the cross so the sins of men would be forgiven by God. When Jesus came to earth to be born of a woman and to live as a man, He committed Himself to God's cause. He came to live a martyr's life and to die a martyr's death because of God's incomprehensible love for the world and the people He created. That redemption restored God's relationship with us and gave us the power to take back control from Satan. Even though Satan remains the god of this world in things pertaining to the world, he has no control over us other than what we foolishly relinquish to him through undisciplined lifestyles.

God gave the prophets knowledge concerning the coming of Christ. But they couldn't imagine the glory that awaited humankind after the death of Jesus on the cross, when the Holy Spirit would come to live in individuals who accepted Christ as their Savior.

Paul talked to the Colossians about being ministers to fulfill the Word of God, and about the mystery that was hidden from past generations but now has been revealed to His saints. "To them God willed to make known what are the riches of the glory of this mystery among the Gentiles: which is Christ in you, the hope of glory" (Colossians 1:27).

Our hope of glory comes not from men but through the power of the Holy Spirit, who takes up residence in the spirits of men who believe on the name of Jesus Christ. Speaking to His disciples, Jesus said, "I still have many things to say to you, but you cannot bear them now. However, when He, the Spirit of truth, has come, He will guide you into all truth; for He will not speak on His own authority, but whatever He hears He will speak; and He will tell you things to come" (John 16:12–13).

We generate the same self-sacrificing love back to Jesus when we follow Him. "You are My friends if you do whatever I command you" (John 15:14).

Marriage to the Lamb: Cause Greater than Self

Developing a cause greater than self is motivated by the sacrifice of love. This act is completely alienated from the world because there is a natural instinct in each person to love self. We nourish and cherish our flesh the way the Lord does the church. "We are members of His body, of His flesh and of His bones. 'For this reason a man shall leave his father and mother and be joined to his wife, and the two shall become one flesh.' This is a great mystery, but I speak concerning Christ and the church" (Ephesians 5:30–32).

Even though many good people are willing to die martyr's deaths, it is difficult to lead martyr's lives that require us to be married to the Lamb and follow the disciplines of Jesus Christ.

Marriage was meant to represent God's love for mankind, and that love was poured out on two people, Adam and Eve, in the form of marriage as a way to populate the earth and bring glory to God with their offspring. However, Satan intervened, and he has been intervening ever since.

Some Christian marriages are no different from earthly marriages. They start out focusing on fun, sex, and acquiring material things. But battles soon arise, usually centered on money or unfaithfulness or a perception of rights being violated. Jesus told His disciples that Moses allowed people to divorce because of the hardness of their hearts (Mark 10:4–5). But His kind of love can change hearts and make human marriages as sacred as His marriage is to the church.

Revelation 19:7–8 says, "Let us be glad and rejoice and give Him glory, for the marriage of the Lamb has come, and His wife has made herself ready. And to her it was granted to be arrayed in fine linen, clean and bright, for the fine linen is the righteous acts of the saints."

Before the church can become a good wife to the Lamb, we have to obey the disciplines left to us by Jesus. We are to put God's will first, regardless of feelings, and learn to walk in love. Then we can have good earthly marriages and produce godly offspring for the kingdom. We will be able to persevere in the cause greater than self for which we were created: our marriage to the Lamb.

Learning Perseverance

Perseverance is a learning process starting from birth. A baby learns how to walk through the hard knocks of falling, bumping into furniture, and using strong objects for crutches as she goes around a room. Then she is ready to take her first step standing alone. Even though she falls, she keeps taking more steps as she gains confidence. She has to develop a sense of humor; otherwise, she will spend all her time crying and nursing her wounds. However, in time, she learns to walk, run, and jump. As she grows older she learns to exercise her body in many ways, including swimming and other sports. None of her goals in life can be reached unless she develops a persevering spirit.

Learning to operate in the ten disciplines that God has given us requires the same tenacity a baby must develop before she can walk. The benefits we will derive from following God's ways of thinking, speaking, and acting will outweigh the hard knocks we have to take before we can develop the "mouse-free house" that self-discipline and perseverance enables us to have.

Exercising godly self-control is not a choice, but our duty to Jesus. He came to show us how to walk in godliness and enjoy an abundant life.

The wisdom of God does not fall upon us like raindrops. We get it through persevering in God's Word. His righteousness helps us overcome the corruption and lust of the world. Without the divine intervention and wisdom of God, we would become bond-slaves to sin, for the lust of the flesh will lure us into ungodly and unrighteous behavior.

Peter says of those who have forsaken the way, "These are wells without water, clouds carried by a tempest, for whom is reserved the blackness of darkness forever" (2 Peter 2:17). Christians are the sons and daughters of Light, and we are looking forward to a heavenly home with our Creator.

Staying the Course

Before we can stand firm and endure the race set before us, we must develop a steady heartbeat of faith and persevere in the ten disciplines that God has outlined for us. God's ten disciplines will enable us to escape the pollution of the world and develop the hinds' feet we need to walk with joy through the valleys of trials and tribulation. Then we can have the mountaintop experiences with God that will help us restore our spiritual vitality and enable us to have mouse-free spiritual houses.

Perseverance will help us develop self-control and produce godliness. From godliness we will be able to increase in brotherly kindness, which in turn helps us to walk in love. Walking in love is not a choice, but a commandment from Jesus (John 15:12). Godly love is the hinge to the Door of Life.

Our Prayer

Father, as we plod through the valleys of our lives, we purpose in our hearts to develop a steady heartbeat of faith that will impregnate our lives with joy and peace. We will respect our bodies, be good stewards of our finances, pray without ceasing, persevere in godliness, and develop hinds' feet to walk in high places so that You can revive, restore, and renew our spirits. Then, with the help of the Holy Spirit, we will continue to abide in You, walk in Your love, and do the works that Jesus has called us to do. Amen.

You Don't Have to Climb Those Mountains

You don't have to climb those mountains.

You don't have to tunnel through.

God will level them before you.

Trust in Him; His Word is true.

Each new day brings joy and sadness.

Hills and valleys are everywhere.

But God says, "Come, I'll walk them with you.

You're not alone; I am always there."

MAINTAINING A MOUSE-FREE HOUSE

We need to walk in God's disciplines to maintain a "mouse-free" house.

He has shown you, O man, what is good;
and what does the Lord require of you but to do justly,
to love mercy, and to walk humbly with your God?
(Micah 6:8)

Chapter 63

Walking in the Way

Paul tried to teach people in the synagogue about the kingdom of God, "but when some were hardened and did not believe, but spoke evil of the Way before the multitude, he departed from them and withdrew the disciples, reasoning daily in the school of Tyrannus" (Acts 19:9). Paul persevered in teaching the Way to the Gentiles and Jews even when he was in prison.

A few years before God gave me the ten disciplines in this book, He asked me one night during my prayer time if I had heard of the Road of Gold, and I said no. He proceeded to give me images of people engaged in various activities such as picnics and games, but warned me against participating in them.

After two or three nights meditating on the scenes, I wrote them down, and with the Holy Spirit's help I put them into a poem. I threw the poem into my file of spiritual thoughts and forgot about it. Many years later, after I married Andy, I was going over old notes and came across the poem. When I realized its importance, I shared it with others. This poem represents what it is like to persevere in faith, walk with Jesus as our guide, and allow Him to direct our paths.

The Road of Gold

Have you not heard of the Road of Gold?

It seems to go on forever.

It's a long road, a hard road made from precious gold metal,

And it leads us into heaven.

I have traveled the Road of Gold,

And my journey did seem endless.

Without the Companion who walked beside me,

It's a journey I could never have finished.

As we traveled down the Road of Gold,

The sun grew hotter and hotter.

Many roads crossed our paths,

And they all looked very inviting.

When we came to a road lined with cool shade trees,

I exclaimed, "Let's walk in their shade!"

Nay, My child, that road ends in miry clay,

And it would impede our journey.

While walking along on the Road of Gold, I gazed at the horizon.

"Oh, look! There's a sea! Let's walk in the sand and watch the sea
gulls flying."

Nay, My child, the sea is cruel and the tide rises ever so swiftly.

You could be carried out to sea and lost from Me for eternity.

Onward we traveled down the Road of Gold, until I spied an artistic
fountain.

"Let's refresh ourselves," I begged, "and have a cool drink of water."

Nay, My child, the water is polluted. You would become ill

And never finish your journey.

We continued on down the Road of Gold, then came to a beautiful
meadow.

Friendly people were waving to us and calling us to join in their
pleasure.

"Let's tarry awhile and join in their games. They look very exciting."

*Nay, My child, our time is limited and we would lose precious
moments.*

As we trudged more slowly down the Road of Gold,

My Friend revealed its mystery,

Telling me stories of people who had built the road,

Of their hardships, struggles, and history.

Soon my feet were drawn to the Road of Gold,

And other roads paled beside it.

They were no longer enticing with cool shade trees

And the promise of things exciting.

But I grew weary as we walked along.

And my steps grew shorter and shorter.

My Friend gave me His staff to lean upon.

Then He encouraged me to go farther.

Carefully and slowly down the road we walked,

And my eyes grew dim and dimmer.

Finally, my Companion put His arm around me

And said, *Lean on Me.*

As we continued on the Road of Gold,

It grew darker and darker. Then I cried, "I'm finished!"

With a soothing voice my Companion replied,

Don't fret, My child, for now I will carry you.

So in utter darkness we traveled on.

Then my Companion spoke ever so softly.

Open your eyes, My child,

For now we have finished our journey.

In front of me were huge shade trees

Swaying slightly in the cool breeze.

"May I rest under these trees?"

Of course, My child, they are yours to enjoy for eternity.

As I gazed around, I saw a meadow of exotic flowers.

I asked my Companion if I could walk among the flowers.

Of course, My child. They are yours to enjoy,

For their blooms will last forever.

While basking in their sweet fragrance, I heard the sound

Of rippling water and beheld a magnificent fountain.

"Oh! May I wash my face and drink that crystal clear water?"

Of course, My child. It's the Water of Life and yours to drink forever.

Once more I gazed at the horizon and saw the splendor of a sea.

"May I walk along the beach and watch the seagulls flying?"

Yes, My child. The sea is calm now and has no cruel tides to harm
you.

It's yours to enjoy for eternity.

As we walked along in the soft, warm sand,

We heard people laughing and singing. "Will I be able to join
them?"

Yes, My child, for they helped to build the Road of Gold

That you have traveled on, and they're anxious to hear of your
journey.

"Oh, I'm not worthy to meet them," I cried.

"They are the noblest of men!"

Nonsense, My child. You are ready to join them,

For you have walked the Road of Gold, and you have finished your
journey!

Christians truly are heaven bound, but we must use God's disciplines to stay on the Road of Gold, because the obstacles in the roads of the world will greatly hamper our journey.

God reminded me recently, while I was meditating on some of my failures, *Life is not about faults, but the Word of God.* He doesn't notice our failures, but He does notice when we don't concentrate on His Word.

The Word tells us to focus on whatever things are true, noble, just, pure, lovely, and beautiful. If there is any virtue or anything praiseworthy or of good report, we are to meditate on those things, not on our faults or someone else's failures. Then the God of peace will be with us as we persevere through the world's trials and tribulations (Philippians 4:8–9).

Our goal as Christians is to attain the fullness of Christ (Ephesians 4:13). This helps us to be fruitful and meet the needs of others. However, we cannot attain the fullness of Christ without perseverance. And without perseverance we cannot stay full of God's knowledge and wisdom, because the Word evaporates from our spirits the way water evaporates from an earthen vessel. To attain the fullness of God we have to keep refilling our spirits through prayer and the Word. This may seem like an impossible mission for us, but "with God all things are possible" (Matthew 19:26).

Satan's goal is to cause us to walk in unbelief. He is a sneak and a thief. Just like a mouse will find ways to creep into a physical house, steal food, and defile it, Satan will find ways to sneak into our spiritual houses to steal the Word from us. He defiles our spirits with negative thoughts and negative emotions. Our prayer life, health, finances, and relationships are affected.

Peter tells us to resist Satan, knowing that the same suffering we are experiencing is being experienced by other Christians throughout the world. He gives the churches a benediction:

May the God of all grace, who called us to His eternal glory by Christ Jesus, after you have suffered a while, perfect, establish, strengthen, and settle you. To Him be the glory and the dominion forever and ever. Amen. (1 Peter 5:10–11)

Perseverance helps us stay on the Road of Gold until we have finished our journey and are safe in our heavenly home, where God will wipe away all tears from our eyes (Revelation 7:17).

In heaven all mansions will be mouse-free houses!

About the Author

Mary Ellen High was born in Drumwright, Oklahoma, on July 23, 1926. Her family moved to Missouri when she was eleven. She married Norman Toon while they were both in college at Missouri State University in Springfield. Norman became a civil engineer for the United States Coast Guard. His tours of duty took them many places, including Alaska and Greece. Norman retired after thirty years of military service, and they made their home in St. Louis, Missouri.

Mary Ellen's activities included helping charitable organizations, teaching Sunday school, and raising four children. She finished her degree in secondary education when her first two children were small. She taught home-bound students in St. Louis County for several years.

Norman's death in 1988 ended their marriage of thirty-nine years. On a mission trip to Israel and Egypt, Mary Ellen met her second husband, Andrew Stewart, a retired businessman whose forty-three year marriage ended with the death of his wife, Ila.

Mary Ellen and Andy now make their home in Chino Hills, California. They have gone to China, Russia, and Africa on mission trips. In 1994, they traveled by bus with Andy's fellow glider veterans and their wives across Europe from Germany to England, revisiting countries the 82nd Airborne Division helped liberate during World War II. It was a time of sadness and healing for the veterans as they shared war memories.

It's Hard to Have a Mouse-Free House: But with God All Things Are Possible is a culmination of the many ways the Lord has impacted Mary Ellen's life with counsel from the Holy Spirit. God's passion to see His people walk in His disciplines has become her passion. She hopes to see more of God's people enjoy an intimate relationship with Him before He calls her home.

"Even so, come, Lord, Jesus!" (Revelation 22:20)

Notes

Notes

Notes